TrailBlazer

Last Minute Guide

BIOLOGY

for

CBSE XII

R.K. Srivastav

UNICORN BOOKS

Publisher
UNICORN BOOKS
F-2/16, Ansari Road, Daryaganj, New Delhi-110002
E-mail: info@unicornbooks.in • Website: www.unicornbooks.in
☎ 011-23275434, 23262683

Branch : Mumbai
23-25, Zaoba Wadi Thakurdwar, Mumbai-400002
☎ 022-22010941, 022-22053387
E-mail: rapidex@bom5.vsnl.net.in

ISBN 978-81-7806-283-9

Edition: 2015

Printed at : *Param Offsetters, Okhla, New Delhi-110020*

Preface

This TRAILBLAZER Series presents CBSE plus-2 preparatory materials for exam preparation, which includes everything that students need to pass the exams with flying colours. This is a unique solution series which is intended to be the most valuable guide to enable the students brush up the concepts.

The series comprises four subjects — Maths, Physics, Chemistry, and Biology.

UNIQUE FEATURES

- The Series is based on the latest CBSE prescribed Exam pattern.
- All the chapters have been designed in Q & A format as per guidelines of CBSE.
- Each chapter contains three sections, such as VSA (Very Short Answer), SA-I & SA-II (Short Answer I & II) and LA (Long Answer).
- At the end of each chapter is a – NUTSHEET (MIND MAP) which includes flow charts.
- HOTS questions at the end of each chapter are given to enhance thought process of the students.
- Solved Mock Sample Question Papers have been included along with four unsolved sample question papers for practice.
- Value based questions have been included.

Students are advised to prepare themselves strictly following the CBSE question papers. The answers have been outlined in a very simple language and kept up to the mark as per the requirement of the questions.

This Book is prima facie an essential and useful compendium for all students aspiring to secure high marks in the exams.

Any suggestions, comments and criticisms from the students & teachers towards improving the book will be highly appreciated.

The Publisher

Content

TOTAL QUESTIONS AT A GLANCE

UNIT WEIGHTAGE	VSA	SA I, II	LA	HOTS
UNIT VI. REPRODUCTION — 14				
Chapter 1. Reproduction in Organisms	20	20	02	07
Chapter 2. Sexual Reproduction in Flowering Plants	20	20	04	09
Chapter 3. Human Reproduction	24	21	04	06
Chater 4. Reproductive Health	10	20	01	05
Total	**74**	**81**	**11**	**27**
UNIT VIII. GENETICS AND EVOLUTION — 18				
Chapter 5. Principles of Inheritance and Variation.	22	21	04	10
Chapter 6. Molecular basis of Inheritance	21	21	02	15
Chapter 7. Evolution	12	05	—	05
Total	**55**	**47**	**06**	**30**
UNIT VIII. BIOLOGY IN HUMAN WELFARE — 14				
Chapter 8. Human Health and Disease				
Chapter 9. Strategies for Enhancement in Food Production	20	15	02	05
Chapter 10. Microbes in Human Welfare	25	15	01	08
Total	**45**	**30**	**03**	**13**
UNIT IX. BIOTECHNOLOGY — 10				
Chapter 11. Principles and Processes	15	13	04	08
Chapter 12. Biotechnology and its Applications	15	11	02	05
Total	**30**	**24**	**06**	**13**
UNIT X. ECOLOGY AND ENVIRONMENT — 14				
Chapter 13. Organisms and Populations	28	16	02	10
Chapter 14. Ecosystem				
Chapter 15. Biodiversity and Conservation	11	12	02	03
Chapter 16. Environmental Issues	20	16	02	06
Total	**59**	**44**	**06**	**19**

DESIGN OF THE CBSE QUESTION PAPER
BIOLOGY-CLASS XII

Hrs : 3 Hours **Max. Marks : 70**

The weightage of the distribution of marks over different dimensions of the question paper shall be as follows:

Weightage to content/subject units

Units	Content	Marks
1.	Reproduction	14
2.	Genetics and Evolution	18
3.	Biology and Human Welfare	14
4.	Biotechnology and its applications	10
5.	Ecology and environment	14
	Total	**70**

Weightage to different forms of questions

S.No.	Forms of Questions	Marks for each	No. of Questions	Total Marks
1.	Very Short Answer (VSA)	1	8	08
2.	Short Answer (SA I)	2	10	20
3.	Short Answer (SA II)/Value Based Question	3	09	27
4.	Long Answer (LA)	5	3	15
	Total	**–**	**30**	**70**

Scheme of Options

1. There will be no overall option.
2. Internal choices (either/or type) on a very selective basis has been provided. This choice has been given in one question of 2 marks, one question of 3 marks and all the three questions of 5 marks weightage.

Weightage to difficulty level of questions

S.No.	Estimated difficulty level	Percentage
1.	Easy	15
2.	Average	70
3.	Difficult	15

The question paper will include value based question(s) to the extent of 3 – 5 marks.

Typology of questions

S.No.	Typology	Weightage in Marks	Weightage in Percentage
1.	Knowledge Based	14	20%
2.	Conceptual Understanding	21	30%
3.	Inferential Type	14	20%
4.	Reasoning Based	11	15%
5.	Skill Based	10	15%
	Total	**70**	**100 %**

Scheme of Options

There will be no overall choices. However, internal choice in any one question of two marks, any one question of three marks and all the three questions of five marks weightage has been provided.

CHAPTER 1

REPRODUCTION IN ORGANISMS

Chapter Outline

- Reproduction
- Asexual reproduction
- Sexual reproduction
- Prefertilization events—gametogenesis, gamete transfer
- Fertilisation
- Post-fertilisation events-zygote, embryogenesis

ASSESSMENT QUESTIONS

VERY SHORT ANSWER TYPE QUESTIONS (VSA)

Q. 1. Name the period from birth to the natural death of an organism.

Ans. Life span.

Q. 2. Which type of organisms are immortal? Multicellular or single cellular organisms?

Ans. Single cellular organisms.

Q. 3. Why is reproduction essential for organisms?

Ans. Reproduction is essential for organism because it enables the continuity of the species, generation after generation.

Q. 4. Why is the offspring formed by asexual reproduction referred to as clone?

Ans. It is referred to as 'clone' because the offspring is morphologically and genetically identical to the parent.

Q. 5. Mention the mode of reproduction in protists and monerans.

Ans. Cell division.

Q. 6. Name the vegetative propagule used for commercial propagation of banana and ginger.

Ans. Rhizome.

Q. 7. Which simple plants during favourable conditions reproduced by asexual mode but during unfavourable conditions shift to sexual mode of reproduction?

Ans. 1. Algae   2. Fungi

Q. 8. Mention the flowering period in—

1. Bamboo   2. *Strobilanthus kunthiana* (neela kuranji)

Ans. 1. Bamboo— 50–100 years *i.e.* once in its life time.

2. *Strobilanthus kunthiana*—12 years.

Q. 9. Some animals are called as seasonal breeders. Why?

Ans. Many mammals that live in natural conditions (wild) exhibit cyclic changes in reproduction, only during favourable seasons in their reproductive phase, hence they are seasonal breeders.

Q. 10. Give two examples of each:

(*a*) Seasonal breeders (*b*) Continuous breeders.

Ans. (*a*) Seasonal breeders—cows, rats. (*b*) Continuous breeders—human, monkey.

Q. 11. Mention the stages of sexual reproduction.

Ans. 1. Prefertilisation, 2. Fertilisation, 3. Post-fertilisation.

Q. 12. What are homogamates or isogamates?

Ans. The gametes (male & female) that are so similar in appearance that it is difficult to differentiate between them are called as homogamates/isogamates.

Q. 13. Give one example to each—

1. Organisms producing homogamate 2. Organism producing heterogamete.

Ans. 1. Homogamate - *Cladophora* (Algae) 2. Heterogamate—Human

Q. 14. Human being is a diploid organism. What is the number of chromosomes present in its sperm cell?

Ans. 23 (*n*).

Q. 15. The meiocyte cell of fruit fly (*Drosophila*) has 8 chromosomes. What will be the number of chromosome in the egg cell?

Ans. 4 (*n*).

Q. 16. The gamete of rice plant has 12 (*n*) chromosome number? What must be the chromosome number in a meiocyte?

Ans. 24 (2n).

Q. 17. Name the medium required for the gametes to transfer in case of algae, bryophytes and pteridophytes.

Ans. Water.

Q. 18. What is bisexual flower?

Ans. Flower that has both male and female reproductive structures is called bisexual flower.

Q. 19. What is zygotic meiosis?

Ans. The meiosis division in zygote produces haploid spores to form haploid individuals. It takes place in haplontic life-cycle and such a division is called zygotic meiosis.

Q. 20. Give a suitable reason why reptiles and birds give/lay shelled eggs and mammals give eggs without shell?

Ans. In first case, the eggs need protection from environment and care, where as, in second case, the eggs are produced inside the animal body; hence, they need no protection from environment.

SHORT ANSWER TYPE QUESTIONS (SA I, SA II)

Q. 1. Define reproduction and its modes in organisms.

Ans. The biological process in which the organism gives rise to offspring similar to itself is called reproduction.

Reproduction in organisms is of two types.

(*a*) **Asexual reproduction:** The reproduction process in which only one parent is involved in producing offsprings.

(*b*) **Sexual reproduction:** The reproductive process in which two parents of opposite sexes are involved in producing organisms.

Q. 2. Which is a better mode of reproduction : sexual or asexual? Why?

Ans. Sexual reproduction is considered as a better mode of reproduction. Because there is morphological and genetic variation among the individuals/offsprings. This enables them of better chances of survival in the environment.

Q. 3. Offsprings formed due to sexual reproduction have better chances of survival? Why? Is this statement always true?

Ans. Because there is morphological and genetic variation among the individuals/offsprings. They get better adopted to the changes in the environment & diseases etc. that risk their survival. Hence, this enables them of better chances of survival in the environment. Yes, it is always true.

Q. 4. How does the progeny formed from asexual reproduction differ from those formed by sexual reproduction?

Ans. Differences between asexual and sexual reproduction progeny.

Asexual-progeny	*Sexual-progeny*
1. The individuals produced are morphologically similar to parents.	1. The individuals produced are morphologically dissimilar to parents.
2. The individuals are genetically similar to the parent.	2. The individuals are genetically dissimilar the parents.
3. They are produced from a single parent.	3. They are produced from two parents of of opposite sexes.
4. All the offsprings are alike and called clones of parent.	4. All the offsprings are not alike.

Q. 5. Distinguish between asexual and sexual reproduction. Why is vegetative reproduction also considered as a type of asexual reproduction?

Ans.

Asexual reproduction	*Sexual reproduction*
1. It is the reproductive process in which only one parent is involved in producing offsprings.	1. It is the reproductive process in which two parents of opposite sexes are involved.
2. All the offsprings produced are morphologically and genetically similar to parent and are called clones.	2. All the offsprings produced are morphologically and genetically dissimilar to parents and are called variants.
3. It is common in single-celled organisms, and plants and animals that have relatively simple organisation.	3. It is common to multicellular plants and animals.
4. Gametes are not produced.	4. Two types of gametes are produced.

Vegetative reproduction is also considered as a type of asexual reproduction because there is in variation among the progenies of the parent and are all alike.

Q. 6. What do you understand by vegetative propagules? Give examples to it. Draw the figure of any one.

Ans. Those structures of plants that have the ability to give rise to new plantlets are called as vegetative propagules. These structures are used for vegetative propagation. Some examples are — rhizome, sucker, offset, bulb, runner.

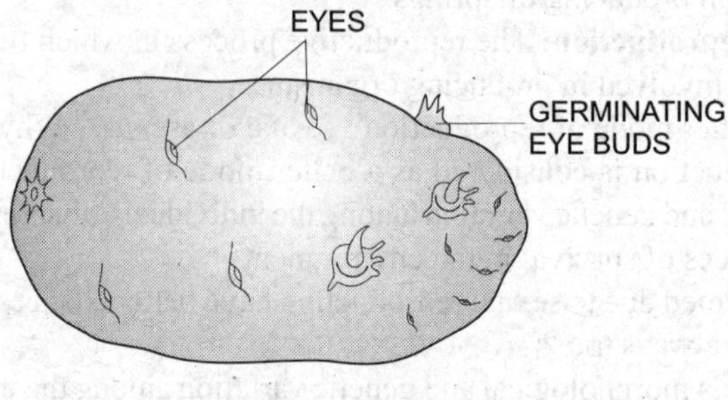

Fig. 1.1 Potato tuber has eye (Vegetative propagule)

Q. 7. What is vegetative propagation? Give two suitable examples.

Ans. The process of producing plants from the vegetative propagules of plants is called vegetative propagation.

1. **Onion bulb :** The bulb is used for propagation of onion by planting it in soil.
2. **Potato tuber :** The potato tuber is used for propagation of potato by planting it in soil. Each eye has the ability to give rise to a plant.

Q. 8. Define—

(*a*) Juvenile phase (*b*) Reproductive phase (*c*) Senescent phase.

Ans. (*a*) **Juvenile phase:** The period of growth and development of an individual until it becomes sexually mature to reproduce is known as juvenile phase/period e.g. a human child upto an age of puberty.

This phase in plants is called vegetative phase i.e. stage of plant before flowering.

(*b*) **Reproductive phase:** The period during which the individual is sexually active/ capable of reproduction is known as reproductive phase.

(*c*) **Senescent phase:** The post reproductive phase or the period during which the individual ceases to reproduce is known as senescent phase/old age.

Q. 9. How you can recognise a flowering plant whether it is mature or not?

Ans. A flowering plant when completes its vegetative growth and enters the reproductive growth it gives flowers/flowering takes place. This indicates that the plant is now mature and suitable/fit for reproduction.

Q. 10. What is the similarity or dissimilarity between oestrus cycle and menstrual cycle?

Ans. Both the cycles are the same process in different animals. In non-primate animals like- deers, dogs, cows, sheep etc. the cyclic changes during reproduction is called oestrus cycle. Where as, in primates like- monkeys, apes and humans it is called menstrual cycle.

Q. 11. Higher organisms have resorted to sexual reproduction in spite of its complexity. Why?

Ans. It is so because this type of reproduction provides the chance of mixing of various types of genes and provides variations among the individuals. It helps in developing better chances of survival and evolution of species.

Q. 12. Briefly explain what is gametogenesis. Mention the types of gametes produced by individuals.

Ans. The process of formation of gametes by the organism is called gametogenesis. It takes place by cell division mitosis or meiosis. In alga like *cladophora* meitotic cell division produces gametes that are similar and are called as disogametes/homogametes. In human being meiotic cell division produces gametes from male and female gonads respectively. The gametes in human are heterogametes and are called sperm and ova respectively.

Q. 13. Which type of cell division occurs during gamete formation in heterogametic and homogametic individuals?

Ans. Species with two morphologically distinct types male and female individuals are called heterogametic species/diploid individuals. In such individuals, gametes produced by them is by meiotic cell division. But in haploid parent/individuals gametes producéd is by mitotic cell division.

Q. 14. Study the following figure—

Write in short about the labelled parts of the figure.

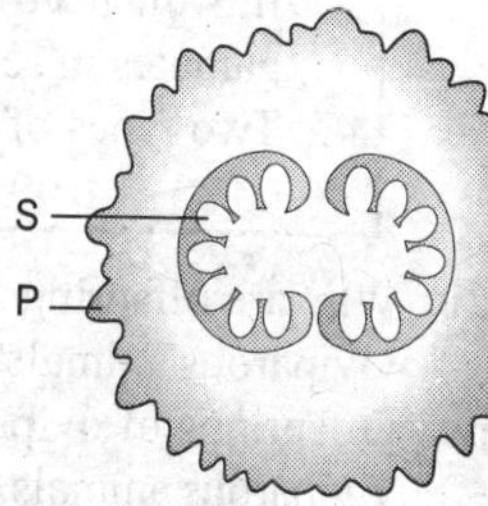

Fig. 1.2

Ans. 1. **S**—It is seed. The seed is formed from the ovule. It has an embryo which in turn is produced from zygote.

2. **P**—It is pericarp. The protective covering of the fruit. Fruit is formed from the ovary after development.

Q. 15. Explain why meiosis and gametogenesis are always interlinked?

Ans. Gametogenesis is the process of formation of gametes by the individual. This process takes place by meiotic cell division in diploid individuals like human being. Without this meiotic cell division gametes with haploid set of chromosome number cannot be produced. Hence both the processes are interlinked.

Q. 16. Identify each part in a flowering plant and write whether it is haploid (n) or diploid (2n).

(*a*) Ovary ________ (*b*) Anther ________
(*c*) Egg ________ (*d*) Pollen ________
(*e*) Male gamete ________ (*f*) Zygote ________

Ans. (*a*) Ovary — $2n$ (*b*) Anther — $2n$
(*c*) Egg — n (*d*) Pollen — n
(*e*) Male gamete — n (*f*) Zygote — $2n$

Q. 17. Define external fertilisation. Mention its disadvantages.

Ans. The process of gametic fusion (sperm and ovum) outside the body of a female organism is called external fertilisation.

Disadvantages

(*i*) Large number of both male and female gametes are released.
(*ii*) All female gametes (ova) are not fortunate to be fertilised.
(*iii*) The fertilised egg (zygote) and offsprings are extremely vulnerable to predators and this threatens their survival upto adulthood.

Q. 18. Differentiate between zoospore and a *x* zygote.

Ans.

Zoospore	*x zygote*
1. It is the reproductive structure or a gamete.	1. It is the fusion product of the gametes.
2. The gamete with mobility is called zoospore. It is a male gamete.	2. It is a single celled structure.
3. It fuses with oospore (female gamete) to form zygote.	3. It is the link between gametes and individual. It ensures the continuity of a species between organisms of one generation and the next.

Q. 19. Differentiate between gametogenesis and embryogenesis.

Ans.

Gametogenesis	*Embryogenesis*
1. It is the process of formation of gametes.	1. It is the process of development of embryo.
2. This process may involve one or both types of cell division *i.e. mitosis/meiosis.*	2. This process involves only mitosis cell division.
3. It is the need of formation of gametes in sexual reproduction.	3. It is the need of formation of adult like individual in sexual reproduction.
4. Two types of gametes are produced.	4. It may take place inside or outside the body of female parent.

Q. 20. Why are offsprings of oviparous animals at a greater risk as compared to offsprings of viviparous animals?

Ans. Offsprings of oviparous have poor embryonic care and protection as compared to the viviparous animals offspring. Hence, they are at greater risk survival because of predators and environment.

LONG ANSWER QUESTIONS (LA)

Q. 1. What are the events that take place in sexual reproduction? Briefly describe any *one.*

Ans. The events that take place in sexual reproduction can be described as follows:

Events in sexual reproduction
- 1. Pre-fertilisation events
- 2. Fertilisation
- 3. Post-fertilisation events

1. **Pre-fertilisation events :**

It includes all those events that take place before the fusion of gametes. These are:

Events in sexual reproduction
- (*a*) Gametogenesis
- (*b*) Gamete transfer

(*a*) **Gametogenesis:** It is the process of formation of gametes by sexually mature (parent) individual. There are two individuals (parents) of opposite sex involved in sexual reproduction. Therefore, two types of gametes are produced by individuals. *i.e.* male gamete and female gamete.

Gamete
- Male gamete — These are often called sperms or antherozoids in (plants).
- Female gamete — These are often called egg/ovum.

It happens in *heterogametes*.

In homogametes. The two gametes are so similar in appearance that it is not easily possible to identify them as male/female gamete. Hence, they are called homogametes/isogametes *e.g. cladophora* (alga).

The production of gametes is done by mitotic cell division in a haploid (n) parent and by meiotic cell division in diploid (2n) parent. Gametes produced by either ways of cell division have a single set (n) of chromosomes.

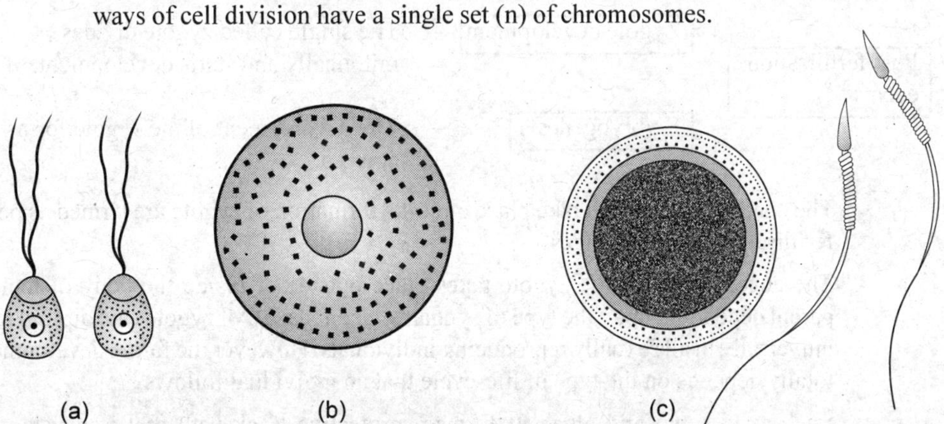

Fig. 1.3 Types of gametes: (*a*) Isogametes of cladophora, (b) Heterogametes of Fucus, (*c*) Heterogametes of human.

(*b*) **Gamete transfer:** After the formation of gametes the next step is their transfer. To ensure it, plants and animals have developed and are adopted to different types of methods. In plants like algae, broyophytes and pteridophytes, the plant need water medium for gamete transfer. Also the male gametes are usually motile and female gametes stationery; male gametes may have flagella to help the mobility (*e.g.* isogamete of cladophora). In higher plants (seed plants), gamete transfer is done by pollination process by various pollinating agencies.

In case of dioecious animals, animals mate or copulate. During this process in frogs the sperms are released outside the female body but in dog/cattle it is released inside the female reproductive track.

OR

2. **Fertilisation (Syngamy) event.**

The process of fusion of gametes (male & female) is called syngamy/fertilisation. During this male and female nuclei fuse to form restore 2n status. This act can be of 2 types.

Fertilisation → External fertilisation — The syngamy takes place outside the female body e.g. frogs, bony fishcs.

Fertilisation → Internal fertilisation — The syngamy takes place inside the female body *e.g.* dog, cattle, human.

In case of external fertilisation the organisms show great synchrony between the sexes and release large number of gametes (male and female) in order to increase the chances of syngamy. In second case, however, the number of eggs produced is significantly reduced but the number of sperms released is more. In plants pollen grains germinate and give out pollen tube that carries male gametes to the egg inside the ovary in seed plants. Their fusion results in triple fusion and double fertilisation. It results in formation of *zygote* (2n).

OR

3. **Post-fertilisation events.**

Post-fertilisation events → Zygote development — The single celled zygote divides mitotically and starts development.

Post-fertilisation events → Embryogenesis — The development of the zygote forms embryo.

The changes/events that take place after the formation of zygote are termed as post-fertilisation events/changes.

The development of the zygote takes place outside or inside the body of female parent depending upon the type of syngamy taken place. All zygotes are diploid (2n) universally in all sexually reproducing individuals. However the future development totally depends on the type of life-cycle that an individual follows.

Such as in fungi and algae. It forms a protective thick wall that is resistant to dessication and damage by decay and it rests before its germination.

In haploid individuals—zygotic meiosis takes place to form haploid spores that germinate as haploid individuals. In animals the zygote develops into an embryo by mitosis cell division.

Embryogenesis involves cell division (mitosis) and cell differentiation. This results in formation of germinal layers (3 layers) in higher animals, human to form various organs of the body in an embryo. It is called morphogenesis. In viviparous embryo forms foetus and then adult like individual that develops inside the body of the female parent (mother) *e.g.* human, cow, etc. In reptiles and birds the embryo develops inside an egg that has a protective hard calcareous shell. Such animals are called *oviparous*/ egg layers.

In flowering plants, following changes are seen.

The zygote is formed inside the ovule.

1. Sepals (calyx) — shed off in most cases.
2. Petals (corolla) — dry and shed off.
3. Stamens — dry and shed off.
4. Pistil — ovary develops into the fruit and the ovules develop into seeds.

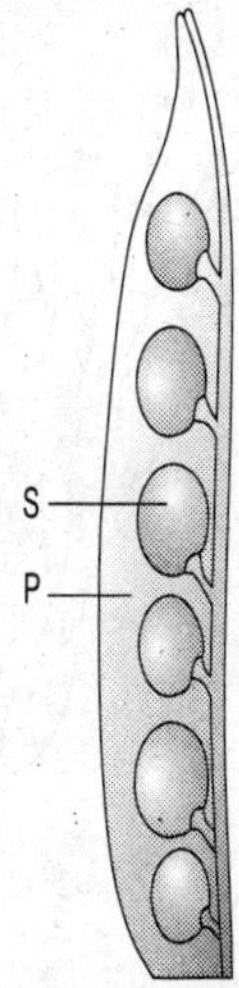

Fig. 1.4 Fruit pea-pod with seeds.

Q. 2. Describe the post-fertilisation changes in a flower.

Ans. Refer to above answer.

NUTSHELL | MINDMAP

Asexual reproduction

Individual —(Cell division / Propagules)→ Offsprings

Sexual reproduction

Male individual → Male gamete

(Gametogenesis) → Fertilization → Zygote → Embyo → Offspring

Female individual → Female gamete

HIGHER ORDER THINKING SKILLS QUESTIONS (HOTS)

1. Mention the factors that are responsible to decide how an organism reproduce. (VSA)
2. Study the following figures—

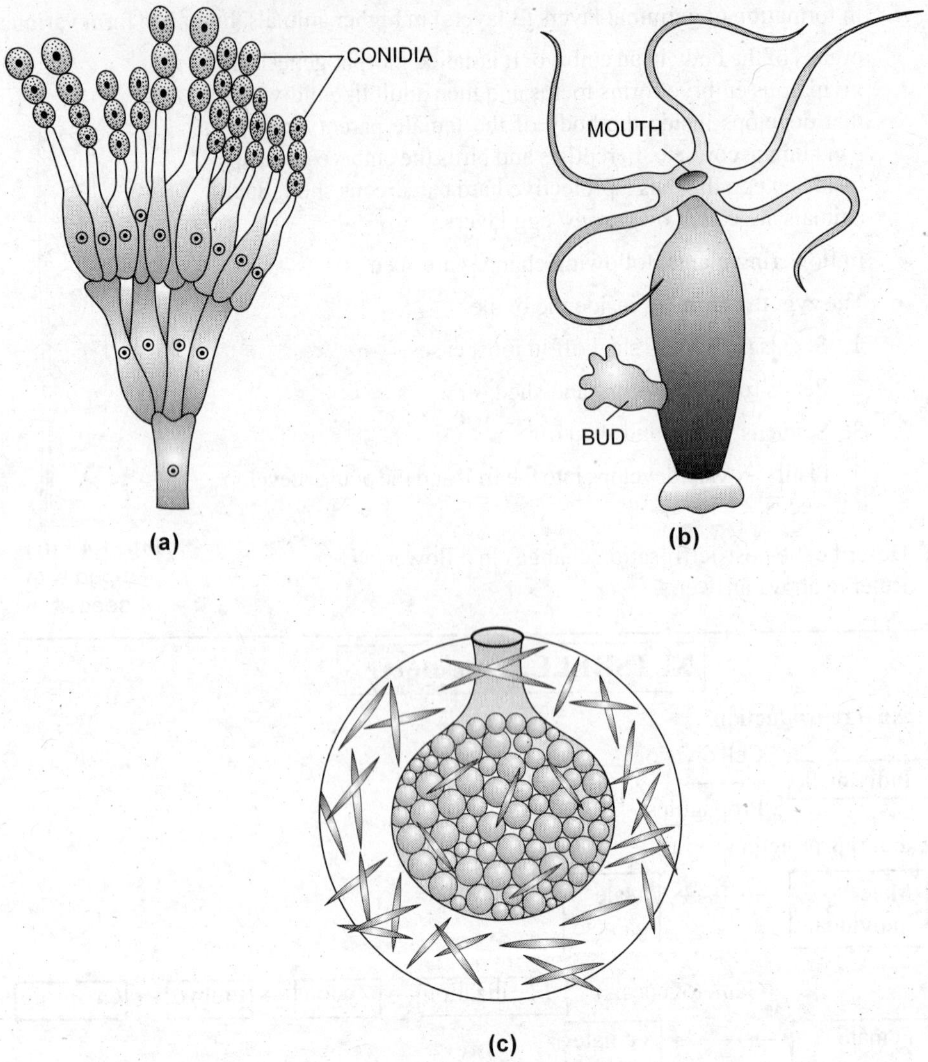

Fig. 1.5

   (*i*) What is common to these structures or organisms?

   (*ii*) Name the structures that help in reproduction. (SAII)

3. What is 'Terror of Bengal'? Mention in brief why this saying is prevalent for which plant & why? (SAII)
4. Birds are seen to lay eggs during particular season only *i.e.* they are seasonal layers. But poultry birds in captivity lay eggs throughout the year. How and why? (SAII)
5. What is common to cucurbits and coconuts, papaya and date palm? (VSA)
6. Briefly comment on the following figure shown in reference to its sexuality.

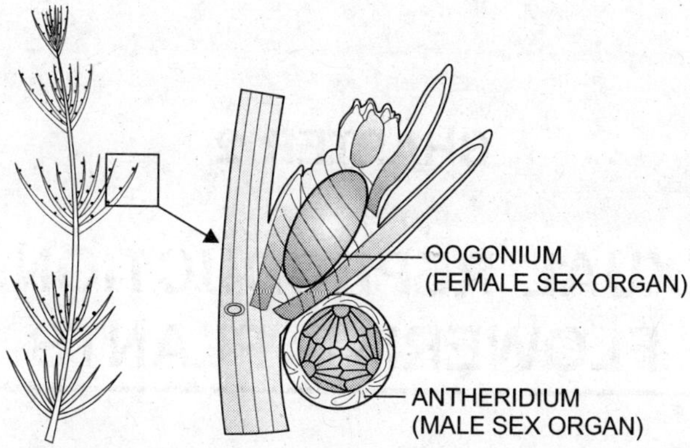

Fig. 1.6

7. Name the phenomenon that is common to these organisms in reference to absence of syngamy. (Honey bee, rotifer, turkey). (VSA)

❑❑❑

CHAPTER 2

SEXUAL REPRODUCTION IN FLOWERING PLANTS

Chapter Outline

- Flower:—A fascinating organ of angiosperms
- Pre-fertilisation:—Structure and events
- Double fertilisation
- Post-fertilisation: Structure and events
- Apomixis and polyembryony

ASSESSMENT QUESTIONS

VERY SHORT ANSWER TYPE QUESTIONS (VSA)

Q. 1. How would you define a flower being a biologist?

Ans. A flower is a reproductive structure of a flowering plant, which is a morphological and embryological marvel and a site of sexual reproduction.

Q. 2. Define the term dithecous.

Ans. Dithecous means a structure having two layers or theca.

Q. 3. Name the tissue present in young anther.

Ans. Sporogenous tissue.

Q. 4. Name the processes that help the release of pollen grains.

Ans. Dehydration of anther tissue and dehiscence of anther.

Q. 5. Which organic materials constitute exine and intine of a pollen grain?

Ans. (*i*) Exine — sporopollenin (*ii*) Intine — cellulose, pectin.

Q. 6. Name the plant responsible for pollen allergy in India.

Ans. **Parthenium** (carrot grass).

Q. 7. Define the terms— Syncarpous or Apocarpus.

Ans. **Syncarpous :** The fused condition of pistils is called syncarpous.

Apocarpus : The free condition of pistils is called apocarpus.

Q. 8. Which cell division forms embryo sac or female gametophyte?

Ans. Meiosis — reduction division.

Q. 9. What is the number of megaspores produced in a ovule (megasporangium)? How many are functional?

Ans. Four, one.

Q. 10. Name the parts of an angiospermic flower in which development of male and female gametophyte takes place.

Ans. Anther and ovule.

Q. 11. Arrange the following terms in the correct developmental sequence.

Pollen grain, sporagenous tissue, microspore tetrad, pollen mother cell, male gametes.

Ans. Sporagenous tissue, microspore tetrad, pollen mother cell (PMC), pollen grain, male gametes.

Q. 12. What is egg apparatus?

Ans. The three cells grouped together at the micropolar end of the embryo sac is called egg apparatus.

Q. 13. Mention the nucleus and cell status of an anigiosperm embryo sac at maturity.

Ans. 8-nucleated and 7-celled.

Q. 14. Mention one difference between chasmogamous and cleistogamous flower.

Ans.

Chasmogamous	*Cleistogamous*
A flower with exposed anther and stigma is chasmogamous flower.	A flower that does not open (*i.e.* anther and stigma is not exposed) is cleistogamous flower.

Q. 15. What are corn cob tussles/silk hair like structures?

Ans. These structures are stigma and style of corn cob (that wave in wind to trap pollen grains).

Q. 16. Mention two strategies evolved to prevent self-pollination in flowers.

Ans. 1. Release of pollens is not synchronised with maturity of stigma in a flower.
2. Different positions (height) of anthers and stigma in a flower.

Q. 17. What is meant by monosporic development of female gametophyte?

Ans. The method of formation of embryo sac from a single megaspore is called monosporic development.

Q. 18. If emasculation is to be done, in which flower it can be done, unisexual or bisexual?

Ans. Bisexual flower.

Q. 19. Define scutellum.

Ans. The single cotyledon in the embryo of grass family is called scutellum.

Q. 20. Define perisperm.

Ans. The residual, persistant nucellus present in a seed is called perisperm .*e.g.* black pepper, beet.

SHORT ANSWER TYPE QUESTIONS (SA I, II)

Q. 1. Explain the role of tapetum in the formation of pollen grain wall.

Ans. The microsporangium has four walls. The innermost wall/layer is called tapetum. It nourishes the developing pollen grains.

Q. 2. What is pollen grain? How long are they viable? Mention its economic importance.

Ans. Pollen grain is the representative-male gametophyte. The viability of the pollen depends on the pepleices. Some pollens live for 30 mins of their release *e.g.* wheat, rice. Others live for months as in some members of leguminoseae, solanceae, etc.

Pollen grains are rich in nutrients such as honey and pollen tablets used as food supplements.

Q. 3. Differentiate between microsporogenesis and megasporogenesis. Which type of cell division occurs during these events? Name the structured formes at the end of these two events.

Ans.

Microsporogenesis	*Megasporogenesis*
1. The formation of microspores (pollen) from pollen mother cell (PMC) is called microsporogenesis.	1. The formation of megaspores from megaspore mother cell (MMC) is called megasporogenesis.
2. It takes place in sporogenous tissue in anther (male reproductive part) of a flower.	2. It takes place in ovule of pistil (the female part) of a flower.

3. Meiotic cell division takes place during both the processes. Microsporogenesis results in formation of pollen grains and megasporogenesis results in formation of embryo sac.

Q. 4. Label the following figure by using the terms given. Mention the role of each part labelled. Embryo sac, micropyle, funicle, nucellus, integuments.

Ans.

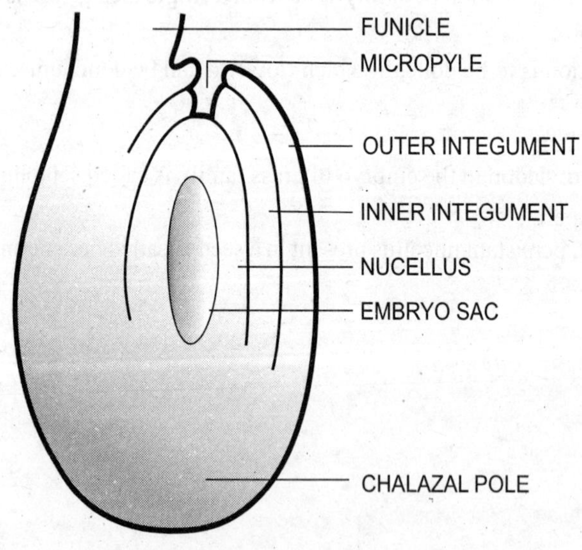

Fig. 2.1

Role of parts of ovule:

1. **Funicle:** The stalls that attaches the ovule to placenta.
2. **Integuments:** One/Two protective envelopes that protect the ovule.
3. **Nucellus:** The reserve food store for developing embryo sac..
4. **Micropyle:** The aperture for oxygen and water during germination.
5. **Embryo sac:** The female gametophyte that develops into embryo.

Q. 5. Define pollination. Briefly mention the different kinds of pollination.

Ans. The (process of) transfer of pollen grains from the anther to the stigma of a pistil is called pollination.

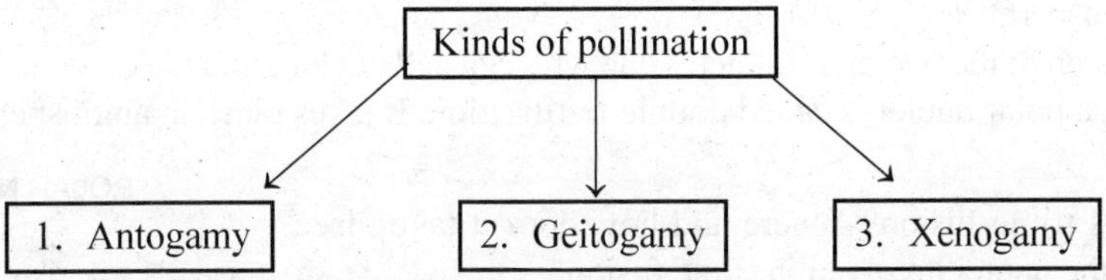

1. **Autogamy:** The pollination process that takes place within the same flower is called autogamy. (auto-self, gamy-marriage). It takes place when both anthers and stigma mature at same time and they lie close to each other.
2. **Geitogamy:** The pollination in which the pollen transfer takes place from anther of a flower to stigma of another flower of same plant.
3. **Xenogamy:** The pollination in which the pollen transfer takes place from anther of a flower to stigma of a flower of a different plant. Only this type of pollination brings genetically different pollens.

Q. 6. What are chasmogamous flowers? Can cross pollination occur in cleistogamous flowers? Give reasons for your answer.

Ans. The flowers that have exposed anthers and stigma are called as chasmogamous flowers. Cross pollination does not occur in cleistogamous flowers. As for the cross pollination to take place both anthers and stigma must be exposed. But in these flowers the flowers does not open, it is closed. Hence the process of cross pollination does not take place.

Q. 7. What is pollen-pistil interaction? What is its significance?

Ans. Pollen-pistil is a dynamic process. It involves the transfer of right pollen (compatible pollen of the same species as the stigma) to right stigma and the acceptance of the stigma. It leads to fertilisation process. It is of significance because compatibility leads to fertilisation and seed formation incompatibility does not allow the fertilisation process and hence the seed formation. Both wrong type of pollen (in compatible) and right type (compatible) of pollen lands on stigma but the chemical communication–interaction only promotes/prevents the post-pollination changes.

Q. 8. What is self-incompatibility? Why does self-pollination not lead to seed formation in self-incompatibility species?

Ans. It is a genetic mechanism in flowers that prevents the self-pollen (from the same flower or other flowers of the same plant) from fertilising the ovules by inhibiting pollen germination or pollen type growth in the pistil of the flower.

This mechanism does not lead to seed formation. Because the pollen germination does not take place or if it does, pollen tube growth is inhibited in pistil as a result of its the male gametes which are carried by the pollen tube do not reach the female gamete and fertilisation does not take place.

Q. 9. What is bagging technique? How is it useful in a plant breeding programme?

Ans. The method of covering with a bag the emasculated flowers is called bagging technique. It's useful as it prevents contamination of stigma with unwanted pollens. When the flower/stigma attains maturity then nature pollens are collected and dusted on it and rebagged.

Q. 10. What is meant by emasculation? When and why does a plant breeder employ this technique?

Ans. Emasculation is the process of removal of anthers from the flowers bud with the help of forceps. If plant breeder uses this technique during artificial hybridisation, it is done so to ensure that only the desired pollen grains are used for pollination and the stigma is protected from unwanted pollen *i.e.* contamination.

Q. 11. Define double fertilisation? In which plants does it take place, bryophytes, pteridophytes or angiosperms?

Ans. The fusion of the two male gametes one with egg cell nucleus and the other male gamete with two polar nuclei is called double fertilisation. It takes place in angiosperms.

Q. 12. What is triple fusion? Where and how does it take place? Name the nuclei involved in triple fusion.

Ans. The process of fusion of a male gamete with two polar nuclei in the central cell is called triple fusion. It takes place in the embryo sac. It takes place by fusion of one male gamete (n) and two polar nuclei (n). Polar nuclei, male gamete nuclei.

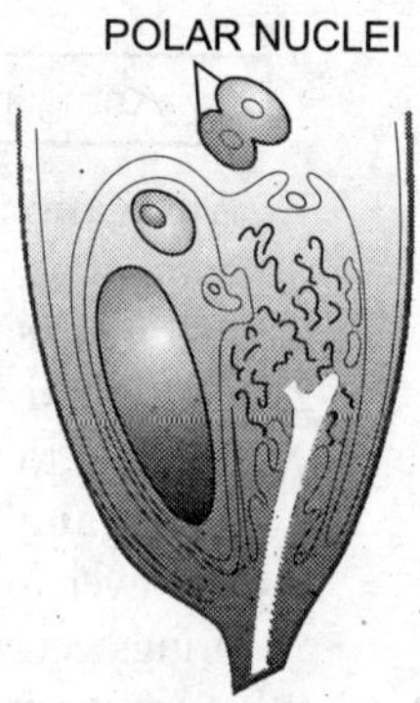

Fig. 2.2

Q. 13. Mention the end products of—

(*i*) Syngamy (*ii*) Triple fusion, ploidy and their fate.

Ans.

Activity	*End products*	*Ploidy*	*Fate*
(*i*) Syngamy	Zygote	2n	It gives rise to embryo.
(*ii*) Triple fusion	Primary endosperm nucleus (PEN)	2n	It gives rise to endosperm.

Q. 14. Why do you think the zygote is dominant for sometime in a fertilised ovule? (*NCERT*)

Ans. It is so because it has to divide and give rise to embryo only after formation certain amount of endosperm. If not done so it will not give rise to embryo because of deficiency of nutrients.

Q. 15. Draw a section of a monocot seed and label the following— coleoptile, coleorrhiza. What are these structures?

Ans. (*i*) **Coleopitile :** The hollow foliar structure that encloses few leaf primodia and shoot apex is called coleoptile.

(*ii*) **Coleorhiza :** The undifferentiated sheath that encloses the radical and root cap is called coleorhiza.

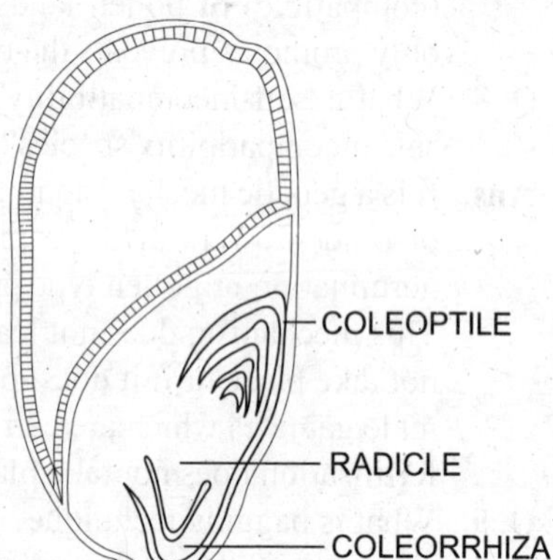

Fig. 2.3

Q. 16. Reason out why some fruits are categorised as—

(*a*) False fruits (*b*) True fruits

(*c*) Parthenocarpic fruits. Give one example to each category.

Ans.

Category	*Reason*	*Example*
(*a*) False fruit	Fruit formation is due to inclusion of other part of flower other than ovary, such as thalamus.	Apple
(*b*) True fruit	Fruit formation is from ovary.	Guava
(*c*) Parthenocarpic fruit	Fruit formation is without the event of fertilisation.	Banana

Q. 17. Why is apple called a false fruit? Which part(s) of the flower forms the fruit?

Ans. Apple is called a false fruit because it is thalamus of the flower that involved in its formation. Normally the fruit formation is only from ovary.

Q. 18. If one can induce parthenocarpy through the application of growth substances, which fruits would you select to induce partharocary and why?

Ans. Banana. These fruits do not have seeds. Such fruits are of economical value and liked by human as some are seedless and edible.

Q. 19. What is apomixis and what is its importance?

Ans. The method of formation of seeds without the event of fertilisation is called apomixis. It is used for production of less expensive hybrid seeds that can be used to raise crops.

Q. 20. Define polyembryony. Name a few examples of it.

Ans. The occurance of more than one embryo in a (ovule) seed is called polyembryony. Citrus fruits (lemon, orange), mango.

LONG ANSWER TYPE QUESTIONS (LA)

Q. 1. With a neat, labelled diagram, describe the parts of a typical angiosperm ovule. (*NCERT*)

Ans.

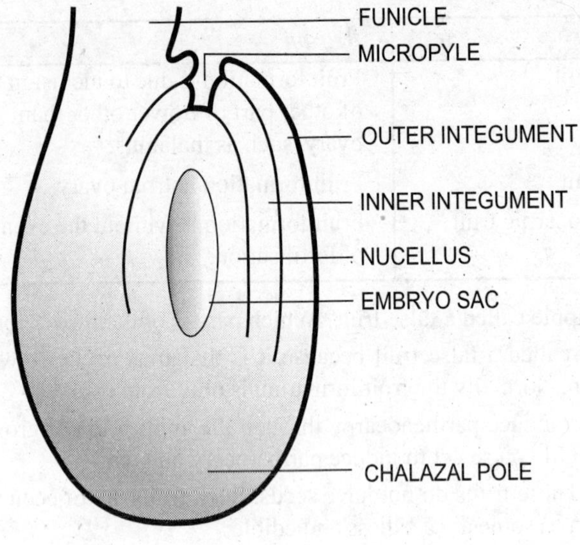

Fig. 2.3

Parts of a typical angiosperm ovule.

Inside the ovary of the pistil is one or many ovules in an angiospermic flower. The ovule is also called as megasporangium. A sectional view of a typical anatropous ovule shows following parts.

1. **Hilum :** It is the region where the body of the ovules fuses with the funicle. It represents the fusi between these two.
2. **Funicle :** This is the stalk by means of which the ovule remains attached to the placenta.
3. **Integuments :** The ovule has one or two protective covers/envelops called integuments. (They encircle the ovule completely except at the tip (in anatropos) where a small opening is formed.) The integument towards inside or which is closer to ovule is inner integument and the one away from it is called outer integument.
4. **Micropyle :** The small opening is called micropyle. It is formed by the space left by integuments.
5. **Nucleus :** The integument encloses the mass of cells. These cells are laden with rich reserve food materials that is utilised by the developing embryo sac or female gametophyte. This part is called nucellus.
6. **Chalaza :** The portion opposite to the micropylar end is chalaza. In an antropous ovule it forms the basal part.

Q. 2. With a neat diagram explain the 7-celled, 8-nucleate nature of the female gametophyte.

Ans. Female gametophyte or embryo sac

In side the nucleus is present the female gametophyte or embryo sac in an angiospermic ovule. An ovule generally has a single embryo sac which is formed from a single megaspore through reduction division.

In general out of the 4 megaspores (tetrad) only one is functional as female gametophyte and it has 7-cells and 8 nuclei. The detailed structure is—

1. **Mitotic divisions :** In a functional megaspore the first mitotic division takes place to form 2 nuclei that move to opposite poles. (*2 nucleate embryo sac stage*). It is followed by 2 more sequential mitotic nuclear divisions resulting in the formation of (4 nucleated and then) *8-nucleated embryo sac stage.*

   Note : No cell wall is laid before these stages. After the 8-nucleated stage cell walls are laid to form the embryo sac.

2. **Distribution of nuclei :** 6 nuclei from the eight nuclei formed are organised into cells at micropyler end and chalazal ends as—

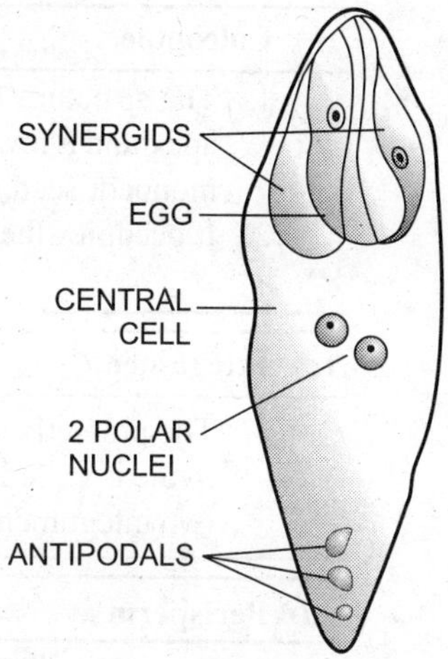

Fig. 2.4

   (*i*) **Micropylar end** - 2 synergids and 1 egg cell this assembly is called egg apparatus.

   (*ii*) **Chalazal end** - 3 antipodal cells.

The 2 polar nuclei in the centre form the central cell.

This complete structure of embryo sac/female gametophyte is a typical embryo sac at maturity with 8-nuclei and 7-cells.

Q. 3. Define the terms—

(*a*) Seed (*b*) Albuminous seed (*c*) Non-albuminous seed

What are the advantages of seeds to angiosperms?

Ans. (*a*) **Seed :** It is the final product of sexual reproduction that encloses a futenistic embryo.

(*b*) **Albuminous seed :** A seed that retains a part of endosperm during embryonic development is called albuminous seed. *e.g.* wheat.

(*c*) **Non albuminous seed :** A seed that does not retain endosperm due to its complete consumption by the developing embryo is called non-albuminous seed .*e.g.* pea.

Advantages of seed to angiosperms

1. Seeds are dependable on water for its germination.
2. They are adapted for dispersal to new habitats and help the species to colonise in other areas.
3. Store reserve food required for developing seedlings.
4. They protect the embryo within by a protective hard seed coat.
5. They are the source of genetic variations
6. Dormant seeds are source of food to human and used to raise crop.
7. Some seeds have long life span.
   (*e.g.* 100 to 1000-10,000 years).

Q. 4. Differentiate between—

(*a*) Hypocotyl and epicotyl. (*b*) Coleoptile and coleorrhiza.

(*c*) Integument and testa. (*d*) Perisperm and pericarp.

Ans. (*a*)

Hypocotyl	**Epicotyl**
1. The portion of embryonal axis below the level of cotyledons is called hypocotyl.	1. The portion of embryonal axis above the level of cotyledons is called epicotyl.
2. This region has root tip or radicle at the lower end.	2. This region has shoot tip or plumule at the tip.

(*b*) **Coleoptile**	**Coleorrhiza**
1. The structure that covers the shoot apex and a few leaf primordia in monocot seed is called coleoptile. 2. It occupies the upper portion of the seed.	1. The structure that covers the radical and root cap in monocot seed is called coleorrhiza. 2. It occupies the lower portion of the seed.

(*c*) **Integument**	**Testa**
1. The protective covering of the ovule is called integument. There are two integuments.	1. The outermost integument harden and forms a tough protective covering called testa.

(*d*) **Perisperm**	**Pericarp**
1. The residual, persistant nucellus of a seed is called perisperm.	1. The ovary wall that forms the fruit wall is called pericarp.

NUTSHELL MIND MAP

1. Flower → Anther → Microsporogenesis → Pollen grains
   Flower → Pistil → Megasporogenesis → Egg cell

2. Pollen grains → Stigma → Pollen tube → Male gametes

3. Male gamete (n) → Egg cell (n) → Zygote cell (2*n*) → Embryo

   Male gamete (n) → 2 Polar nuclei (n) → Primary endosperm cell

   Triple fusion PEC ↓ Endosperm

4. Zygote → Embryo → Seed
   Primary endosperm cell → Endosperm → Seed

5. Ovule → Seed → Fruit
   Ovary → Fruit → Fruit

HIGHER ORDER THINKING SKILLS QUESTIONS (HOTS)

Q. 1. Name the changes that take place in a shoot/floral primordium, responsible for formation of a flower. (VSA)

Q. 2. Label the section of microsporangium showing these structures: Tapetum, epidermis, microspore mother cell, endothecium. Write their role. (SAII)

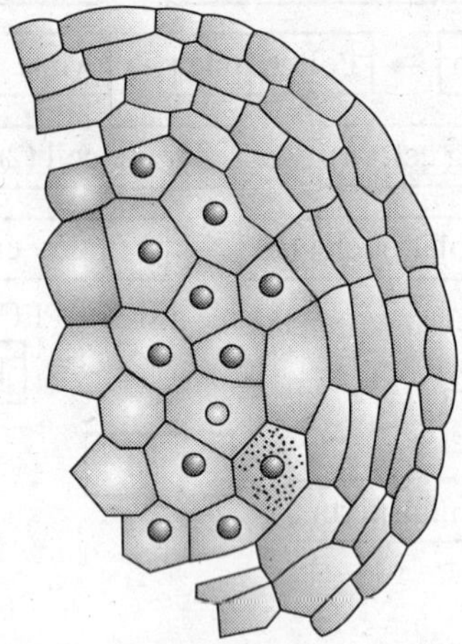

Fig. 2.5

Q. 3. What is exine chemically made of? Mention the importance of this chemical material. (SAI)

Q. 4. Study the following figure. Answer the questions that follow. (SAII)

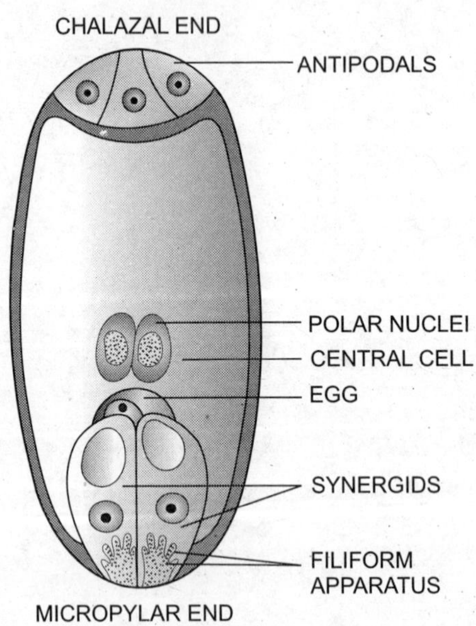

Fig. 2.6

(*a*) What is this structure called?

(*b*) Where does this structure develop?

(*c*) What does the fertilisation of polar nuclei lead to and how?

(*d*) What is the end product after fertilisation of egg?

Q. 5. Mention the location and function of filiform apparatus. (VSA)

Q. 6. Which type of pollination can bring genetically different pollens? (VSA)

Q. 7. What do you understand by inbreeding depression? Briefly give the out breeding devices in angiosperms. (LA)

Q. 8. Write in brief about the following. (SAII)

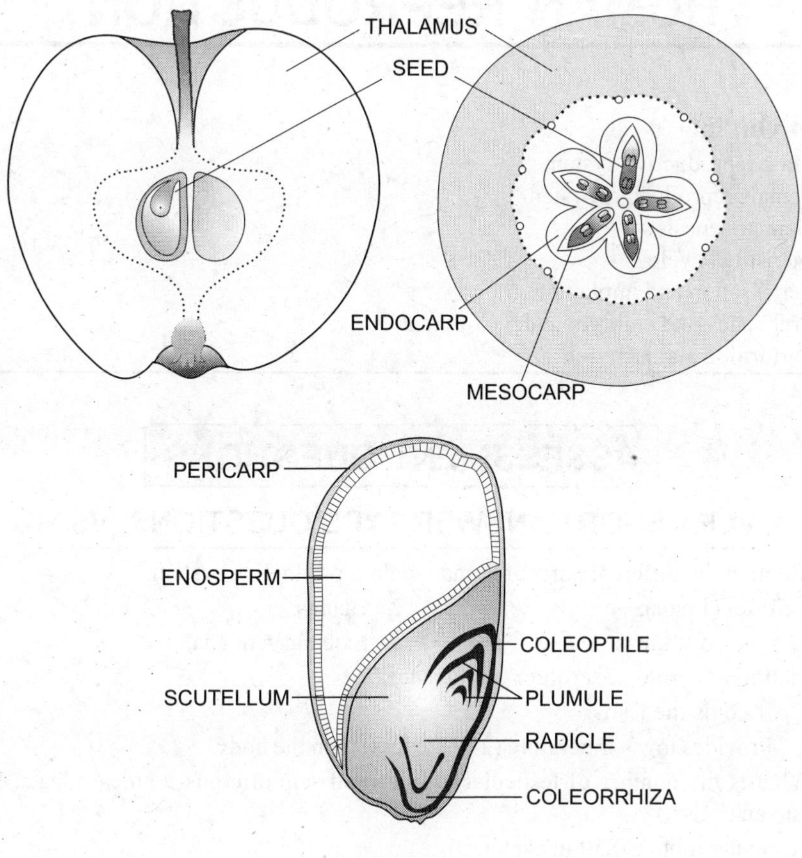

Fig. 2.7

Q. 9. Define hybrids. Mention its one disadvantage regarding its cultivation or use. (VSA)

❑❑❑

CHAPTER 3

HUMAN REPRODUCTION

Chapter Outline

- Male reproductive system
- Female reproductive system
- Gametogenesis
- Menstrual cycle
- Fertilisation and implantation
- Pregnancy and embryonic development
- Parturition and lactation

ASSESSMENT QUESTIONS

VERY SHORT ANSWER TYPE QUESTIONS (VSA)

Q. 1. Mention the different parts of human male reproductive system.

Ans. 1. Testes (1 pair), 2. Glands, 3. Accessory ducts 4. External genitalia.

Q. 2. Mention the role of scrotum/scrotal sacs.

Ans. 1. It holds the testis.

2. Provides low temperature (2-2.5°c less) than the body.

Q. 3. What is the number of testicular lobules and seminiferous tubules in each lobule in human testis?

Ans. Testicular lobules-250 in each testis.

Semineferous tubules in each lobule-1-3.

Q. 4. Mention the cells that are present on inner layer of semineferous tubules.

Ans. 1. Male germ cells (spermatogonia) 2. Sertoli cells.

Q. 5. What are these structures collectively called?

Vasa efferentia, rete testis, epididymis and vas deferens.

Ans. Human male sex accessory ducts.

Q. 6. What is urethral meatus?

Ans. It is the external opening of urethra at the penis.

Q. 7. What are the two zones of stroma of human ovary?

Ans. 1. Peripheral cortex 2. Inner medulla.

Q. 8. How is birth canal formed?

Ans. The birth canal is formed from—

1. Cervical canal and
2. Vagina.

Q. 9. Write the function of: 1. Endometrium 2. Myometrium in human female.

Ans. Uterine wall Function:

1. **Endometrium**—cyclic changes during menstrual cycle.
2. **Myometrium**—strong contration during delivery of the child. (child birth).

Q. 10. What are these structures/parts collectively known?

Mons pubis, labia majora, labia minora, hymen and clitoris.

Ans. Human female external genitalia.

Q. 11. At what age or stage does the spermatogenesis start in a male individual?

Ans. At puberty.

Q. 12. Name the hormones that maintain the functions of male sex accessory ducts and glands.

Ans. Testicular hormones (androgens).

Q. 13. At what stage/age does the oogenesis initiate in human female?

Ans. Embryonic development.

Q. 14. Name the ovarian hormone that is high during ovulation in human female.

Ans. Esterogen.

Q. 15. At which phase of menstrual cycle the hormone level of progesterone is high?

Ans. Leutal phase (secretory phase).

Q. 16. Mention the hormone released by pituitary that induces rupture of Graafian follicle and then its release.

Ans. LH (Luteinising hormone).

Q. 17. Which event does block the entry of additional sperms into an ovum?

Ans. Fertilisation process.

Q. 18. Mention the end products of second meiotic division of secondary oocyte.

Ans. 1. Second polar body

2. A haploid ovum (ootid).

Q. 19. Fill in the blanks:

(*a*) Humans reproduce ——— (asexually/sexually).

(*b*) Humans are ——— (oviparous, viviparous, ovoviviparous).

(*c*) Fertilisation is ——— in humans (external/internal).

(*d*) Male and female gametes are ——— (diploid/haploid).

(*e*) Zygote is ——— (diploid/haploid).

(*f*) The process of release of ovum from a mature follicle is called ———.

(*g*) Ovulation is induced by a hormone called ———.

(*h*) The fusion of male and female gametes is called ———.

(*i*) Fertilisation takes place in ———.

(*j*) Zygote divides to form ——— which is implanted in uterus.

(*k*) The structure which provides vascular connection between the foetus and uterus is called ———.

Ans. (*a*) sexually (*b*) viviparous (*c*) internal (*d*) haploid

(*e*) diploid (*f*) ovulation (*g*) LH (*h*) fertilisation

(*i*) oviduct (*j*) blastomere (*k*) placenta.

Q. 20. Identify true/false statements. Correct each false statement to make it true.

(*a*) Androgens are produced by sertoli cells. (True/False)

(*b*) Spermatozoa get nutrition from sertoli cells. (True/False) (*c*) Leydig cells are found in ovary. (True/False)

(*d*) Leydig cells synthesis eandrogens. (True/False)

(*e*) Oogenesis takes place in corpus luteum. (True/False)

(*f*) Menstrual cycle ceases during pregnancy. (True/False)

(*g*) Presence or absence of hymen is not a reliable indicator of virginity or no sexual experience. (True/False)

Ans. (*a*) False. It is produced by leydig cells. (*b*) True.

(*c*) False. It is found in human testis. (*d*) True.

(*e*) False. Ovary. (*f*) True. (*g*) True.

Q. 21. Name the hormones involved in regulation of spermatogenesis.

Ans. Gn RH- Gonadotropin releasing hormone → Luteinising Hormone (LH); Follicle Stimulating Hormone (FSH).

Q. 22. What are the major components of seminal plasma?

Ans.

Fluid	*Components*
Seminal plasma	Fructose, calcium enzymes.

Q. 23. What are the major functions of male accessory ducts and glands?

Ans.

Structures	*Major functions*
1. Male accessory ducts. 2. Glands.	1. Store and transport sperms from testis to the outside. 2. Secretion of seminal plasma.

Q. 24. How many eggs do you think were released by the ovary of a female dog which gave birth to 6 puppies?

Ans. 6 eggs.

SHORT ANSWER TYPE QUESTIONS (SA I, SA II)

Q. 1. Draw a labelled diagram of male reproductive system.

Ans.

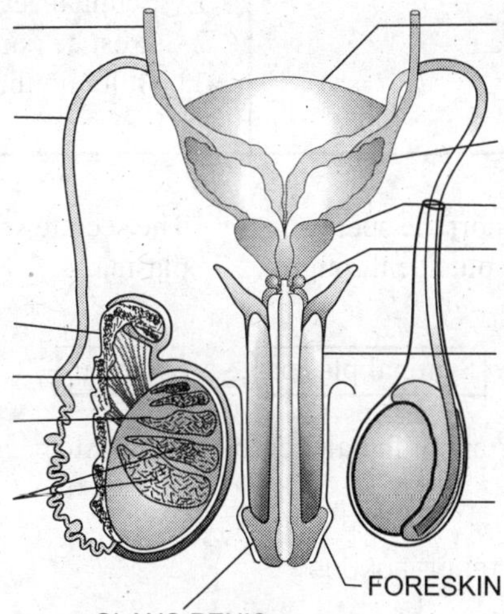

Fig. 3.1

Q. 2. Write the function of the structures labelled in the following figure.

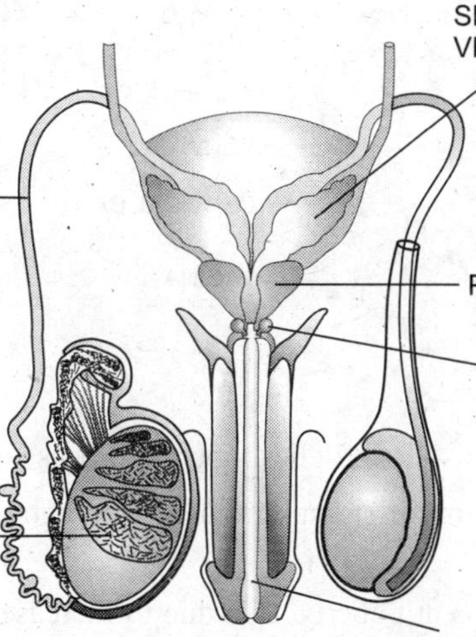

Fig. 3.2

Ans.

Structures	*Functions*
1. Testicular lobules	1. Produce sperms
2. Vas deferens	2. Carry sperms to abdominal cavity
3. Seminal vesicle, prostate and bulbourethral glands	3. Seminal plasma
4. Urethra	4. Conduct sperms outside the body

Q. 3. Mention the human male sex accessory ducts and glands. What is their overall function/ role in reproduction?

Ans.

Male sex accessory ducts	*Male sex accessory glands*
1. Rete testis 2. Vasa efferentia 3. Epididymis 4. Vas deferens	1. Seminal vesicles (paired) 2. Prostate (single) 3. Bulbourethral (paired)
↓	↓
They store and transport the sperms from the testis to the outside through urethra.	The secrete secretion that forms seminal plasma.

Note. Sperms + Seminal plasma → Semen

Q. 4. Draw a labelled diagram of female reproductive system.

Ans.

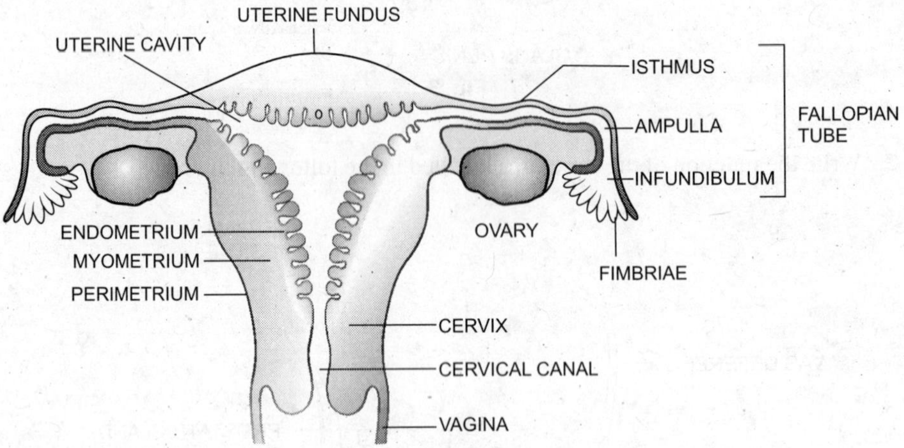

Fig. 3.3

Q. 5. What is spermatogenesis? Briefly describe the process of spermatogenesis.

Ans. The process of formation of sperms from spermatogonia (male germ cells) is called spermatogenesis.

Spermatogenesis begins at puberty. It is due to increase of secretion of gonadotropin releasing hormone (Gn RH). This stimulates the secretion of LH-The luteining hormone and FSH-Follicle Stimulating Hormone. These hormones produce other hormone to stimulate the process.

The spermatogonia present inside the wall of seminiferous tubules multiply by mitotic division and increase in number, some of these under go meiosis division. These are primary spermatocytes. As a result two haploid cells called secondary spermatocytes are formed from each primary spermatogonium. Secondary spermatocytes give rise to 4 haploid spermatids by 2 meiotic division. These cells get transformed into spermatozoa.

Q. 6. Define spermiogenesis and spermiation.

Ans. 1. **Spermiogenesis :** The process of formation of sperms from spermatogonia is called spermatogenesis.

2. **Spermiation :** The process of release of sperns from seminiferous tubules is called spermiation.

Q. 7. Draw a labelled diagram of sperm.

Ans.

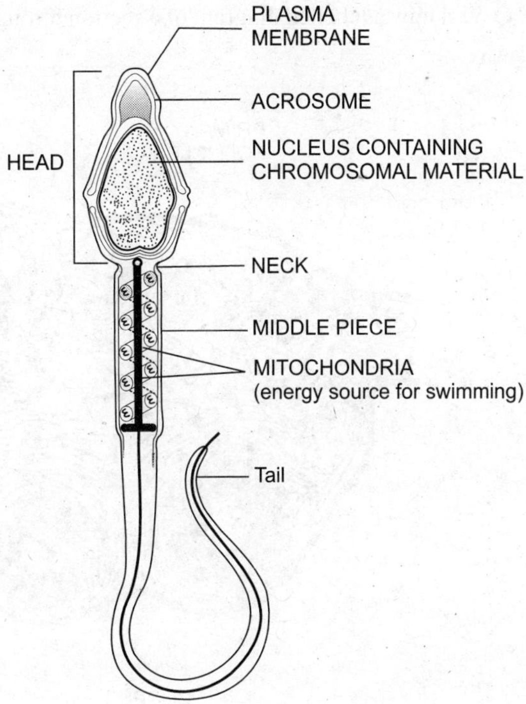

Fig. 3.4. Structure of a sperm.

Q. 8. Study the following figure. Swati had drawn the sectional view of the female reproductive system and labelled it incorrect. Label the same correctly.

Ans.

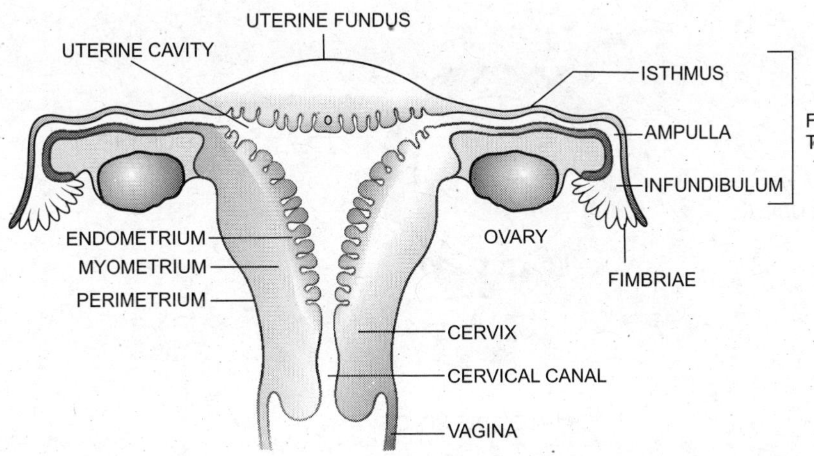

Fig. 3.5

Q. 9. Draw a labelled diagram of a section through ovary.

Ans.

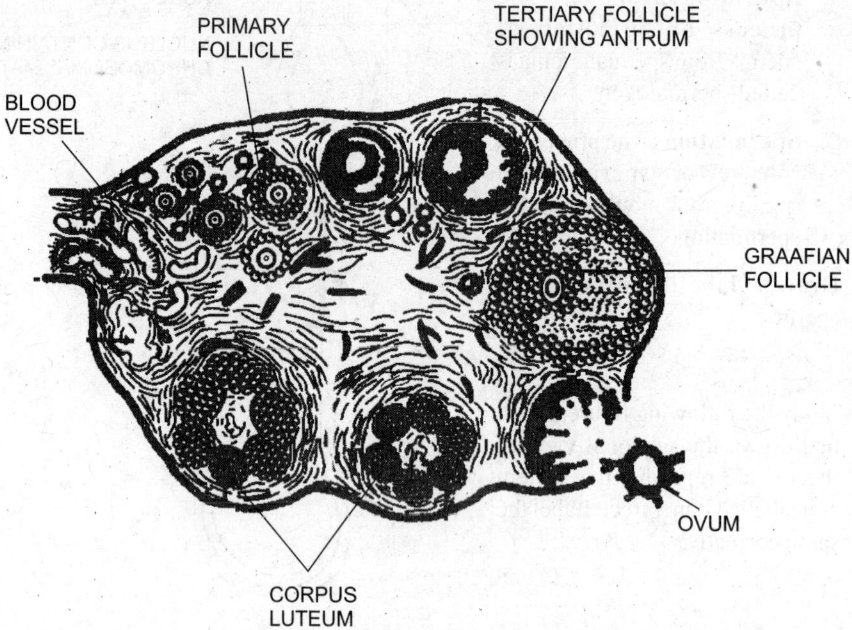

Fig. 3.6. Sectional view of ovary

Q. 10. Draw a labelled diagram of a Graafian follicle.

Ans.

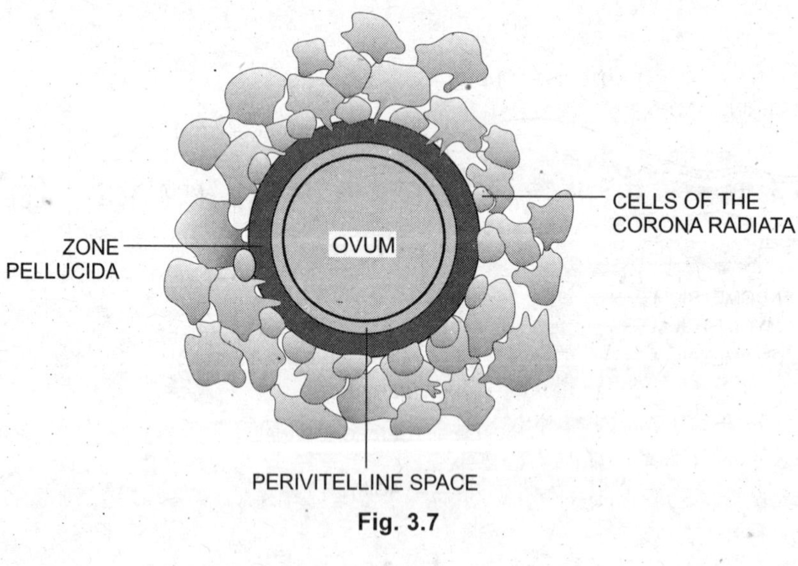

Fig. 3.7

Q. 11. Name the functions of the following.

(*a*) Corpus luteum (*b*) Endometrium (*c*) Acrosome
(*d*) Sperm tail (*e*) Fimbriae

Ans.

Structure	*Functions*
(*a*) Corpus luteum	Secretion of progesterone (ovarian hormone) necessary for maintenance of the endometrium for implantation of fertilised egg (zygote).
(*b*) Endometrium	This develops a cusion for implantation of the fertilised egg.
(*c*) Acrosome	Releases enzymes that dissolve the zonapellucida and the plasma membrane of ovum and helps the sperm to enter into the cytoplasm of ovum. *e.g.* penetration of sperm into ovum.
(*d*) Sperm tail	It helps in the motality of sperm to the ovum.
(*e*) Fimbriae	It helps in collection of ovum after ovulation process.

Q. 12. What is menstrual cycle? Which hormones regulate the menstrual cycle?

Ans. The cyclic events that take place in a human female at an interval of about 28/29 days is called menstrual cycle. It involves—

1. Menstruation 2. Follicular phase 3. Luteal phase 4. Next cycle

Hormones that regulate menstrual cycle

- Ovarian hormones
  - Estrogen
  - Progesterone
- Pituitary Hormones
  - Luteirising hormone (LH)
  - Follicle Stimulating Hormone (FSH)

  (Gonadotropins).

Q. 13. What is the role of trophoblast and inner mass cells?

Ans. 1. **Trophoblast :** It gets attached to the endometrium of uterus.

2. **Inner cell mass :** It gets differentiated in an embryo.

Q. 14. What is the fate of inner cell mass of the blastocyst? Draw a labelled diagram of blastocyst.

Ans. The inner cell mass gets differentiated into embryo. This further differentiates into three germ layers—

1. Ectoderm the outer layer.
2. Endoderm the inner layer.
3. Mesoderm the middle layer.

These layers are called germ layers which give rise to various body organs of the developing embryo. Stem cells are present in this inner cell mass.

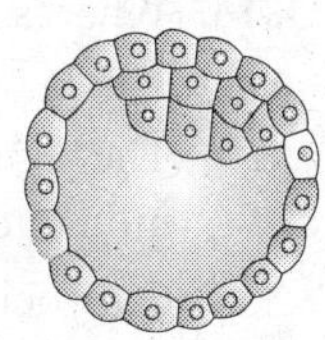

(BLASTOCYST)

Fig. 3.8

Q. 15. What is placenta? Mention its components. Which hormones are secreted by it?

Ans. The tissue that connects between the foetus and maternal body (uterus) is called placenta. It consists of

(*a*) **Chorionic villi** — the part of trophoblast (foetus) and

(*b*) **Uterine tissue** — the part of uterus with maternal blood vessels.

Hormones produced by placenta

1. Human chorionic gonadotropin (HCG)
2. Human placental lactogen (HPL)
3. Oestrogen
4. Progesterone

Q. 16. Draw a figure to show following structures.

(*a*) Developing embryo (*b*) Umbilical cord (*c*) Yolk sac (*d*) Placental villi

Ans.

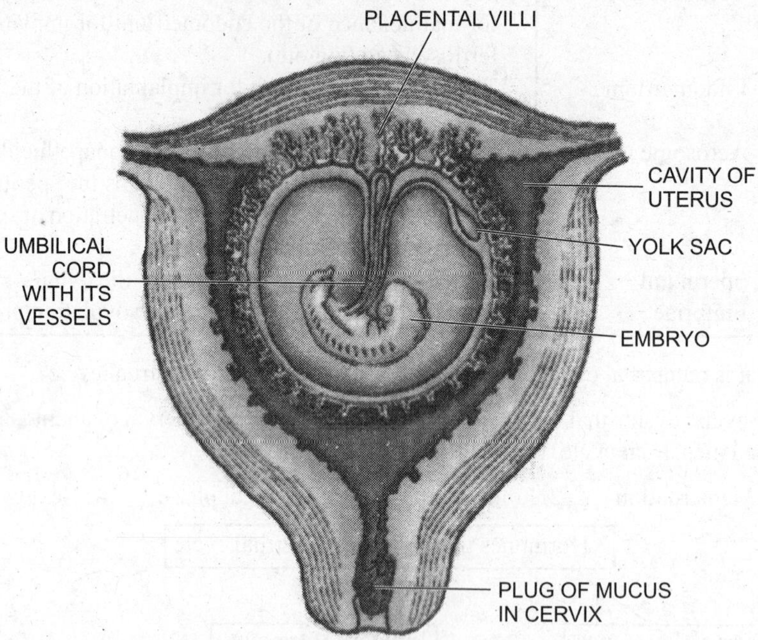

Fig. 3.9. The human foetus within the uterus.

Q. 17. Define the terms— lactation, colostrum. Mention the significance of colostrum.

Ans. The process of production of milk by the mammary glands at the end of pregnancy is called lactation.

The milk produced during the initial days of lactation is called colostrum.

Significance of colostrum.

1. It has antibodies that are essential for the new born babies to develop resistance.
2. It improves the health of the baby.

Q. 18. What is parturition? Which hormones are involved in the induction of parturition?

Ans. The process of child birth is called parturition. It is a complex neuroendocrine process. The signals for this originate from a fully developed foetus and placenta which induce mild interine contractions called foetal ejection index.

Oxcyocin from maternal pituitary gland.

Q. 19. In our society the women are often blamed for giving birth to daughters. Can you explain why this is not correct?

Ans. The sex of the child is determined by the chromosomes that the sperms have. There are two types of sperms—

(*a*) Sperms with *x*-chromosome.

(*b*) Sperms with *y*-chromosome.

When the sperms with x-chromosome fertilises the egg then a zygote with xx chromosomes is formed and this zygote will form a female foetus. On the other hand when the sperm with y-chromosome fertilises the egg then a zygote with xy chromosomes is formed and this zygote will form a male foetus. Therefore, this myth is wrong. The female is not responsible for it.

Q. 20. How many eggs are released by a human ovary in a month? How many eggs do you think would been released if the mother gave birth to identical twins? Would you answer change if the twins born were fraternal?

Ans. Normally one egg is release by a human ovary in a month .

Q. 21. Write two major functions each of testis and ovary.

Ans.

Organs	*Major Functions*
1. Testis	(*i*) **Spermatogenesis** - producing sperms. (*ii*) **Secretion of hormones** - testosterone.
2. Ovary	(*i*) **Oogenesis** - production of ova. (*ii*) **Secretion of hormones** - oestrogen, progesterone.

LONG ANSWER TYPE QUESTIONS (LA)

Q. 1. Describe the structure of seminiferous tubule.

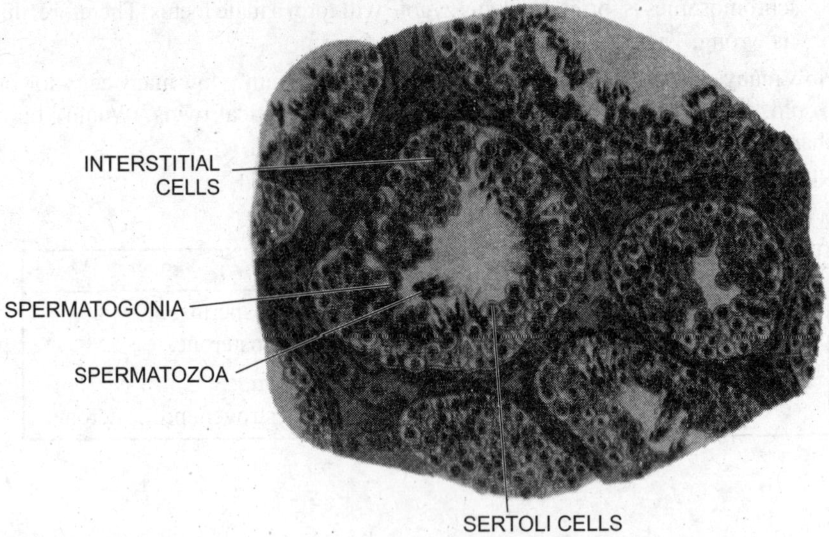

Fig. 3.10(A). Diagrammatic sectional view of seminiferous tubule (Microscopic view).

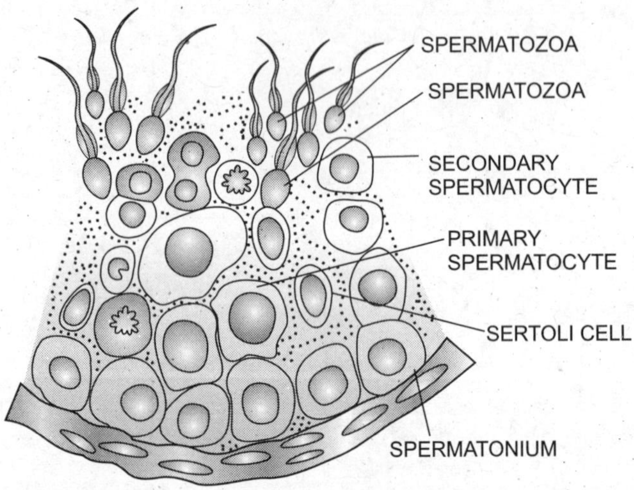

Fig. 3.10(B). Diagrammatic sectional view of a seminiferous tubule (enlarged).

Ans. Testis is a male gonad that produces sperms and male sex hormones. Each testis consists of—

(*i*) **Testicular lobules:** There are about 250 compartments called testicular lobules in each testis.

(*ii*) **Seminiferous tubules:** Each lobule has 1-3 seminiferous tubules.

Section of seminiferous tubule.

1. **Inside the tubule:** Each seminiferous tubule is lined by two types of cells on the inside cavity portion.

(*i*) **Male germ cells:** These cells form the single layer of germinal epithelium cells. These cells are responsible for formation of sperm cells by meiotic division. They are called spermatogonia.

(*ii*) **Sertoli cells:** They are long, conical shaped cells present in between the mass of germ cells. These cells are responsible for providing nutrition to the germ cells and developing spermatids. Spermatids remain attached to these nursing cells.

(*iii*) **Spermatids and spermatozoa:** These are the cells that are produced during the process of spermatogenesis spermatids are products of second meiotic division and remain attached to sertoli cells. Spermatozoa are sperms formed from transformation of spermatids. They occupy the cavity of tubule and are with tail.

2. **Outside the tubule :** The region outside the tubules is called as interstitial spaces. These spaces are packed with interstitial cells (Leydig cells) that secrete testicular hormones (androgens) and immunological competent cells. Blood vessels are also found in these spaces.

Q. 2. Draw a flow chart diagram to represent the scheme of spermatogenesis or oogenesis.

Ans.

	Spermatogenesis	*No. of cells*	*Chromosome No.*
	Spermatogonium	01	46
Mitosis division differentiation	↓		
	Primary Spermatocytes	02	23
1st Meiotic division	↓		
	Secondary Spermatocytes	04	23
2nd Meiotic division	↓		
	Spermatids	04	23
Differentiation	↓		
	Spermatozoa	04	23

Fig. 3.11

OR

	Oogenesis	*Chromosome no.*
	Oogonium	46
Mitosis division and differentiation	↓	
	Primary Oocyte	
1st Meiotic division before ovulation	↓	
	Secondary Oocyte	23
	↓	
	Ovum	

Fig. 3.12

Q. 3. Briefly describe the following events.

(*a*) Menstruation (*b*) Follicular phase (*c*) Luteal phase

Ans. (*a*) **Menstruation:** It is a cyclic event that takes place in human females after every 28/29 days. It starts from the age of puberty till the age of 50 yrs. During the process the disintegrated endometrium, blood vessels and degenerated ovum (unfertilised) is released as a menstrual flow. It lasts upto 3-4 days. The fluid comes out through vagina. The cyclic menstruation is an indicator of normal reproductive phase/and it is in between menarche and menopause. It occurs only when the ovum is unfertilised and if fertilised then it results in pregnancy and absence of menstruation.

(*b*) **Follicular phase:** This phase comes after menstruation. During this phase the primary follicles in the ovary grow to become a fully mature Graafian follicle. The endometrium of uterus regenerates through proliferation. These changes take place under the influence of pituitary and ovarian hormones. These hormones stimulate the development of follicles and attains the peak level in the middle of the cycle-the 14th day. The rapid secretion of LH leads to maximum level during mid cycle and is called LH surge. This induces the release of ovum (ovulation). It marks the end of this follicular phase.

(*c*) **Luteal phase:** After the follicular phase starts the luteal phase. The remaining parts of the Graafian follicle in the ovary gets transformed into corpus luteum. It is yellow in colour. This secretes large amounts of progesterone which is needed for maintenance of the endometrium. It is requirement for implantation of the fertilised egg and then pregnancy. In case of absence of fertilisation, the endometrium degenerates, egg and then pregnancy. In case of absence of fertilisation, the endometrium degenerates, egg degenerates and blood vessels transforms into liquid-menstrual flow. The corpus luteum also degenerates and new menstrual cycle starts.

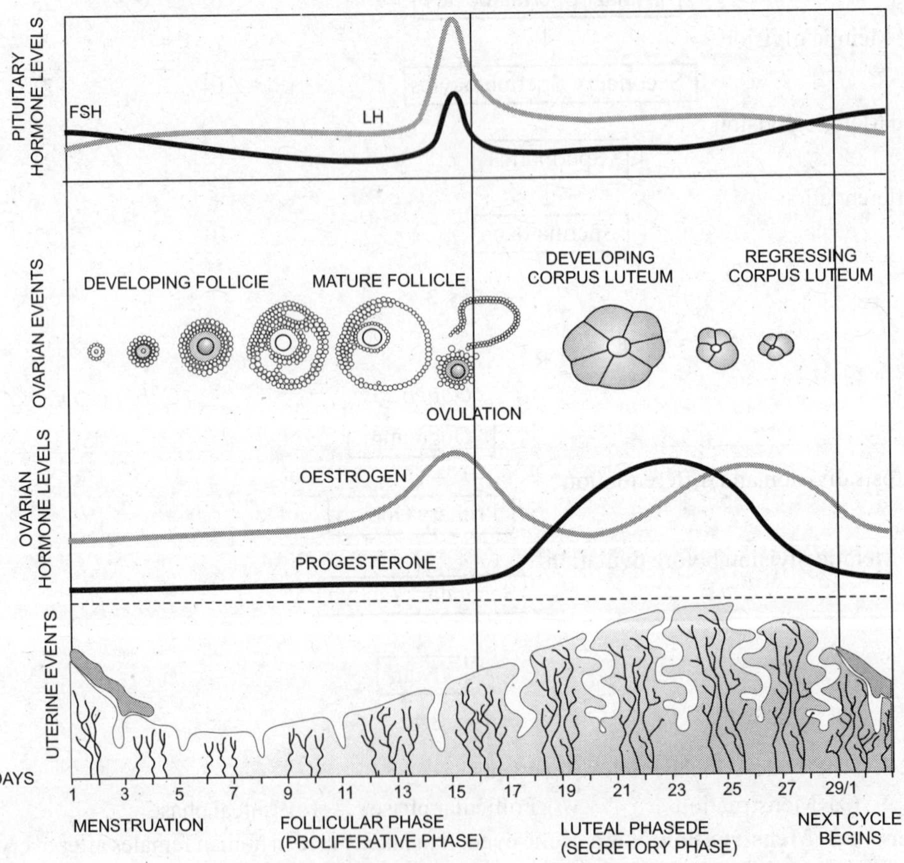

Fig. 3.13

Q. 4. Give a flow chart representation of major features of embryonic development at various months of pregnancy.

Ans.

Pregnancy → 9 months (30 weeks)

One month of Pregnancy ↓	Formation of embryonic heart. Heart sounds produced and can be heard by stethoscope. Indication foetus developing.	Ist Timester By end of this most of the major organs formed.
Second month of Pregnancy ↓	Formation of limbs and digits.	(12 weeks)
5th month of Pregnancy ↓	Formation of hair. First Foetus movements	2nd Timester Fine hair on body, eye lids separate, eye lashes formed.
9th month of Pregnancy	Fully formed foetus. Ready for delivery.	(24 weeks) ↓ Parturition

NUTSHELL MINDMAP

Human Male Reproductive System → Sex accessory ducts; Sex accessory glands

Human Female Reproductive System → Sex accessory ducts; Mammary glands

Menstruation → Follicular phase → Luteal phase → Next cycle starts

Sperm + Ovum → Fertilisation → Implantation → Pregnancy → Pasturition → Lactation

HIGHER ORDER THINKING SKILLS QUESTIONS (HOTS)

Q. 1. Give a suitable reason for presence of testis in scrotal sacs in human male. (VSA)

Q. 2. Mention the roles of- sertoli cells and leydig cells of testis. (VSA)

Q. 3 Name the membrane that envelops the sperm. (VSA)

Q. 4. How does the sperm gets its entry into the ovum? (VSA)

Q. 5. Mention the hormones essential for support of foetal growth metabolic changes in mother and maintenance of pregnancy. (SA I)

Q. 6. Label the following figure and write the role of each labelled part.

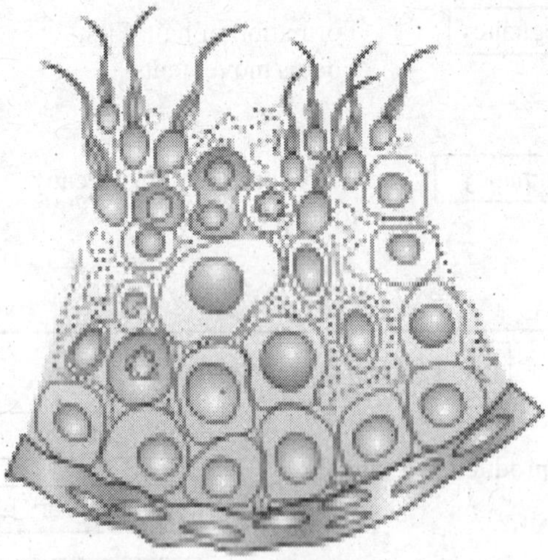

Fig. 3.13

❑❑❑

CHAPTER 4

REPRODUCTIVE HEALTH

Chapter Outline

- Reproductive health: Problems and strategies
- Population explosion and birth control
- Medical termination of pregnancy (MTP)
- Sexually transmitted diseases (STD)
- Infertility

ASSESSMENT QUESTIONS

VERY SHORT ANSWER TYPE QUESTIONS-(VSA)

Q. 1. Define aminocentesis.

Ans. A foetal sex determination test based on the study of chromosomal pattern in the aminotic fluid surrounding the developing embryo is called aminocentosis.

Q. 2. Mention the ideal features of a contraceptive.

Ans. It should be user friendly, easily available, effective and reversible. It should not have any side effects or least side effects.

Q. 3. Mention the natural methods of contraception.

Ans.

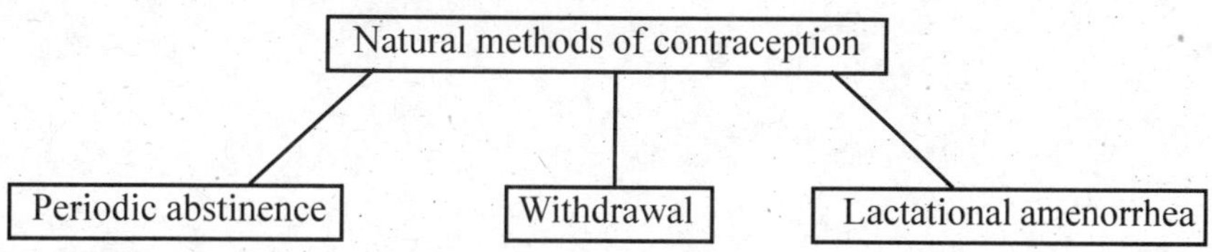

Q. 4. Name any two intra uterine devices.

Ans. CuT, LNG–20.

Q. 5. How does a contraceptive pill show its effect?

Ans. It inhibits the ovulation and implantation processes. Also it alters the quality of cervical mucus to prevent the entry of sperms so that fertilisation is checked.

Q. 6. Define the term MTP.

Ans. It is an intentional/voluntary medical termination of pregnancy before the full term is completed. It is also called induced abortion.

Note : It is safe only during 1st trimester *i.e.* upto 12 weeks of pregnancy.

Q. 7. Mention a few STDs.

Ans. (1) Gonorrhoea, (2) Syphillis, (3) Genital herpes, (4) AIDS.

Q. 8. Which STDs are serious and at present incurable?

Ans. (1) Hepatitis-B, (2) Genital herpes, (3) HIV infection

Q. 9. How one can avoid STDs?

Ans. (*i*) Avoid sex with unknown partners/multiple partners.

(*ii*) Always use condom during coitus.

Q. 10. Expand the terms — ZIFT, GIFT.

Ans. **ZIFT** — Zygote intra fallopian transfer.

GIFT — Gamete intra fallopian transfer.

SHORT ANSWER TYPE QUESTIONS (SA-I, SA-II)

Q. 1. What do you think is the significance of reproductive health in a society?

Ans. Health is of prime importance to an individual so is reproductive health. It is for well being in all the respects of reproduction *i.e.* physical, emotional, behavioural and social. This will provide functionally normal reproductive organs, normal emotional and behavioural interactions among individuals, sex related diseases free society and healthy people.

Q. 2. Suggest the aspects of reproductive health which need to be given special attention in the present scenario.

Ans. There are 4 aspects of reproductive health.

1. Physical 2. Emotional 3. Behavioural 4. Social

Behavioural and social aspects of reproductive health need special attention in the present scenario because if proper attention is given then misconception about sex related aspects, social evils such as sex abuse and sex-related crimes and sex related diseases can be controlled.

Q. 3. What is family planning? At present which programmes related to reproduction are run by government. What are its objectives?

Ans. As early as 1951, reproductive health programmes were carried out as a social goal to achieve healthy society. These programmes were called family planning. At present such improved programmes related to reproductive health are being carried out by government under the name of — Reproductive and Child health care (RCH). Its objectives are—

(*a*) Creating awareness among people about various reproduction health related aspects.
(*b*) Building up a reproductively healthy societies.

Q. 4. Is sex education necessary in schools? Why?

Ans. Yes, sex education is necessary in schools so that the children can be educated for having good reproductive health when they grow up and make a healthy society. It will also help to—

(*a*) Obtain correct information about reproduction and discourage— myths and misconceptions, such as, mother is responsible for a daughter child etc.
(*b*) Correct information about reproductive organs, adolescence related changes.
(*c*) Safe and hygienic sexual practices when they grow up as adults and.
(*d*) Keep themselves away from sexually transmitted diseases (STDs)
(*e*) Birth control measures, marriageable age and to limit the family size.

Q. 5. Do you think that reproductive health in our country has improved in the past 50 years? If yes, mention some areas of improvement.

Ans. Yes. **Some areas of improvement are:**

(*a*) Better awareness about sex-related matters.
(*b*) Increase in number of medically assisted deliveries.
(*c*) Better pre-and post-natal care resulting in decrease in infant mortality rate and maternal mortality during delivery.
(*d*) Increased number of couples with small-sized families.
(*e*) Better detection and cure of STDs.
(*f*) Overall better medical facilities for sex related problems. Improved reproductive health of the society.

Q. 6. What are the suggested reasons for population explosion?

Ans. Some reasons for population explosion are.

(*a*) All round development in various fields.

(*b*) Increase in health facilities.
(*c*) Better living conditions.

Q. 7. Is the use of contraceptives justified? Give reasons.

Ans. Yes, the use of contraceptives is justified, because it
(*a*) helps to keep the family size/space between children.
(*b*) is safe and user friendly.
(*c*) checks the STD, in case of sexual relationship with unknown partner.
(*d*) helps to retain reproductive health of couples.

Q. 8. Which principle works for natural methods of contraception? Mention the various methods in brief.

Ans. The natural methods of contraception work on the principle of avoiding the chances of meeting sperms and ovum. It can be done by any of these following methods.

Natural methods of contraception

1. **Periodic abstinence :** In this method the coitus/intercourse is avoided during the *10 to 17 days* of the menstrual cycle by the couple. This is called periodic abstinence. As ovulation takes place on 14th day and chances of sperms meeting the ovum are nil if this is practised.
2. **Withdrawal :** In this method, the coitus/intercourse is done but the penis is withdrawn from vagina just before the ejaculation of the semen. Hence, once again the sperms meeting the ovum are nil. It is also called coitus interruptus.
3. **Lactational amenorrhea :** It is also known as absence of menstruation due to lactation after parturition. It is based on ovulation as it does not occur due to intense lactation of mother. As long as the child is breast fed the chances of conception is almost nil. It is effective only upto the maximum of 6 months following parturition.

Q. 9. What are contraceptives? Classify them with examples.

Ans. Those methods/practices that check the meeting of sperms with ova or interrupt in the ovulation or supress the fertility of sperms or kill then or obstruct their transport/conduct all are called as contraceptives.

Contraceptive methods

1. **Natural methods/Traditional methods** — Periodic abstinence.
2. **Barrier methods** — Condoms, cervical caps.
3. **Intra uterine devices** — Loop, CuT.
4. **Oral contraceptive** — Saheli.
5. **Injectables and implants** — Progesterone and estrogen.
6. **Surgical methods** — Vasectomy for male, tubectomy for female

Q. 10. What is IUD? Mention the different types/categories. Also mention their mode of action.

Ans. IUD — Intra uterine device. These are effective and popular devices used for contraception by a reproductively active human female.

IUDs →
- IUD → Non-medicated, *e.g.* Lippes loop.
- IUD → Copper ions releasing, *e.g.* CuT, Cu7, Multiload 375.
- IUD → Hormone releasing, *e.g.* Progestasert, LNG-20.

These devices are inserted into the uterus of the female through vagina. Expert medical practioner does this job. Different IUDs act differently.

The IUDs increase the phagocytosis of sperms within the uterus. Copper ions releasing IUDs release Cu ions which subpress the mobility and fertilising capacity of sperms. Whereas hormone releasing IUDs release hormones that change the uterine layer and makes it unsuitable for implantation of the zygote/embryo. Also it makes the cervix hostile to sperms.

Q. 11. State the advantages and disadvantages of use of contraceptives.

Ans. **Advantages of contraceptives**

1. It helps to prevent or space or delay pregnancy.
2. It helps to maintain the family size and health of female.
3. It helps to control the population growth.

Disadvantages of contraceptives

1. Abdominal pain, break through bleeding, irregular menstrual bleeding.
2. Nausea, breast cancer.

Q. 12. Removal of gonads cannot be considered as a contraceptive option. Why?

Ans. The characteristics of contraceptive is that it should be effective, reversible and with no or least side effects. Removal of gonads cannot be considered as a contraceptive option because once it is removed the reproductive process cannot be reversed/done.

Q. 13. Aminocentesis for sex determination is banned in our country. Is this ban necessary? Comment.

Ans. Yes, this ban is necessary because some sections of our society prefer male child due to which they abort the female foetus after knowing the sex. This has caused a misuse of this technique. It has also caused an imbalance in the sex ratio.

Q. 14. Suggest some methods to assist infertile couples to have children.

Ans. Childless couples can follow any one of these measures. They can go for assisted reproductive technologies such as-IVF-a technique of fertilisation outside the body, embryo transfer, and in vivo fertilisation. Also donor's gamete and sperms can be used for artificial insemination processes.

Another method is legal adoption of child as it is permitted by law in our country.

Q. 15. What are the measures one has to take to prevent from contracting STDs?

Ans. 1. Avoid sex with unknown partners/multiple partners.

2. Always use condom during coitus.

Q. 16. State True/False with explanation.

(*a*) Abortions could happen spontaneously too. (True/False)

(*b*) Infertility is defined as the inability to produce a viable offspring and is always due to abnormalities/defects in the female partner. (True/False)

(*c*) Complete lactation could help as a natural method of contraception. (True/False)

(*d*) Creating awareness about sex-related aspects is a method to improve reproductive health of people. (True/False)

Ans. (*a*) True.

(*b*) No. Infertility is defined as the inability of the couple to produce offspring. It may be due to any of the partner.

(*c*) True.

(*d*) True.

Q. 17. Correct the following statements:

(*a*) Surgical methods of contraception prevent gamete formation.

(*b*) All sexually transmitted diseases are completely curable.

(*c*) Oral pills are very popular contraceptives among the rural women.

(*d*) In E.T. techniques, embryos are transferred into the uterus.

Ans. (*a*) No surgical methods only check the transfer of gametes and not their formation.

(*b*) No, some sexually transmitted diseases are not curable genital herpes, hepatitis-B, HIV infections – AIDS.

(*c*) Oral pills are very popular contraceptives among urban women.

(*d*) Early embryos (upto 8 blastomeres) are transferred into fallopian tube and embryo with more than 8 blastomeres are transferred to uterus of women in E.T. techniques.

Q. 18. Expand the terms and what is it? GIFT and MTP.

Ans. **GIFT :** Gamete intra fallopian transfer. It is done in female who is unable to produce viable gametes.

MTP : Medical termination of pregnancy. It is done to abort defective foetus.

Q. 19. What is the difference between coitus interruptus and periodic abstinence?

Ans. Coitus interruptus involves the process of coitus (intercourse) and before ejaculation the penis is withdrawn from vagina.

Periodic abstinence does not involve the process of coitus *.i.e.* coitus does not take place during the specified period.

Q. 20. Define sterlisation. What is this method called?

Ans. Surgical methods of contraception is called sterlisation. It is called contraceptive method.

LONG ANSWER TYPE QUESTIONS (LA)

Q. 1. What is assisted reproductive technologies? Describe them.

Ans. Couples who have infertility problem they can undergo assisted reproductive technologies.

These technologies used different methods for the processes of fertilisation, implantation and help in conceiving the embryo. These are.

ART → In vitro fertilisation | Gamete intra. fallopian transfer | In vivo fertilisation

In vitro fertilisation
↓
Embryo transfer
↓
Test tube baby
↓
Zygote intra fallopian transfer

In the in-vitro fertilisation, the fertilisation is done outside the body. The zygote formed is then transferred to the fallopian tube (ZIFT) the blastomeres upto 8, and more than this blastomeres are transferred to uterus. Both these methods are called embryo transfer and also called test tube baby that is formed.

Gamete transfer is done from donor to a recipient and also artificial insemination donor sperms is done in cases.

In-vivo fertilisation cases embryo is transferred which can not be conceived by the female, inspite of fertilisation in body.

NUTSHELL MINDMAP

Contraception → avoid meeting of sperm and ovum.

Aminocentesis → foetal sex determination based on chromosomal pattern.

MTP → First trimester → Upto 12 weeks of pregnancy → SAFE.

MTP → Second trimester → After 12 weeks-24 weeks of pregnancy → UNSAFE

ABBREVIATIONS

ART	—	Assisted Reproduction Technologies.
WHO	—	World Health Organisation.
RCH	—	Reproductive and Child Health.
STD	—	Sexually Transmitted Diseases.
IMR	—	Infant Mortality Rate.
MMR	—	Maternal Mortality Rate
IUD	—	Intra Uterine Device.
CuT	—	Copper T.
PIDs	—	Pelvic Inflammatory Diseases.
MTP	—	Medical Termination of Pregnancy.
HIV	—	Human Immuno Deficiency Virus.
VD	—	Veneral Disease.
RTI	—	Reproduction Tract Infection.
IVF	—	In Vitro Fertilisation.
ET	—	Embryo Transfer.
IUT	—	Intra Uterine Transfer.
GIFT	—	Gamete Intra Fallopian Transfer.
ICSI	—	Intra Cytoplasmic Sperm Injection.
AI	—	Artificial Insemination.
IUI	—	Intra Uterine Insemination.
ZIFT	—	Zygote Intra Fallopian Transfer.

HIGHER ORDER THINKING SKILLS QUESTIONS (HOTS)

1. Which type of contraceptives are – spermical creams, jellies and foams? (*VSA*)
2. Select the odd one out from this category. (*VSA*)
   (*a*) CuT (*b*) LNG—20 (*c*) Lipper loop (*d*) Saheli
3. Study the figures and answer the questions that follow: (*SA II*)

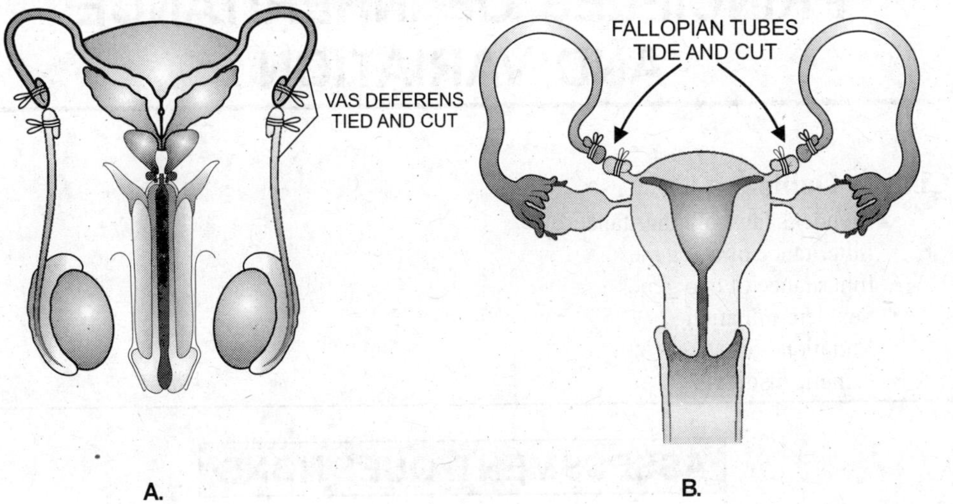

Fig. 4.1

   1. Which methods of contraception are these?
   2. What are these methods known?
   3. How is their efficiency and reversibility?
4. What stage of MTP is risky and why? (*SA I*)
5. Distinguish between in vitro and in vivo fertilisation-which is practised by doctors?

❑❑❑

CHAPTER 5

PRINCIPLES OF INHERITANCE AND VARIATION

Chapter Outline

- Mendel's laws of inheritance
- Inheritance of one genes
- Inheritance of two genes
- Sex determination
- Mutation
- Genetic disorders

ASSESSMENT QUESTIONS

VERY SHORT ANSWER TYPE QUESTIONS (VSA)

Q. 1. Name the process by which the traits (characters) are passed on from parent to progeny.

Ans. Inheritance.

Q. 2. Define variation.

Ans. It is the degree by which progeny differs from their parents.

Q. 3. Give one example to state that humans knew as early as 8000-1000 BC the causes of variation and exploited it.

Ans. Sahiwal cows in Punjab.

Q. 4. What is a true-breeding line?

Ans. A true-breeding line is that, which has undergone continuous self pollination (*e.g.* pea plant) *i.e.* it is pure and does not have any cross pollination/contamination.

Q. 5. What is the phenotypic ratio of monohybrid cross in F_2?

Ans. 3:1.

Q. 6. What is the removal of anthers from a flower called?

Ans. Emasculation.

Q. 7. Where do you think that information required to be expressed for a particular trait is stored?

Ans. Genes.

Q. 8. Distinguish between— genotype and phenotype.

Ans. The genetic representation (*e.g.* TT) for a trait is called genotype and descriptive terms (*e.g.* Tall) for a trait is called phenotype.

Q. 9. Which type of cross is termed as monohybrid cross?

Ans. A cross between plants/parents alleles where one trait is studied is called monohybrid cross.

Q. 10. Under which condition you will recommend a test cross?

Ans. To determine the unknown genotype of a dominant phenotype.

Q. 11. State the 1st law of inheritance.

Ans. The law of dominance states that the expression of only one of the parental characters in the F_1 and expression of both in F_2, (in case of monohybrid cross) in a ratio of 3:1 in F_2.

Q. 12. A monohybrid cross produced similar ratios of phenotype and genotype in F_2. The genotype ratio is similar to monohybrid Mendelian cross. Name the phenomenon.

Ans. Incomplete dominance.

Q. 13. Give an example of multiple alleles in human.

Ans. ABO blood grouping.

Q. 14. Name the scientists who used chromosome movement to explain Mendel's Laws.

Ans. Walter Sutton and Theodour Bovesi.

Q. 15. Who had proposed the chromosomal theory of the inheritance?

Ans. Walter Sutton.

Q. 16. Briefly mention the contribution of T.H. Morgan in genetics.

Ans. Experimental verification of chromosomal theory of inheritance was done by T.H. Morgan which led to discovery of the basis of the variation due to sexual reproduction.

Q. 17. Which type of sex determination is present in grasshopper? Mention the chromosomes of male and female grasshopper.

Ans. XO type sex determination. Male grasshopper has XO and female grasshopper has XX.

Q. 18. Name a phenomenon that results in alternation of DNA sequences.

Ans. Mutation (or also recombination).

Q. 19. What is point mutation? Give one example.

Ans. The change in a single base pair of DNA is called point mutation *e.g.* Sickle cell anemia.

Q. 20. Mention the significance of pedigree study in human genetics.

Ans. It provides a strong tool, which is utilised to trace the inheritance of a specific trait, disease or abnormality of an individual.

Q. 21. A diploid organism is heterozygous for 4 loci, how many types of gametes can be produced?

Ans. 4 types of gametes.

Q. 22. When a cross is made between tall plant with yellow seeds (Tt Yy) and tall plant with green seed (Tt yy), what proportions of phenotype in the offspring could be expected to be—

(*a*) tall and green (*b*) dwarf and green

Ans. (*a*) 50% (*b*) 25%

SHORT ANSWER TYPE QUESTIONS (SA-I, SA-II)

Q. 1. Mention the advantages of selecting pea plant for experiment by Mendel.

Ans. *Advantages are.*

(*a*) Pea plant shows self pollination.

(*b*) It shows stable trait inheritance.

(*c*) The expression of traits is for several generations.

(*d*) The plants selected were true breeding.

Q. 2. Give the phenotypic representation of monohybrid cross of pea plant.

Ans.

Parent Tall × Dwarf

↓ (crossing)

F_1 generation — Tall × Tall

(selfing)

F_2 generation — Tall Tall Tall Dwarf

Q. 3. (*a*) What is Punnett square?

(*b*) Mention its one use.

Ans. (*a*) It is a graphical representation to calculate the probability of all possible genotypes of offspring is a genetic cross.

(*b*) It is used to represent the possible genotypes of offspring of a genetic cross.

Q. 4. Using a Punnett Square, workout the distribution of phenotypic features in the first filial generation after a cross between a homozygous female and a heterozygous male for a single locus.

Ans. Homozygous female (tt) × Heterozygous male (Tt)

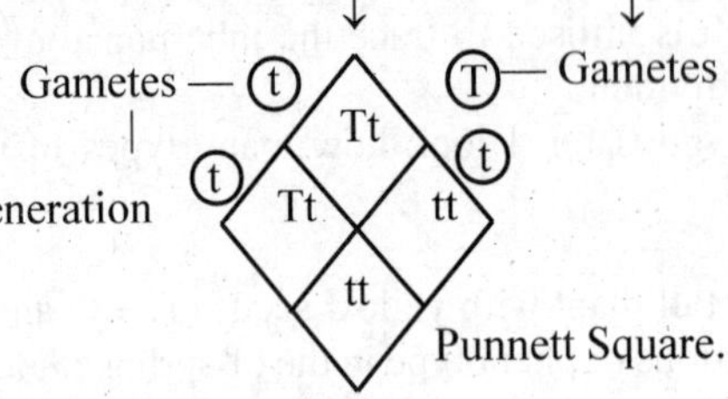

Punnett Square.

Q. 5. Define and design a test-cross.

Ans. The cross which helps us to determine the unknown genotype of a dominant phenotype by crossing it with the recessive parent is called a test cross.

For example.

Tall × Drawf
(unknown genotype)

	t	t
T	Tt	Tt
T	Tt	Tt

All are Tall hybrid.

	t	t
T	Tt	Tt
t	tt	tt

50% Tall hybrid 50% Dwarf.

Q. 6. What was the opinion of Mendel regarding the law of dominance?

Ans. 1. The characters are controlled by discrete units called factors.

2. Factors occur in pairs.

3. In a dissimilar pair of factors (heterozygous) one member of the pair dominates (dominant) and the other is recessive.

Q. 7. Differentiate between the following.
(*a*) Dominance and Recessive. (*b*) Homozygous and Heterozygous.
(*c*) Monohybrid and Dihybrid.

Ans.

(*a*) *Dominance*	*Recessive*
1. The trait expressed by the gene in an individual by suppressing the other one is called dominance. The gene/allele is represented in capital alphabet.	1. The trait that remains hidden in an individual by dominant gene is said to be recessive. The gene/allele is represented in lower case of alphabet.
(*b*) *Homozygous*	*Heterozygous.*
The existence of genes is in pairs. If both the alleles of a gene are same, the condition is termed as homozygous. Such as— TT, tt, RR, etc.	If the alleles of a gene are dissimilar, the condition is termed as heterozygous. Such as— Tt, Rr etc.
(*c*) *Monohybrid*	*Dihybrid*
An individual with two dissimilar allele for a gene of a trait is called monohybrid. (it is also called heterozygous). Such as— Tt or Rr.	An individual with dissimilar alleles for two genes or two traits is called dihybrid. (it is also a heterozygous). Such as— Rr Yy.

Q. 8. A child has blood group *O*. If the father has blood group *A* and mother blood group *B*, work out the genotypes of the parents and the possible genotypes of the other offsprings.

Ans. Father's blood group *A* - genotype IAi° or IAIB.
Mother's blood group *B* - genotype IBi° or IBIB.
Child's blood group *O* - genotype ii.
Other child's blood group is AB genotype I^AI^B.

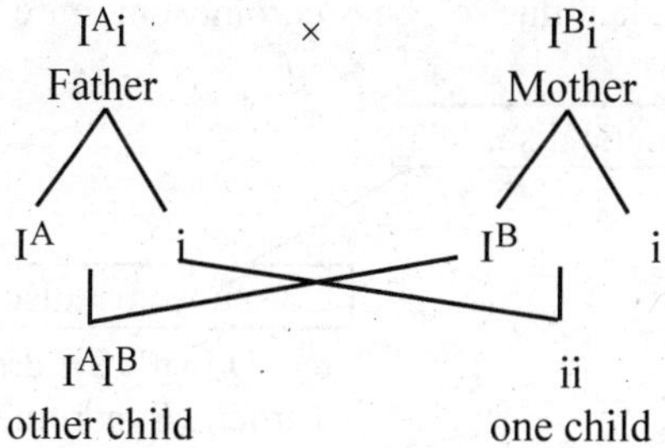

Q. 9. Mention any two autosomal genetic disorders with their symptoms.
Ans. Autosomal genetic disorders Sickle cell anemia and Phenylketonuria

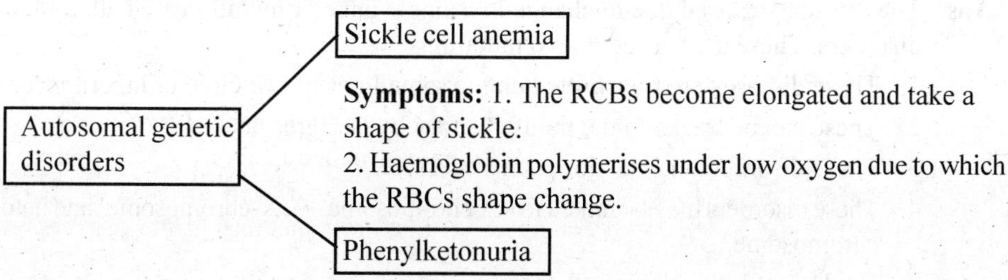

Symptoms:

1. Phenylalanine is accumulated and is converted into phenylpyruvic acid and other derivatives.
2. These are accumulated in brain leading to mental retardation.
3. These are excreted in urine because of its poor absorption by the kidney.

Q. 10. Define the term— sex chromosome and autosome.

Ans. **Sex chromosomes :** Chromosomes that are involved in determination sex of an individual are called sex chromosomes. Such as — X and Y in human.

Autosomes : Chromosomes other than sex chromosomes are called autosomes. They are 22 pairs in human.

Q. 11. How is sex determined in human beings?

Ans. Sex determination in human is of *xy* type.

The male and female individual has the same number of chromosomes *i.e.* 22 pairs autosomes and 1 pair sex chromosomes. The males are heterogametes and responsible for production of two types of gametes— sperms. Sperms with *x* chromosome and sperms with *y* chromosome. Females are homogametic and produce ovum with *x* chromosome only.

Condition 1 — Combination/fertilisation of sperm with *y* chromosome with ovum results in male zygote. *i.e.* xy.

Condition 2 — Fertilisation of sperm with *x* chromosome with ovum results in female zygote. *i.e.* xx.

Therefore, the 1st zygote will form male child and the 2nd zygote will form female child.

Sperm with chromosome *Y* is responsible for male child and not the women as she is blamed in the society for bearing female child.

Q. 12. What are genetic disorders? Classify them with 2 examples to each.

Ans. The disorders caused in the individual due to genes/chromosomes are broadly called gametic disorders.

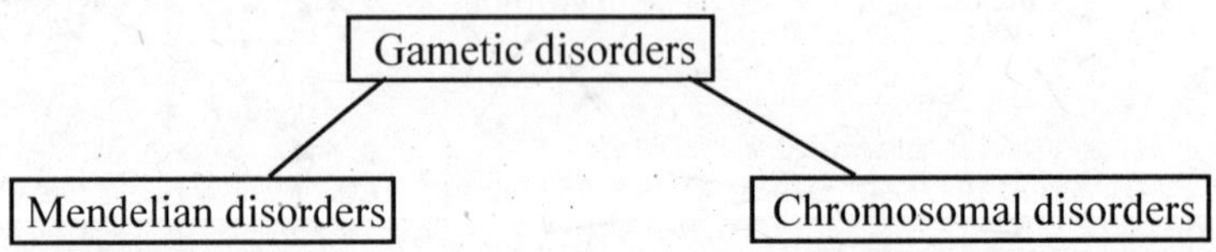

Mendelian disorders: *e.g.* Hemophilia. Sickle cell anemia.

Chromosomal disorders: *e.g.* Down's Syndrome Turner's Syndrome.

Q. 13. What are Mendelian disorders? How are they caused? Mention their characteristics and give examples.

Ans. The disorders caused due to change in a single gene or mutation are called Mendelian disorders. These are caused due to mutations.

1. These diseases are transmitted on the same lines of principle of inheritance.
2. These can be traced in the family history by pedigree analysis.
3. These disorders may be dominant/recessive.
4. These disorders may be linked to sex chromosome — (X-chromosome) and autosomal chromosome.

   e.g. Hemophilia, sickle cell anemia.

Q. 14. Study the following figures:

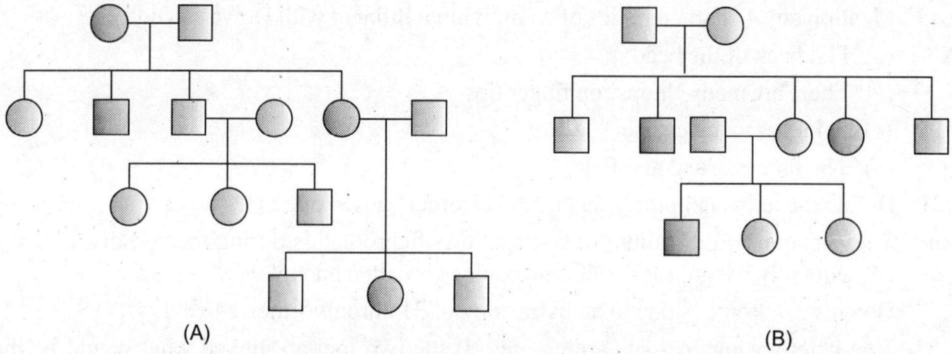

Fig. 5.1. Representative pedigree analysis of (a) Autosomal dominant trait (for example, Myotonic dystrophy) (b) Autosomal recessive trait (for example, Sickle-cell anaemia).

(*a*) What is this type of analysis called?
(*b*) Which disease is being represented by it? Name them.
(*c*) It is autosomal or sex linked disease?

Ans. (*a*) This type of analysis is called pedigree analysis.
(*b*) Mendelian disorder. It is myotonic dystrophy and sickle cell anemia.
(*c*) It is autosomal dominant trait— myotonic dystrophy and autosomal recessive trait— sickle cell anemia.

Q. 15. What is pedigree analysis? Suggest how such an analysis can be useful?

Ans. The pattern of inheritance of Mendelian disorder in (human) family can be traced by study of family history is called pedigree analysis.
Such an analysis is useful to know whether the trait is— dominant/recessive, autosomal/ sex linked.

Q. 16. (*i*) Who used Mendelian principles and united the knowledge with chromosomal segregation?
(*ii*) Who verified the chromosomal theory of inheritance?
(*iii*) Name the organism used for the experiment and why?

Ans. (*i*) Sutton.
(*ii*) T.H. Morghan.
(*iii*) *Drosophila melanogaster*
(*a*) Organisms can be grown in simple synthetic medium in the lab.
(*b*) They produce large number of progeny flies in a single mating.

Q. 17. Which type of sex determination is shown by—
(*a*) Human beings, (*b*) Drosophila,
(*c*) Grasshopper, (*d*) Hen.

Ans. (*a*) Human beings - XY type. (*c*) Grasshopper - XO type.
(*b*) Drosophila - XY type. (*d*) Hen - XO type.

Q. 18. Draw the symbols used to represent the following in a pedigree analysis.
(*a*) Male (*b*) Unspecified sex (*c*) Mating (*d*) Consanguineous mating

Ans. (*a*) Male — □
(*b*) Unspecified sex — □—O
(*c*) Mating — ◇

(*d*) Consanguineous mating — □═○

Q. 19. Mention any 4 characteristics of an individual inflated with Down's syndrome.

Ans. (*a*) Flat back of the head.

(*b*) There are many 'loops' on finger tips.

(*c*) Palm has many crease.

(*d*) The face is broad and flat.

Q. 20. Define the term aneuploidy. Name the disorder caused due to it.

Ans. The phenomenon of failure of segregation of chromatids during the cell division and consequently the gain/loss of chromosomes is called aneuploidy.

Down's syndrome is due to an extra copy of 21 chromosomes. (46 + 1 = 47)

Q. 21. Two heterozygous parents are crossed. If the two loci are linked what would be the distribution of phenotypic features in F_1 generation for a dihybrid cross?

Ans. Suppose two loci linked are— TtYy, TtYy in parents. As they are linked the segregation of traits (dominant and recessive) will not occur and will go as it is in parents, *i.e.* gametes will have Tt Yy genotype. A cross will result in same phenotype. All the progeny will have same phenotype tall and yellow trait.

LONG ANSWER TYPE QUESTIONS (LA)

Q. 1. Explain the law of Dominance using a monohybrid cross.

Ans. The law of dominance explains that the expression of only one of the parental characters in a monohybrid cross in the F_1 and the expression of both parental characters in the F_2 in the ratio— 3:1. It can be easily expressed by the following cross.

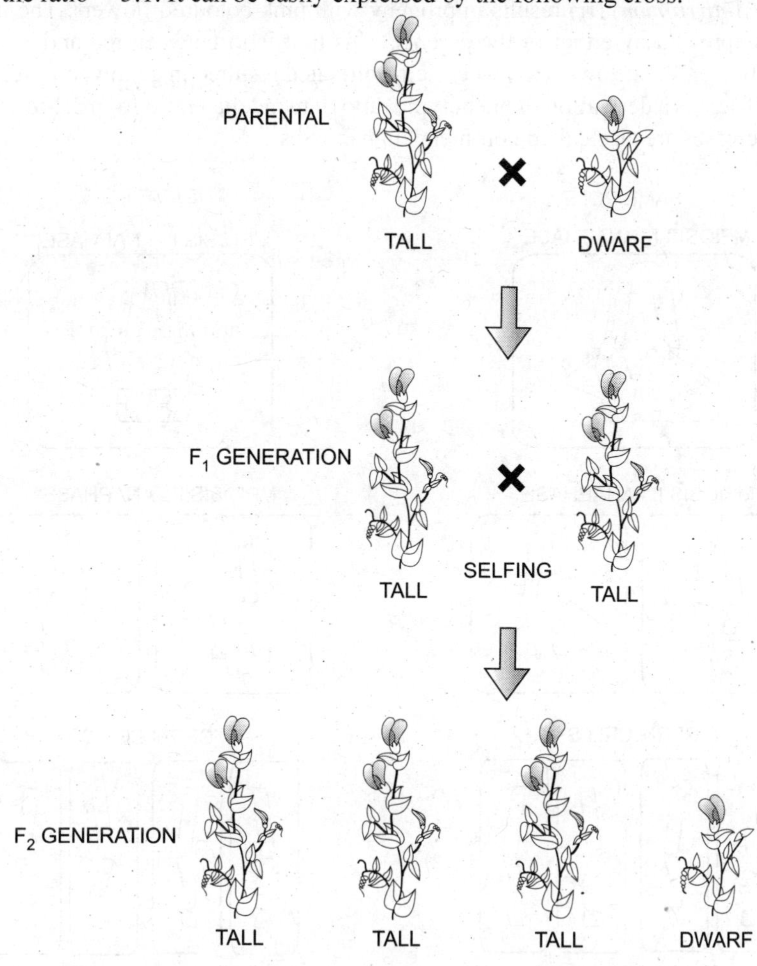

Fig. 5.2. Diagrammatic representation of monohybrid cross.

When the parents with tall (TT) and dwarf (Tt) are crossed, the progeny in F_1 express the dominant trait tall. When the selfing of F_1 tall individuals is done, both the parental traits of previous generation get expressed in F_2 progeny in ratio of 3:1.

Q. 2. Explain the following terms with example.

(*a*) Codominance (*b*) Incomplete dominance.

Ans. (*a*) The cross that gives rise to offspring/progeny of F_1 generation that resembles both parents, such a cross or phenomenon is called co-dominance.

Example of codominance — Expression blood group in human beings.

The blood groups ABO in human are controlled by the gene *I*. It has three alleles I^A, I^B and *i*. I^A and I^B alleles produce a slightly different from each other and *i* does not produce any sugar. As humans are diploid, they have any two genes out of these three gene alleles. I^A and IB are dominant over *i* and if I^AI^B are present then both the alleles express it is because of codominance and blood group will be *AB* in this case.

(*b*) **Incomplete dominance** — The phenomenon of expression of a trait in F_1 progeny that is not expressed by either of the two parents is known as incomplete dominance. For example— The cross between a Red (RR) shape dragon and white shape dragon (*Antirrhinum*) (rr) results in progeny with pink coloured flowers. The trait is not expressed by either of the parents. This trait is in between red and white colour flower. Pink flower (Rr) when self-pollinated resulted in genotype— 1:2:1. There is a derivation of phenotypic ratio of mendelian ratio from 3:1 to 1:2:1. Such crosses are also called non-mendelian crosses.

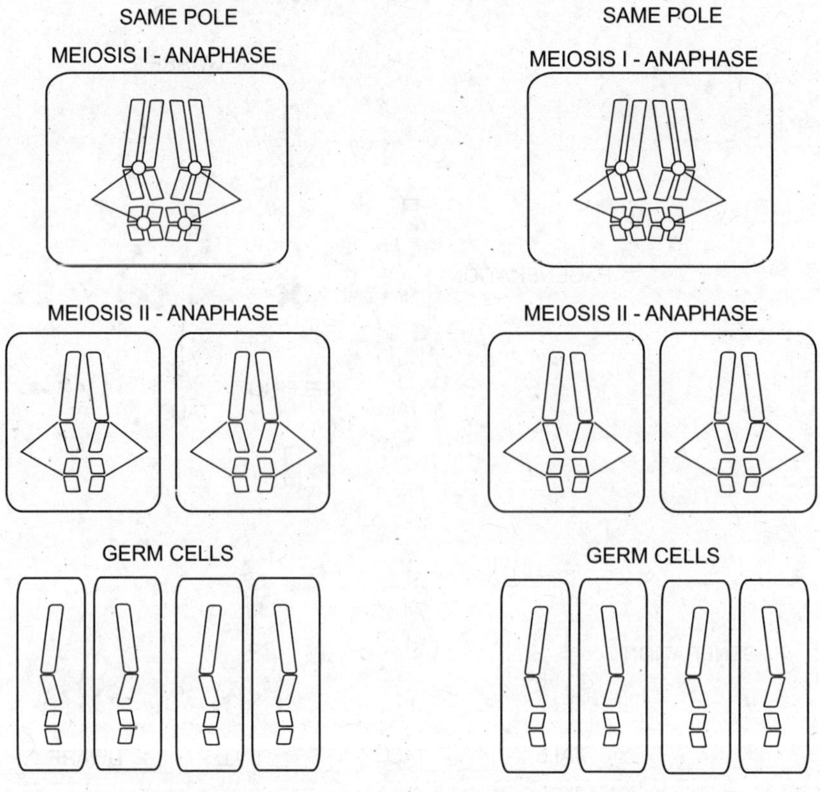

Fig. 5.3. Independent assortment of chromosomes.

Q. 3. (i) What is linkage and recombination? Who coined the terms?

(*ii*) What did the study reveal?

(*iii*) What did his student Alfred Sturtervant do by use of frequency of recombination?

Ans. (*i*) The physical association of two or more genes on the chromosomes is called linkage. The non-parental gene combination on a chromosome is called recombination. The term recombination was termed by T.H.Morgan.

(*ii*) The study of linkage revealed that a group of genes may be linked/associated with each other very tightly that they cannot be separated and moved as a group. These genes show very low recombination. On the other hand, a group of genes may be linked/associated with each other very loosely that they can separate out easily from the group/association. These genes show very high recombinations.

(*iii*) Alfred Sturtervant used the frequency of recombination of between the gene pairs in the same chromosome as a measure of the distance between the genes and 'mapped' their position on the chromosome. This is called gene mapping (of a chromosome). Today this method is used as a starting point in the sequencing of the whole genome.

Q. 4. (*i*) What are chromosomal disorders? Mention their types.

(*ii*) Write the cause and symptoms of Down's syndrome, Klinefelter's syndrome and Turner's syndrome.

Ans. (*i*) The disorders caused due to absence/excess/abnormal arrangement of one or more chromosomes are called chromosomes disorders.

Chromosomal disorders

Aneuploidy

It is the failure of separation of chromatids during cell division. It results in gain/loss of a chromosome. *e.g.* Down's syndrome.

Polyploidy

It is the failure of cytokinesis after telophase stage of cell division. It results in an increase of whole set of chromosomes in an organism. *e.g.* in plants.

(*ii*) **Down's Syndrome**

Cause : Due to additional copy of 21 chromosome *i.e* trisomy of 21.

Symptoms.

1. Short statured individual with small round head, furrowed tongue and partially opened mouth.
2. Palm broad and characteristic palm crease.
3. Physical, psychomotor and mental development is retarded.

Klinefelter's Syndrome

Cause : Due to additional copy of X chromosome *i.e* XXY (47).

Symptoms :

1. Over masculine development, however development of breast is also expressed—Gynecomastia.
   Such individuals are *sterile.*

Turner's Syndrome

Cause : Due to absence of x-chromosome *i.e* *45* with XO.

Symptoms :

1. Such females are sterile. Ovaries are rudimentary.
2. Other secondary sexual characters are also lacking.

Table 5.1: Contrasting Traits Studied by Mendel in Pea

S. No.	Characters	Contrasting Traits
1.	Stem height	Tall/dwarf
2.	Flower colour	Violet/white
3.	Flower position	Axial/terminal
4.	Pod shape	Inflated/constricted
5.	Pod colour	Green/yellow
6.	Seed shape	Round/wrinkled
7.	Seed colour	Yellow/green

Table 5.2: Table Showing the Genetic Basis of Blood Groups in Human Population

Allele from Parent 1	Allele from Parent 2	Genotype of offspring	Blood types of offspring
I^A	I^A	I^AI^A	A
I^A	I^B	I^AI^B	AB
I^A	i	I^Ai	A
I^B	I^A	I^AI^B	AB
I^B	I^B	I^BI^B	B
I^B	i	I^Bi	B
i	i	ii	O

Symptoms : *Description*

□	Male
○	female
◇	sex unspecified
□○◇	affected individuals
□—○	mating
□═○	mating between relatives (consanguineous mating)
□—○ ○ □	parents above and children below (in order of birth-left to right)
□—○ □	parents with male child affected with disease
5	five unaffected offspring

Fig. 5.3. Symbols used in the human pedigree analysis.

NUTSHELL | MINDMAP

1. Mendelian crosses follow Mendelian laws and give the ratio as said.
   Monohybrid cross— Phenotypic ratio 3:1, Genotypic ratio 1:2:1 in F_2 generation.
   Dyhybrid—phenotypic ratio is 9:3:3:1 in F_2 generation.
2. Non-Medelian crosses show derivations from the above ratios.
3. Genes are in pairs/groups loosely or tightly linked.
4. Sex determination types—
   XY type (human, drosophila, insects)—
   XO type grasshopper.
5. Genetic disorders
   - Mendelian disorders
   - Chromosomal disorders

HIGHER ORDER THINKING QUESTIONS (HOTS)

Q. 1. What did Mendel observe in progeny of F_1 generation in a monohybrid cross? (VSA)

Q. 2. Mention the alleles of Tall in pea plant. (VSA)

Q. 3. Give the Genotypes of

1. Heterozygous tall, 2. Homozygous dwarf. (VSA)

Q. 4. Which type of gametes are produced by homozygous and heterozygous parents and in what ratio? (VSA)

Q. 5. Give the alleles of ABO. Which allele does not produce sugar? (SAI)

Q. 6. Briefly mention the synthesis of starch in peas and its control. (SAII)

Q. 7. 1. What is the no. of chromosomes in XY type of individuals?

2. Define male and female heterogamety.
3. How is sex determination different in birds? (SAII)

Q. 8. 1. Which type of mutations are seen in cancer cells?

2. What is frame shift mutations? (SAI)

Q. 9. Which disorder was present in Queen Victoria's family? (VSA)

Q. 10. Study the figure.

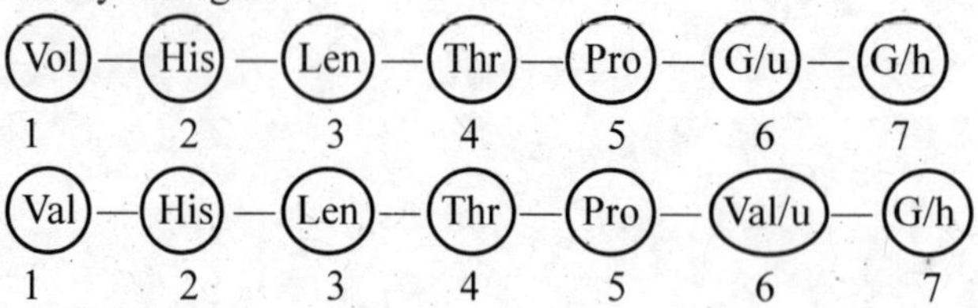

(*i*) What do these represent?

(*ii*) What is this disorder called?

(*iii*) How is this disorder caused/developed? (SAII)

❑❑❑

CHAPTER 6

MOLECULAR BASIS OF INHERITANCE

Chapter Outline

- The DNA
- Transcription
- Human genome project
- The search for genetic material
- Genetic code
- RNA world
- Translation
- DNA finger printing
- Replication
- Regulation of gene expression

ASSESSMENT QUESTIONS

VERY SHORT ANSWER TYPE QUESTIONS (VSA)

Q. 1. What is the basis of DNA length?

Ans. It depends on the number of nucleotide pairs present in it.

Q. 2. Name the molecules that form the backbone of polynucleotide chain.

Ans. (1) Sugar (2) Phosphate.

Q. 3. What are the ratios between Adenine and Thymine and Guanine and Cytosine?

Ans. It is constant and equals to one.

Q. 4. Who identified the acidic nature of deoxyribose nucleic acid?

Ans. Friendrich Meischer.

Q. 5. Who proposed the central dogma of molecular biology?

Ans. Francis Crick.

Q. 6. What is central dogma in molecular biology?

Ans. The flow of information from DNA → RNA → Protein is called central dogma in molecular biology.

Replication ↳ DNA $\xrightarrow{\text{transcription}}$ In RNA $\xrightarrow{\text{translation}}$ Protein

Q. 7. What is the term 'beads-on-a string' stand for?

Ans. It stands for nucleosomes in a chromatin.

Q. 8. What was the conclusion of Griffith's mice experiment?

Ans. When the heat killed S-type bacteria mixed with R-type bacteria was injected to mice it transformed the R type to S type bacteria and killed the mice due to pneumonia.

Q. 9. What was the work of O. Avery, C. Macleod and M. Mccarty?

Ans. They isolated the material that transformed R type bacteria into S type bacteriade. It was DNA.

Q. 10. Whose experiments proved that DNA is the genetic material?

Ans. A. Hershey and Marks chase on bacteriophages.

Q. 11. Mention the dual role/functions of deoxyribonucleotides triphosphates in a cell.

Ans. (1) Act as substrates for polymerisation

(2) Provide energy for polymerisation

Q. 12. Mention two characteristics of polymerisation?

Ans. (1) High speed — 2000 bp/Sec. approximately.

(2) High degree of accuracy.

Q. 13. Mention the regions in the DNA that act as transcription unit?

Ans. (*i*) A promotor, (*ii*) Structural gene, (*iii*) Terminator.

Q. 14. What is the similarity between DNA polymerase and RNA polymerase?

Ans. Both are DNA dependent enzymes and do polymerisation in only one direction, *i.e.* $5' \rightarrow 3'$.

Q. 15. If the sequence of one strand of DNA is written as follows:

TACGTACGTACGTACGTACGT ACGTAÇG

write down the sequence of complementary stand in 5′—3′.

Ans. 5′—ATGCATGCA TGCATG CATGCA TGCATGC—3′

Q. 16. If the sequence of the coding strand in a transcription unit is written as follows:

5′ ATGCATGCATGCA TGCATGCATGCATGC—3′

write down the sequence of complementary strand in RNA.

Ans. UACGUACGUACG UACGUA CGUACGUACG:

Q. 17. What is operon?

Ans. A polycistronic structural gene, promotor and regulator genes of bacteria is called operon.

Q. 18. Expand the terms — HGP, BAC

Ans. Human Genome Project, BAC — Bacterial Artificial Chromosome.

Q. 19. What is satellite DNA?

Ans. The small peaks formed during the DNA finger printing in DNA sequence is called satellite DNA.

Q. 20. What is VNTR in DNA finger printing?

Ans. The use of satellite DNA as probe (that shows very high degree of polymorphism) is called as Variable Number of Tandem Repeats (VNTR).

Q. 21. List two essential roles of ribosome during translation. (NCERT)

Ans. (1) Charging of tRNA or aminocylation of tRNS.

(2) Acts as catalyst for binding of amino acids by forming peptide bond.

SHORT ANSWER TYPE QUESTIONS (SA-I, SA-II)

Q. 1. Mention the different roles performed by RNA.

Ans. (*i*) Genetic material in some of the viruses.

(*ii*) Massenger RNA,

(*iii*) Transfer RNA — adapter, structural RNA,

(*iv*) Catalytic molecule for binding of amino acids.

Q. 2. Draw the structure of a polynucleotide chain and write in short about its components.

Ans.

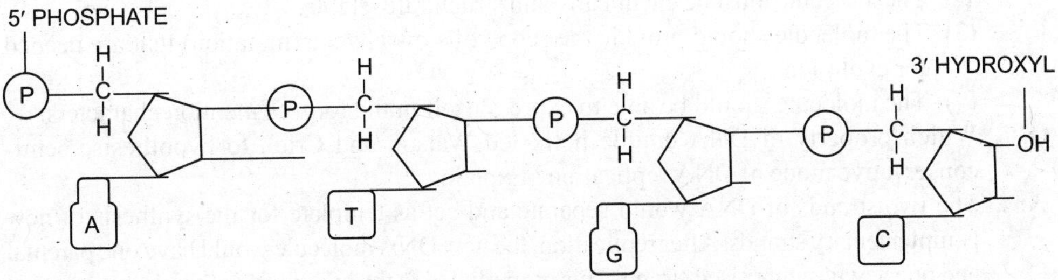

Fig. 6.1. A polynucleotide chain

A polypeptide has a chain of nucleotide. Each nucleotide consists of 3 components.

Nucleotide
- 1) Nitrogenous base
  - Purines — Adenine, Guanine
  - Pyrimidines — Cytosine, Uracil (in RNA) and Thymine (in DNA)
- (2) Sugar (Pentose)
  - Ribose in RNA
  - Deoxyribose in DNA
- (3) Phosphate group

Q. 3. Group the following as nitrogenous bases and nucleosides. Adinine, Cytidine, Thymine, Guanosine, Uracil and Cytosine (NCERT)

Ans.

Nitrogenous bases	*Nucleosides (N-bases+ Pentose sugar)*
1. Adinine 2. Thymine 3. Uracil 4. Cytosine	1. Cytidine 2. Guanosine

Q. 4. What are histones? What is its role in formation of a nucleosome? Draw the figure of a nucleosome.

Ans. The basic proteins are called histones. These are rich in basic amino acid residues lysines and arginines. They carry a positive charge in their side chains. The histones are organised to form a histone octamer consisting of molecules. A negatively charged

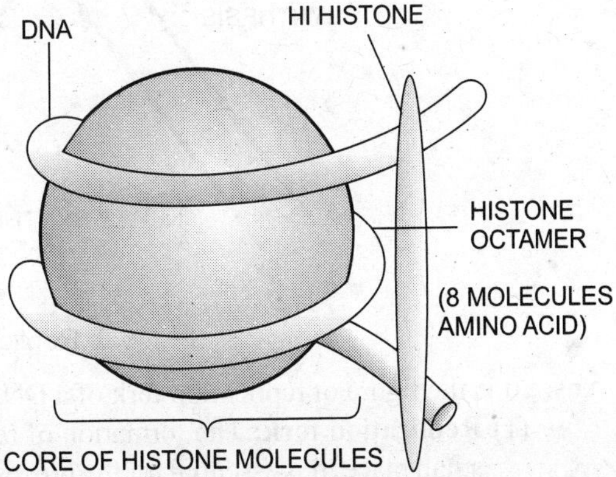

Fig. 6.2. Nucleosome.

DNA is wrapped around the positively charged histone octomer to form a nucleosome. Which are like beads in a string and form a structure called chromatin.

Q. 5. Define the terms — Euchromatin, Heterochromatin.

Ans. (1) **Euchromatin:** The regions of chromatin that are loosely packed and take light stain are called euchromatin.

(2) **Heterochromatin:** The regions of chromatin that are densely packed and take dash stain are called heterochromatin.

Q. 6. Briefly mention characteristics of a molecule to act on a genetic material.

Ans. (1) The molecule should be able to replicate/generate its replica (Replication).

(2) The molecule must be chemically and structurally stable.

(3) The molecule should provide the scope of slow change (mutation) that are needed for evolution.

(4) The molecule should be able to express itself in the form of mention characters.

Q. 7. Which property of DNA double helix led Watson and Crick to hypothesise semi-conservative mode of DNA replication? Explain.

Ans. The two strands of DNA would separate and act as template for the synthesis of new complementary strands. After replication, the new DNA molecule would have one parental and one newly synthesised strand. This property led to the hypothesis of semi-conservative mode of DNA replication.

Q. 8. Who provided the experimental proof for semi-conservative nature of DNA?

Ans. Messelson and Stahl by the use of heavy isotopes of nitrogen and their separation by centrifugation.

Q. 9. Study the given figure comment in brief about the labelled portions.

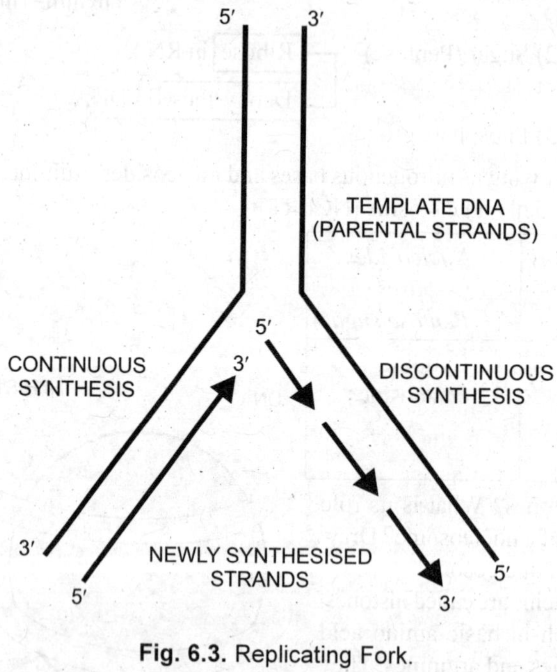

Fig. 6.3. Replicating Fork.

Ans. It is the figure of replication fork of a DNA helix.

(1) **Replication fork:** The formation of replication fork of a DNA helix takes place of small place. It is essential for the process of formation of new DNA strands. This fork is 'Y' shaped.

(2) **Continuous synthesis:** of DNA strand takes place by the polymerisation only in one direction. It is in 5′–3′. It is catalysed by polymerases enzyme.

(3) **Discontinuous synthesis:** of DNA strand takes on the other strand with 5′–3′ polarity. It is discontinuous synthesis because it takes place in small fragments and these are later joined by DNA legase enzyme.

Q. 10. Where does the replication process start? How is it initiated and when does the replication take place in eukaryotes?

Ans. The DNA replication does not initiate at any place on DNA. The vector is required for initiation of origin of replication. This replication process of DNA takes place at S-phase of the cell cycle.

Q. 11. Define the terms:

(1) Menocistron (2) Polycistron (3) Exons (4) Introns.

Ans. (1) **Monocistron:** The structural gene of enkaryote is called monocistron.

(2) **Polycistron:** The structural gene of bacteria or prokaryotes called polycistron.

(3 **Exons:** The coding sequences/expressed sequences of a structural genes is called exons.

(4) **Introns:** The intervening sequences that do not appear in the nature or processed RNA are called introns.

Q. 12. Mention the RNA polymerases of eukaryote nucleus. Write their notes also.

Ans. 3 RNA polymerases in the nucleus.

Types		**Role**
RNA polymerase I	—	transcribes rRNAs,
RNA polymerase II	—	transcribes precursor of m RNA, the heterogeneous nuclear RNA (hn RNA).
RNA polymerase III	—	transcribes t RNA, 5 Sr. RNA, Sr RNA (Small nuclear RNA).

Q. 13. Briefly explain the processes—(*i*) Splicing (*ii*) Capping (*iii*) Tailing

Ans. (*i*) **Splicing:** The transcribed primary transcripts have both exons and introns and are non-functional. To make it functional the introns are removed and exons are joined in a defined order. It is called splicing.

(*ii*) **Capping:** The addition of nucleotide—methyl guanosine triphosphate to 5′end of hn RNA is called capping.

(*iii*) **Tailing:** When adenylate residues (200–300) are added at 3′ end in a template independent manner a fully processed hn RNA then forms in RNA. This process is called tailing.

Q. 14. Mention any four salient features of genetic code.

Ans. (1) **Triplet code:** The genetic codes are is triplets. 61 codons code for amino acids and 3 codons do not. Hence they are called stop codons.

(2) **Specific codon:** One codon codes for only one amino acid i.e. they are specific and unambiguous.

(3) **Degenerate:** Some amino acids are coded by more than one codon.

(4) **Universal:** The codes are universal from bacteria to human with some exceptions.

Q. 15. Study the following figure:

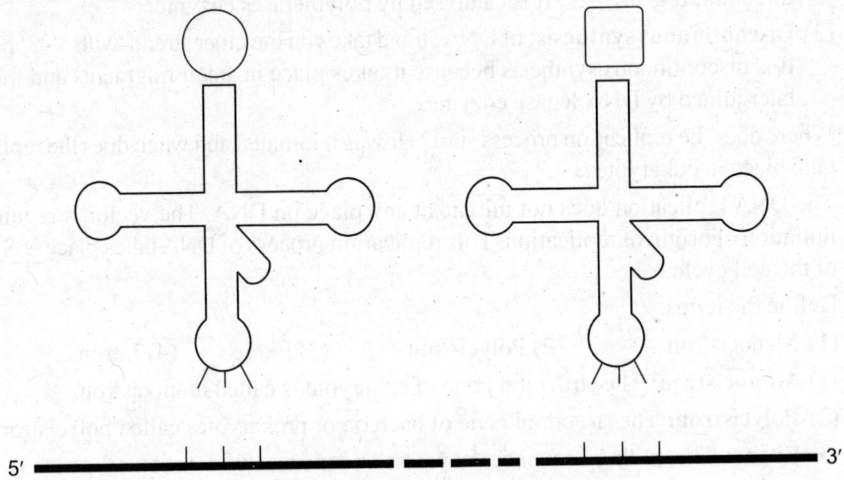

Fig. 6.4. tRNA–the adapter molecule.

(1) Draw and label anticodon and amino acid accepter end.
(2) The model name and the actual structure.
(3) The name of the molecule.

Ans. (1) Anticodon, amino acid accepter end

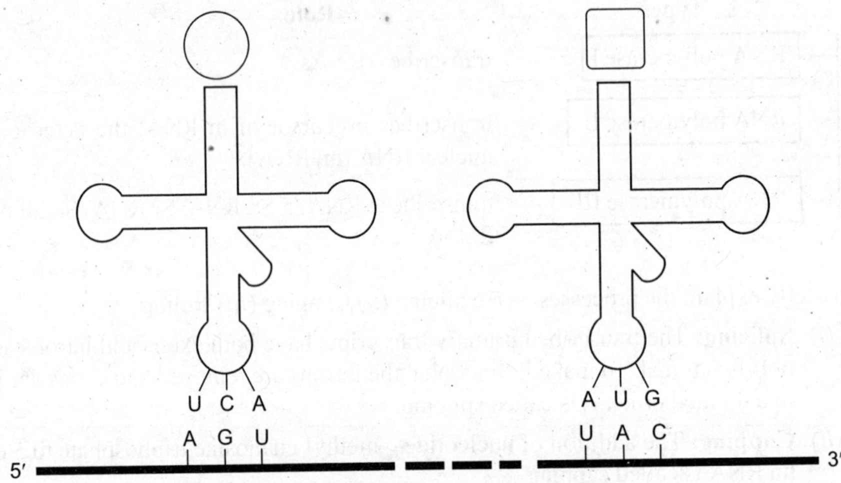

Fig. 6.4. tRNA–the adapter molecule.

(2) It is a clover-leaf model; actual structure is a compact molecule which looks like inverted L.

(3) t RNA— the adapter molecule.

Q. 16. Explain (in one or two lines) the function of the following:

(*a*) Promotor (*b*) tRNA (*c*) Exons

Ans. (*a*) **Promotor.** It is a sequence of DNA that provides the binding site for RNA polymerase. It is located towards 5—end of the structural gene.

(*b*) **t RNA.** It is a adapter molecule. It has an anticodon loop that has bases complementary to the code and are amino acid accepter end which binds to amino acids. tRNA are specific for each amino acid.

(*c*) **Exons.** The coding sequences/expressed sequences of structural genes are called exons. These sequences appear in the nature or processed RNA.

Q. 17. Depending upon the chemical nature of the template (DNA or RNA) and the nature of nucleic acids synthesised from it (DNA or RNA), list the types of nuclei acid polymerases.

Ans. RNA polymerase I, RNA polymerase II, RNA polymerase III.

Q. 18. In the medium where *E. coli* was growing, lactose was added, which induced the **lac** operon. Then, why does lac operon shut down some time after addition of lactose in the medium?

Ans. It is because in the presence of inducer (lactose) the repressor is inactivated by interaction with the inducer. Due to this transcription proceeds 3 enzymes—B-galactosidase, permease and transacetylase are synthesised. These are responsible for the hydrolysis of lactose into its monomer units. Lactose regulates the switching on or off of the operon.

Q. 19. Differentiate between the followings:

(*a*) Repetitive DNA and Satellite DNA.

(*b*) mRNA and tRNA.

(*c*) Template strand and coding stand.

Ans.

(*a*) *Repetitive DNA*	*Satellite DNA*
(1) Specific regions of DNA that are repeated in DNA finger printing is called repetitive DNA.	(1) The small peaks formed in DNA finger printing is called satellite DNA. (2) It can be classified into micro satellites, mini satellites.

(*b*) *mRNA*	*tRNA*
(1) mRNA is called messenger RNA.	(1) tRNA is called transfer RNA or adapter molecule.
(2) mRNA is transcribed from DNA template. It has message for a polypeptide synthesis.	(2) t RNAs are specific for each amino acid.
(3) It is a strand like structure. In the transcription unit.	(3) The compact molecule looks like inverted L.

(*c*) *Template Strand*	*Coding Strand*
(1) The DNA strand that has the polarity 3′ - 5′ is called template strand.	(1) The DNA strand that has polarity of 5′- 3′ as called as coding strand.
(2) The sequence is synthesised in RNA/ complementary DNA strand.	(2) The sequence of codes is same as RNA except for thymine.
(3) 3′—ATGCATGCATGCATGCATC —5′	(3) 5′—TACGTA CGTACGTACGTA CGTAGC—3′

Q. 20. Why is human genome project called a mega project?

Ans. The human genome project (HGP) was called a mega project because of following features:

1. **Number of base pair (bp):** Approximately 3 × 106bp sequencing was supposed to be done in human genome.
2. **Cost factor:** The estimated cost worked out to 9 billion USD.
3. **Storage in book:** If each page with 1000 letters, each book II with 1000 pages then 3300 books would be required.
4. **High speed computational devices:** Required for data processing.
5. **Development of new area:** In biology called 'Bioinformatics'.

6. **Time:** It was a time consuming project—13 years. Coordinated by U.S. Dept. of Energy and National Institute of Health. Contributions from many countries were done. It was launched in 1990 and completed in 2003.

Q. 21. What is DNA finger printing? Mention its application.

Ans. The method of identifying differences in some specific regions in DNA sequence of any two individuals is called DNA finger printing.

(1) It has its application in forensic science to identify the person involved in crime/ victim of crime.

(2) Paternity testing in case of disputes.

(3) Monozygotic twins have same DNA finger printings.

(4) For wider applications in determining population and genetic diversities.

LONG ANSWER TYPE QUESTIONS (LA)

Q. 1. How did Hershey and Chase differentiate between DNA and protein in their experiment while proving that DNA is the genetic material.

Ans.

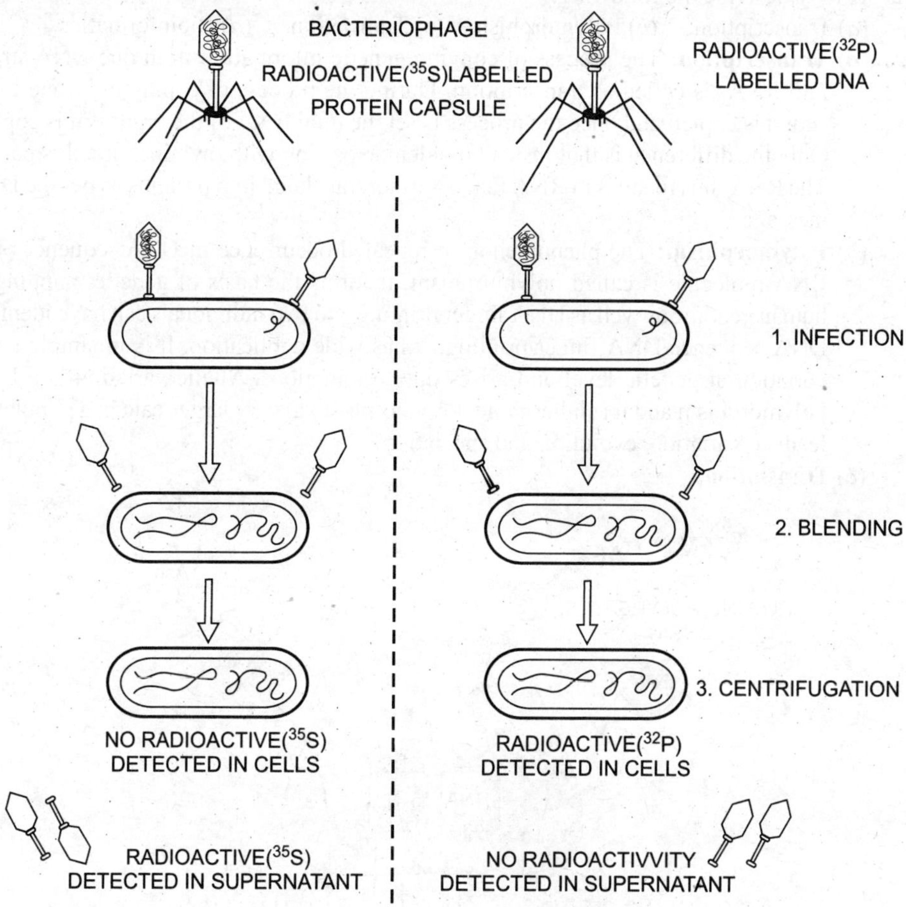

Fig. 6.5. The Hershey-Chase experiment.

Hershey and Chase (1952) worked with viruses that infected bacteria—Such viruses are called bacteriophages.

They studied which material enters into the bacterial cell. When the bacteriophages attach to a bacterium its genetic material enters into it. The bacterial cell treats the viral genetic material as its own and subsequently manufactures more virus particles. What was the genetic material —DNA/Protein.

Step 1. They grew viruses in two medium. One on medium that had radioactive phosphorus. The viruses grown on this medium has radioactive DNA because DNA has phosphorus and not for protein. The viruses grown in second medium having radioactive sulphur has viruses with radioactive protein because protein has sulphur and not in DNA.

Step 2. Radioactive bacteriophages were allowed to attach to *E. coli* as the infection proceeded the viral coats were removed from bacteria by agitating their in blender. The virus particles were separated from bacteria by centrifugation in centrifuge observation.

1. Bacteria which was infected with viruses that had radioactive DNA were radioactive indicating that DNA was the material that was passed from virus to bacteria.

2. Bacteria that was infected with viruses that had radioactive proteins were not radioactive. Indicating that proteins did not enter the bacteria from virus.

Conclusion:

DNA is the genetic material that is passed from virus to bacteria.

Q. 2. Briefly describe the following:

(*a*) Transcription, (*b*) Polymorphism, (*c*) Translation, (*d*) Bioinformatics.

Ans. (*a*) **Transcription:** The process of copying genetic information from one DNA strand into RNA is called as transcription. During the process of coping only one DNA strand is copied and once the process is set the total DNA of the organism is copied. Only the difference is that instead of adenine pairing with thymine, uracil is paired. The RNA thus made is m RNA that is further translated into proteins as per the DNA message.

(*b*) **Polymorphism:** The phenomenon of repeated occurrence of DNA sequences in a DNA molecule is called polymorphism. It forms the basis of genetic mapping of human genome as well as DNA finger printing. No two individuals can have identical DNA sequence/DNA finger printing. It has wide application. It is in simple terms variation at genetic level and arises due to mutations. Allelic variation is a DNA polymorphism and it is inheritable. Polymorphism at very large scale in a population leads to variation, evolution and speciation.

(*c*) **Translation:**

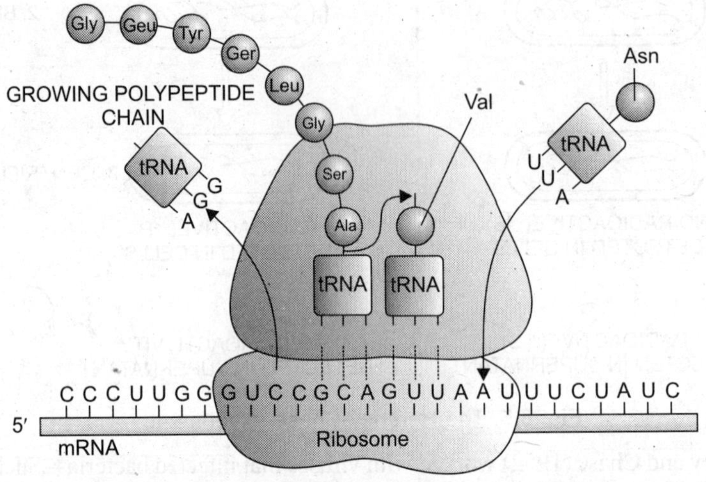

Fig. 6.6. Translation.

Translation in the process of polymerisation of the amino acids to form a polypeptide chain. This is according to the information/message coded on the mRNA from DNA. The formation of peptide bond between 2 amino acids requires energy. First the amino acid is activated in presence of ATP and linked to cognate tRNA — a process called charging of tRNA/aminocylation of tRNA. If two such charged tRNA come close enough then a peptide bond is formed in presence of a catalyst. Ribosomes are the cellular protein factories.

(*d*) **Bioinformatics:** It is the new branch of biology associated with HGP. It provides the study of data collection, methods and analysis.

NUTSHELL MIND MAP

Nucleotide → Nitrogenous base → Pentose sugar → Phosphate group

Nitrogenous bases → Adenine, Guanine, Cytosine (common to DNA, RNA), Thymine (in DNA), Uracil (in RNA)

Nucleoside → Nitrogenous base —(N-glycoside Liakage)— Pentose Sugar

Central Dogma — DNA (Replication) —transcription→ m RNA —translation→ Protein.

DNA helix → Histone → Nucleosome → Chromatin → Chromosome

DNA Finger Printing → Repetitive DNA → Satellite DNA

ABBREVIATIONS

bp	—	base pair
DNA	—	Deoxyribose Nucleic Acid
RNA	—	Ribose Nucleic Acid
NHC	—	Non Histone Chromosomal Proteins
tRNA	—	transfer RNA
SnRNA	—	Small nuclear RNA
hnRNA	—	heterogenous nuclear RNA - (unprocessed mRNA)
mRNA	—	Massenger RNA
UTR	—	Untranslated Regions (present on mRNA)
HGP	—	Human Genome Project (a mega project)
EST	—	Expressed Sequence Tags
BAC	—	Bacterial Artificial Chromosome
YAC	—	Yeast Artificial Chromosome
SNP	—	Single Nucleotide Polymorphism (pronounced as 'Snips')
VNTR	—	Variable Number of Tandem Repeats. (used in DNA)
PCR	—	Polymerase Chain Reaction (finger Printing analysis)

HIGHER ORDER THINKING SKILL (HOTS) QUESTIONS

1. What is the number of bp in *E. coli* and haploid content of human DNA? (*VSA*)
2. What is nucleoid? (*VSA*)
3. Mention the charges of DNA and histone protein. (*VSA*)
4. What do you understand by 'beads-on-string'? (*VSA*)
5. Which is transcriptionally active and inactive?
   (*a*) Heterochromatin, (*b*) Euchromatin. (*VSA*)
6. Name two viruses that have RNA the genetic material. (*VSA*)
7. Which nucleic acid was the first genetic material? (*VSA*)
8. Give one reason to state that DNA cannot be separated for entire length.
9. Mention the function of structural gene. (*VSA*)
10. What is the basic difference between m RNA of bacteria and enukaryoties'. (*SAI*)
11. (*i*) Expand the term-hn RNA active
    (*ii*) How is inactive hn RNA made into inactive m RNA
12. Mention the requirement of peptide bond formation during translation process. (*VSA*)
13. Mention the function of mRNA of a transitional unit and other component. (*SAI*)
14. (*i*) What is 'Snips'? (*SAI*)
    (*ii*) Which material can be lifted from crime scene by forensic experts for DNA finger printing?
15. Expand the following terms. Also mention their role.
    (*i*) bp (*ii*) HGP.

❑❑❑

CHAPTER 7

EVOLUTION

Chapter Outline

- Evolution
- Evolution of life forms A theory
- Hardy—Weinberg principle
- A brief account of evolution
- Origin and evolution of man.
- Biological evolution
- Mechanism of evolution
- What are the evidence for evolution?
- What is adaptive radiation?

ASSESSMENT QUESTIONS

VERY SHORT ANSWER TYPE QUESTIONS (VSA)

Q. 1. When did the life appear on earth?

Ans. Life appeared almost 4 billion years ago.

Q. 2. Which theory of origin of life is accepted by scientists? Who proposed it?

Ans. Chemical evolution by Oparin and Haldane.

Q. 3. What are fossils?

Ans. The remains of hard parts/impressions of life forms found on rocks is called fossil.

Q. 4. Illustrate an example to divergent evolution.

Ans. The presence of forelimbs with similar anatomical structure in different organisms is divergent evolution.

Q. 5. Give one example to homology in plants with names.

Ans. Thorn and tendril of *Bougainvillea* and *Cucurbita*.

Q. 6. What is convergent evolution?

Ans. Organs that perform similar function but are anatomically different shows convergent evolution *i.e.* wings of birds and butterfly.

Q. 7. What is the basis of adaptive ability to be inherited?

Ans. Genetic basis.

Q. 8. Name the person who proposed the idea of mutation causes evolution and what did he call it.

Ans. Hugo de Vries, Saltation. (Single step large mutation)

Q. 9. What is founder effect?

Ans. The drift in original population due to genetic drift is called founder effect.

Q. 10. Name the animal that evolved into amphibian.

Ans. Coelacanth—the lobe fin fish like animal.

Q. 11. Can we call human evolution as adaptive radiation?

Ans. Yes. Because the evolutionary process started in a given geographical area—Africa.

Q. 12. Attempt giving a clear definition of the term species.

Ans. The evolution of an individual due to adaptive radiation is called a species.

SHORT ANSWER TYPE QUESTIONS (SA)

Q. 1. Mention the various evidences for evolution you know.

Ans. (*a*) Paleontological

(*b*) Comparative anatomy and morphology

(*c*) Biochemical evidence

Q. 2. Here are given two plants—one with thorn and the other with tendril. What is this type of structure called? What is this type of evolution?

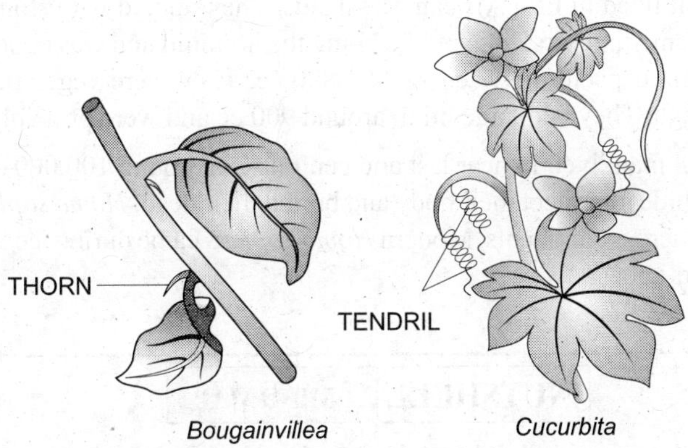

Fig. 7.1. Example of homologous organs in plants.

Ans. These structures are called homologous organs. The evolution is called divergent evolution. The organs indicate a common ancestry. These organs are the result of development in different direction due to adaptation to different needs.

Q. 3. Describe one example of adaptive radiation? (*NCERT*)

OR

Following is the figure of small black birds observed by Darwin in Galapagos Island. What was his observation and conclusion?

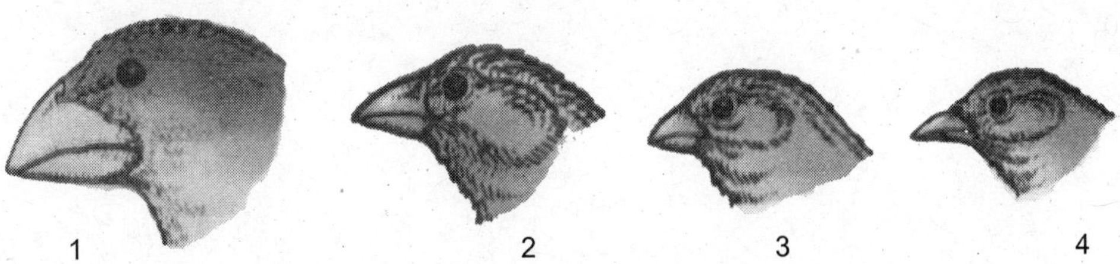

Fig. 7.2. Variety of beaks of finches that Darwin found in Galapagos Island.

Ans. The process of evolution of different species in a given geographical area from a point and literally radiating to other areas of habitats is called adaptive radiation. As observed in case of Darwin's finches, their existed varieties in Galapagos island he observed that small black birds. These birds originally evolved from seed eating to insect-eating birds. The seed eating features in beaks altered to insect eating and vegetarian finches. Another example is of Australian marsupials that evolved on Australian island from on ancestral stock.

Q. 4. (1) What is the basis of Hardy-Weinberg principle?

(2) Define the genetic equilibrium and

(3) What will be effect of disturbance in genetic equilibrium?

Ans. (1) Algebraic expressions.

(2) The total genes and their alleles in a population (gene root) remains constant. This is known as genetic equilibrium.

(3) The disturbance in the equilibrium would result in evolution.

Q. 5. Try to trace the various components of human evolution. (hint: brain size and function, skeletal structure, dietary preference etc.)

Ans. *Dryopithecus* and *Ramapithecus* originated 15 mya. They were hairy and walked like gorillas and chimpanzees. *Ramapithecus* was more man like *Australopithecines* came 2 mya and it lived in East African grasslands. They hunted with stone weapons and ate fruits. By same time first human like being the hominid and was called *Homo habilis*. It had the brain capacity between — 650-800 cc. They were vegetarians. *Homo erectus* came 1.5 mya. They had large brain around 900 cc and were probably non-vegetarians.

Neanderthal man lived in near last and central Asia around 100,000–40, 000 years ago. They used hide to protect their body and buried their dead. *Homo sapiens* arose in Africa and moved across continents. Modern *Homo Sapiens* came during ice age around 75,000–10,000 years ago.

NUTSHELL | MIND MAP

Universe is 20 billion years old. It has galaxies, clouds of gas and dust.
First non-cellular forms of life originated 3 billions years ago
First cellular form of life originated 2000 million years ago (mya)

Big bang ⟶ Universe 20 billion ⟶ O earth a speck 4.5 billion years ⟶ Life originated 4 billion years back

---

HIGHER ORDER THINKING SKILLS QUESTIONS (HOTS)

1. Name the scientist who experimented origin of life from chemicals. (*VSA*)
2. Eye of octopus and upi are homologous or analogous? (*VSA*)
3. What is common to these—

   Sweet potato, potato, flippers of penguins and dolphins? Write in brief about it. (*SAI*)
4. What is common to—

   (*a*) Darwin's finches, (*b*) Australian mammals and (*c*) Placenta mammals? Write in brief it. (*SAI*)
5. Mention the two key concepts of 'Darwinian' Theory of Evolution. (*VSA*)

❑❑❑

CHAPTER 8

HUMAN HEALTH AND DISEASE

Chapter Outline

- Common diseases in human
- Immunity
- AIDS
- Cancer
- Drugs and alcohol abuse.

ASSESSMENT QUESTIONS

VERY SHORT ANSWER TYPE QUESTIONS (VSA)

Q. 1. How you can maintain good health?

Ans. Good health can be maintained by balanced diet, personal hygiene and regular exercise.

Q. 2. What are pathogens?

Ans. The disease causing organisms are called pathogens.

Q. 3. A doctor identified following symptoms in a patient.

(*a*) Respiration problem, fever, cough and headache

(*b*) Gray nails, bluish finger nails and lips.

Name the disease and causative agent.

Ans Disease —Pneumonia, Causative agent —*S. pneumoniae*

Q. 4. What is haemozoin?

Ans. It is a toxic substance released by infected RBCs causing chill and high fever every 3-4 days in case of malaria.

Q. 5. Which stage of *Plasmodium* is introduced into human body, when a female *Anopheles* mosquito bites?

Ans. Sporozoites.

Q. 6. What is the source of contamination of food in case of amoebiasis? Name the vector.

Ans. Faeces of infected person, Housefly.

Q. 7. Which body parts are affected in filariasis?

Ans. Lymphatic vessels of legs (Lower limbs), genital organs.

Q. 8. Define immunity.

Ans. The ability of the body to fight the pathogens conferred/due to immune system is called immunity.

Q. 9. Which WBCs act as cellular barriers in innate immunity?

Ans. (1) Polymorpho-nuclear leukocytes—neutrophils

(2) monocytes

Q. 10. Mention the different types of antibodies produced by our body.

Ans. IgA, IgM, IgE and IgG.

Q. 11. What is the purpose of giving 'vaccine' to a person?

Ans. The two purposes are—

(1) To produce antibodies against the antigens injected/given as vaccine which would neutralise the agents during actual infection.

(2) To generate memory cells—Band cells to recognise the pathogen quickly.

Q. 12. Which type of antibodies are produced against allergy?

Ans. IgE type.

Q. 13. Name a few drugs used to reduce the symptoms of allergy

Ans. (1) Anti-histamine, (2) Adrenalin, (3) Steroids.

Q. 14. Mention the expanded form of MALT.

Ans. Mucosal Associated Lymphoid Tissue.

Q. 15. In which cases—following tests are done—Widal, Elisa?

Ans. (1) Typhoid, (2) AIDS.

Q. 16. What is metastasis?

Ans. It is the property of cells sloughed from malignant tumors to start a new tumor whereever they get lodged in the body.

Q. 17. Which diseases are caused by: (1) Retero virus and (2) Oncogenic virus?

Ans. (1) Retero virus causes AIDS *e.g.* HIV.

(2) Oncogenic virus causes cancer.

Q. 18. Give examples to any two commonly abused drugs.

Ans. (1) Opioids, (2) Cannabinoids or coca alkaloids.

Q. 19. What you understand by the term drug abuse?

Ans. When certain medicines/drugs are taken for purpose of other than medicinal use or in amounts/pregnancy that impairs one's body functions is called drug abuse.

Q. 20. Name the primary and secondary Lymphoid organs.

Ans. (1) **Primary Lymphoid organs**—thymus, bone marrow.

(2) **Secondary Lymphoid organs**—spleen, tonsils.

Q. 21. In which way has the study is biology helped us to control infectious diseases?

Ans. It has enabled us to deal effectively with many infectious diseases, eradicate diseases, control the diseases and effectively treat the infectious diseases.

SHORT ANSWER TYPE QUESTIONS (SA-I, SA-II)

Q. 1. Mention in brief various factors that can affect health.

Ans. Health is affected by:

1. **Genetic disorders**— The disorders developed in an individual which are inherited from either of the parents. It is called congenital disorder.
2. **Infections**— The disorders/diseases caused due to pathogenic organisms.
3. **Life style**— The life style of a person is responsible for developing disorders/diseases.

Q. 2. Define health and its benefits.

Ans. It is the state of complete physical, mental and social wellbeing.

Benefits of health are—

(1) Increase the productivity and brings economic prosperity.

(2) Increases the life (*Longevity*).

(3) It reduces infant and maternal mortality.

Q. 3. What are various public health measures which you would suggest as safeguard against infectious diseases?

Ans. (1) Awareness about diseases and their effect on different body functions.

(2) Vaccination programmes.

(3) Waste disposals.

(4) Control of vectors (mosquito and housefly breeding).

(5) Hygienic food and water resources.

Q. 4. How does transmission of each of the following diseases take place?

(*a*) Amoebiasis, (*b*) Malaria, (*c*) Ascariasis, (*d*) Pneumonia.

Ans.

Diseases	***Mode of Transmission***
(*a*) Amoebiasis	(*a*) Contaminated food and water
(b) Malaria	(*b*) Biting of female anopheles mosquito
(c) Ascariasis	(c) Contaminated vegetables, fruits and water
(d) Pneumonia	(*d*) Inhalation of droplets/aerosols released by infected person during coughing

Q. 5. A patient went to Dr. Swati with following symptoms. Sustained high fever (39°-40° C), weakness headache, loss of appetite and stomach pain. Which test would Dr. Swati recommend? If positive, name the causative agent and the disease. What is the possible mode of infection?

Ans. Test recommented — Widal test.

Causative agent — *Salmonella typhi*

Disease — Typhoid

Mode of infection — Contaminated food and water.

Q. 6. What measures would you like to take to prevent water-borne diseases?

Ans. 1. Consumption of clear drinking water.

2. Proper disposal of waste and excreta.

3. Periodic cleaning and disinfection of water reservoirs.

4. Awareness about diseases.

Q. 7. The following are some well-known abbreviations which have been used in this chapter. Expand each one to its full form:

(*a*) MALT, (*b*) CMI, (*c*) AIDS, (*d*) NACO, (*e*) HIV.

Ans.

Abbreviation	*Expanded form*
(*a*) MALT	Mucosal Associated Lymphoid Tissue
(*b*) CMI	Cell—Mediated Immunity
(*c*) AIDS	Acquired Immune Deficiency Syndrome.
(*d*) NACO	National Aids Control Organisation
(*e*) HIV	Human Immune Deficiency Virus.

Q. 8. Differentiate the following and give examples to each:

(*a*) Innate and acquired immunity (*b*) Active and passive immunity

Ans.

(*a*) ***Innate immunity***	***Acquired immunity***
1. The non-specific type of defence of the body is called innate immunity.	1. Pathogen specific type of defence of the body is called acquired immunity.
2. It is present at the time of birth of the child.	2. It is developed due to infections.
3. It is due to 4 types of barriers. (*a*) Physical *e.g.* skin, mucus, (*b*) Physiological *e.g.* acid in stomach, saliva, tears. (*c*) Cellular *e.g.* WBCs, macrophages. (*d*) Cytokine *e.g.* interferous.	3. It is memory based and of 2 types. (*a*) Antibody mediated *e.g.* antibody produced in response to aniantigen. (*b*) Cell mediated *e.g.* graft rejection.

(*b*) ***Active immunity***	***Passive immunity***
1. The immunity developed in the body due to antigens is called active immunity. 2. It is slow and takes time to develop and gives full effectiveness.	1. The immunity developed in body due to ready made antibodies when given to body is called passive immunity (vaccinations).

Q. 9. Draw a well-labelled diagram of an antibody molecule.

Ans.

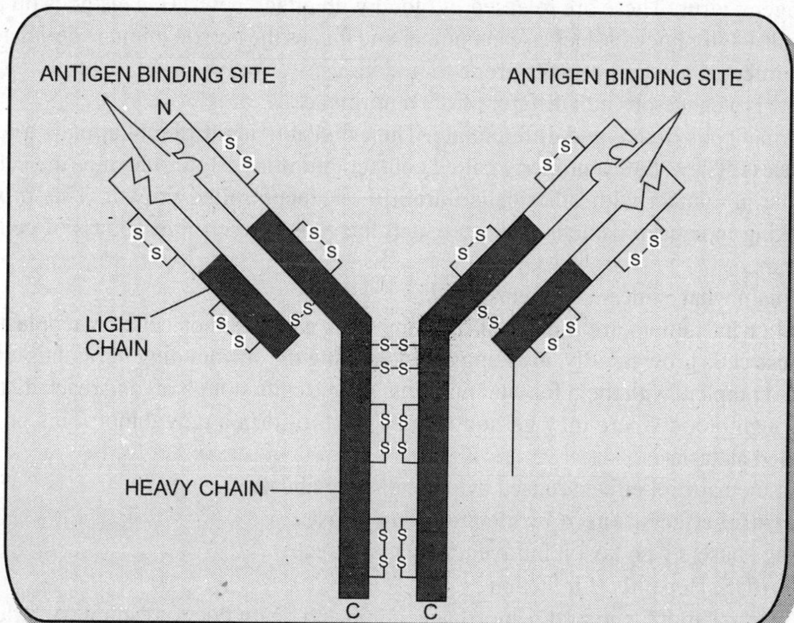

Fig. 8.1. Structure of an antibody molecule.

Q. 10. What is vaccination? What is the role of vaccines in body? Give two examples when immediate response is needed by body to defend it, name this type of immunisation.

Ans. The process of injecting giving vaccine into the body for developing immunity is called **vaccination**. The role of vaccine is to produce memory cells—B and T cells. Vaccines for tetanus, snake bites–this type of immunisation is called passive immunisation.

Q. 11. What is auto immunity? How it is caused? Give one example.

Ans. The body sometimes 'attacks' self cells, this type of activity is called autoimmunity. It is caused due to some unknown and genetic reasons. *e.g.* rheumatoid arthritis.

Q. 12. Which type of organ is spleen? What is its role and function in the body?

Ans. Spleen is a secondary lymphoid organ. It is the site for interaction of lymphocytes with the antigen, which then divide to become effector cells.

It has lymphocytes and phagocytes. It acts as a filter of blood by trapping the blood-borne microorganisms. It also acts as a reservoir of erythrocytes.

Q. 13. What are the various routes by which transmission of human immune deficiency virus takes place? *(NCERT)*

Ans. **Transmission of HIV** takes place following means:

(1) Sexual contact with infected person.

(2) Transfusion of contaminated blood and blood products.

(3) Sharing the infected needles.

(4) From the infected mother to her developing child through placenta.

Q. 14. What is the mechanism by which the AIDS virus causes deficiency of immune system of the infected person?

Ans. The mechanism followed in an infected person by the AIDS virus—HIV is as follows:

1. HIV — Macrophages   virus particles
        \ T-lymphocytes (T_H)   progeniy virus.

2. Progendiy virus → Blood → TH.

The virus enters the body of the person and attacks macrophages which starts producing virus particles. Simultaneously, they also attack T-lymphocytes helper cells that produce progeny virus. These are released in blood with attack new TH. This goes on and as a result T-lymphocytes decrease in number and makes the person immune deficient. Thus, the infected person becomes prone to infections.

Q. 15. How is a cancerous cell different from a normal cell?

Ans. Normal cells divide and differentiate. Their division and differentiation is a regulated process. They show a property called contact inhibition. By virtue of it, the cells when come in contact with other cells inhibit their uncontrolled growth. This property is lacking in cancerous cells. Due to which the cells convert into a mass of cells called tumor.

Q. 16. Explain what is meant by metastasis?

Ans. Malignant tumors are a mass of dividing cells called tumor cells or neoplastic cells. These cells grow rapidly, invading and damaging the surrounding normal tissues. They also complete with them for vital nutrients. These cells slough off and reach distant sites through blood where they get lodged and start to form a new tumor. This property is called metastasis.

Q. 17. List the harmful effects caused by alcohol/drug abuse.

Ans. **Harmful effects caused by alcohol/drug abuse.**

Drug abusers who take it intravenously may cause

(1) AIDS, Hepatitis B infection

(2) Heart failure, cerebral hemorrhage, coma and death due to respiratory failure.

(3) In females—masculisation, aggressiveness, mood swings, enlargement of some organ. During pregnancy it adversely effects the foetus.

Alcohol abusers who become addicts may show:

(1) Damaged nervous system and

(2) Liver-cirrhosis.

(3) Reckless behaviour, vandalism and violence.

Q. 18. Do you think friends can influence one to take alcohol/drugs? If yes, how may one protect himself/herself from such an influence.

Ans. It all depends on an individual's inner strength. If one believes in oneself, accepts the falls and rises in sports academics evenly, happily and can face and cope with such situations, then the answer is **NO.**

If an individual has weak inner strength, then he/she can easily be carried away to overcome the above situations and can get influenced. On the other hand, if he/she is experimental/curiosity mode then a strong will power is needed to keep one-self at bay to reject such things to groups of friends.

Q. 19. In your view what motivates youngsters to take to alcohol/drugs and how can this be avoided?

Ans. Refer ans. to Q. 18 above.

Q. 20. List some preventive and control measures for students regarding alcohol and drugs abuse.

Ans. (1) Avoid undue peer pressure.

(2) Seek help from parents and peers.

(3) Self education and counselling.

(4) Seeking professional and medical help.

(5) Awareness of danger signs, harmful effects on body and life.

Q. 21. Give the information you have under the following heads in reference to the drugs mentioned therein. Answer any **One.**

(*i*) Source

(*ii*) Mode of intake

(*iii*) Effect of drug on body

(*a*) opioids, (*b*) cannabinoids, (*c*) coca alkaloid, (*d*) LSD.

Ans. (*a*) **Opioids**

(*i*) **Source: Paperer somriferum** (Poppy plant). Latex form of this plant. Acetylation of morphine extracted from latex.

(*ii*) **Mode of intake:** By snorting and injection.

(*iii*) **Effect of drug on body:** Depressant and slows down the body junctions.

(*b*) **Cannabinoids**

(*i*) **Source: Cannabis sativa** (Bhang plant). The flower tops, leaves and resin.

(*ii*) **Mode of intake:** By inhalation and oral ingestion.

(*iii*) *Effect of drug on body*: Cardio vascular system.

(*c*) **Coca alkaloid**

(*i*) **Source:** *Erythroxylum coca* (Coca plant)

(*ii*) **Mode of intake:** By snorting

(*iii*) **Effect of drug on body:** Stimulating action on CW System, hallucinations,

(*d*) **LSD**—Lysergic acid diethyl amides.

(*i*) **Source:** Medicines

(*ii*) **Mode of intake:** By injections, oral ingestion.

(*iii*) **Effect on body:** Hallucination, tranquility.

Q. 22. Define the term cancer. Mention its types, causes, detection and diagnosis and preventive measures if any.

Ans. The uncontrolled growth of cells is called cancer. Broadly it is classified as:

Cancer

- **Benign** — The cancer cells are confined to their original location and do not spread to other parts and cause with damage.
- **Malignant** — The cancer cells are on move to reach other parts of the body and start proliferating. These cause damage to normal tissues. They starve the normal cells.

Certain agents called carcinogens, oncogenic virus, cellular oncogenes (C-one) when activated cause cancer. Cancer can be detected by biopsy and histopathological studies, radiography, CT, MRI, antibiotics, molecular biology. Once diagnosis is done the treatment of the same by combination of various therapies is recommended. Preventive measures include the avoidance of carcinogens.

NUTSHELL MINDMAP

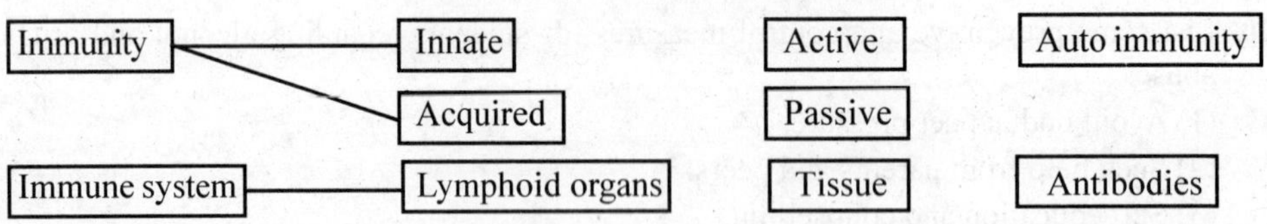

HIGHER ORDER THINKING SKILLS (HOTS)

1. Name the host and organ where material sporozoites are formed. (*VSA*)
2. Name the diseases caused by—
   (*a*) *Trichophyton*, (*b*) *W. bancrofti*
3. What is the role of: (1) Interferon, (2) L-Interferon?
4. What is colostrum? Which antibodies are present in it? What is the immunity developed by it called? (*SA*)
5. Which technology has helped us to produce vaccines by use of bacteria/yeast? Give one example to it. (*VSA*)
6. Name at least two drugs that help to reduce the symptoms of allergy. (*VSA*)
7. Briefly write about mucosal associated lymphoid tissue. (*SAI*)
8. Mention the causes of neoplastic transformation. (*VSA*)
9. Study the following chemical structures.

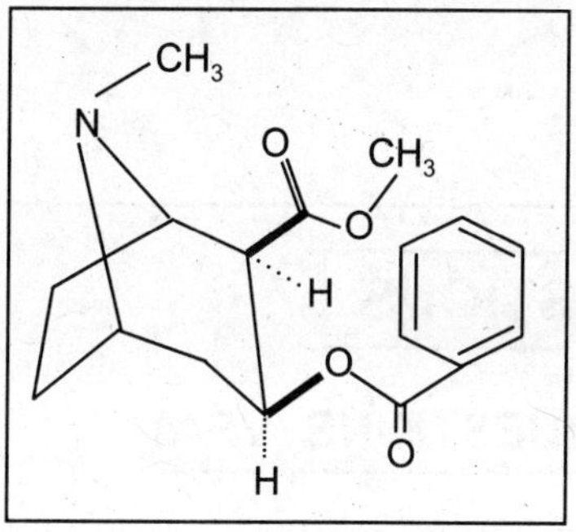

Fig. 8.2(a)

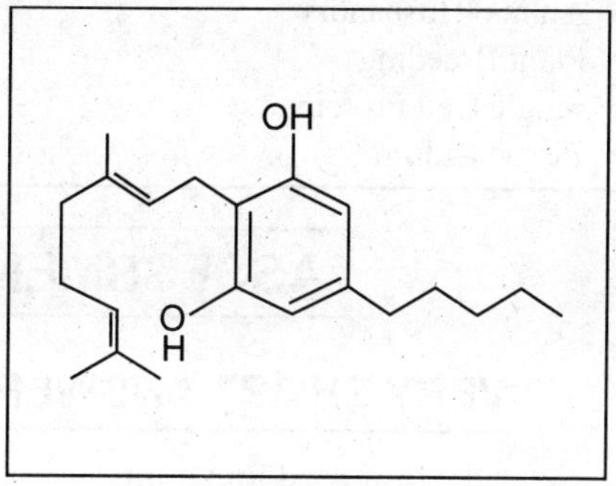

Fig. 8.2(b)

Name the chemical and its category. Mention its effects on the body. (*SA*)

10. What do you understand by withdrawal syndrome? (*SA*)

❑❑❑

CHAPTER 9

STRATEGIES FOR ENHANCEMENT IN FOOD PRODUCTION

Chapter Outline

- Animal Husbandry
- Plant Breeding
- Single Cell Proteins
- Tissue Culture

ASSESSMENT QUESTIONS

VERY SHORT ANSWER TYPE QUESTIONS (VSA)

Q. 1. Name the fowl used for poultry.

Ans. (1) Chicken (2) Duck (3) Turkey (4) Geese.

Q. 2. How is inbreeding different from outbreeding?

Ans. In inbreeding, the breeding is between animals of the same breed whereas in outbreeding the breeding is by crossing animals of different breeds.

Q. 3. What does superior female mean in cow or buffalo?

Ans. Superior female means it produces more milk per lactation period.

Q. 4. What is superior male in cow or buffalo?

Ans. Superior male means the bull which gives rise to superior progeny as compared to other bulls/males.

Q. 5. How does inbreeding depression take place?

Ans. Continued inbreeding (specially close breeding) leads to inbreeding depression. It reduces fertility and production both.

Q. 6. How can inbreeding depression be overcome?

Ans. It can be overcome by breeding of selected animals of the breeding population with unrelated superior animals of same breed.

Q. 7. Name the parent of **Hisardale** a new breed of sheep developed in Punjab.

Ans. Bikaneri ewes and Marino ram.

Q. 8. Expand the term MOET

Ans. **MOET**— Multiple Ovulation Embryo Transfer Technology.

Q. 9. Name any two of each type eaten.

(a) Fresh water fishes (b) Marine fishes in food

Ans. (*a*) Catla, Rohu (*b*) Hilsa, Pomfrets.

Q. 10. Which HYV wheat varieties were introduced in India in 1963, for Green revolution?

Ans. (1) *Sonalika* (2) *Kalyan Sona*

Q. 11. Name the sugar cane varieties of North and South India used to hybrid variety for high yields, sugar and thick stem.

Ans. *Saccharum barberi, Saccharum officinarum*.

Q. 12. Define germ plasm collection.

Ans. The process of entire collection (of plants/seeds) having all the diverse alleles for all genes in a given crop is called as germplasm collection.

Q. 13. Name the bacterial blight disease resistant variety of cowpea.

Ans. Pusa Komal

Q. 14. Which radiations are used to induce mutations in plants.

Ans. Gamma radiations.

Q. 15. Name the insect pest to which *Pusa Gaurav*, a variety of *Brassica* is resistant?

Ans. Aphids.

Q. 16. Expand the term SCP.

Ans. SCP—Single Cell Protein.

Q. 17. Mention one source of alternate proteins for animal and human nutrition.

Ans. Single cell protein.

Q. 18. How are clones produced?

Ans. By tissue culture—micro propagation.

Q. 19. Give two examples to commercial plants produced by tissue culture method.

Ans. (1) Tomato (2) Banana

Q. 20. Mention any one benefit of tissue culture.

Ans. Virus free plants (disease free) from diseased plants.

SHORT ANSWER TYPE QUESTIONS (SA)

Q. 1. Explain in brief the role of animal husbandry in human welfare.

Ans. The agricultural practice of breeding and raising live stock is animal husbandry. It has benefited the human in developing the better breeds of animals. It has improved the quantity and quality of the animal products. The economical condition of people involved in agriculture has improved and their lives have become better.

Q. 2. If your family owned a dairy farm, what measures would you undertake to improve the quality and quantity of milk production?

Ans. Measures to be undertaken to improve the quantity of milk yield are—

(*a*) Selection of good breeds having high yielding potential (HYV) should be choosen.

(*b*) The breeds should be diseases resistant.

(*c*) They should be taken care by giving proper house/shed.

(*d*) They should be hygienically kept, disease free and regular checkup done by a veterinary doctor.

(*e*) They should be given good quality fodder.

(*f*) The handlers should be clean and follow hygiene while milking.

Q. 3. What is meant by the term 'breed''? What are the objectives of animal breeding?

Ans. A group of animals related by descent and similar in most characteristics is called as breed.

Then main objectives of animal breeding are:

1. Produce live stock of that give high yield.
2. Produce live stock of desired qualities of produce.
3. Produce/increase the hard size in a short time.

Q. 4. Name the methods employed in animal breeding. According to you which of the methods is best? Why?

Ans. Broadly there are two methods employed in animal breeding

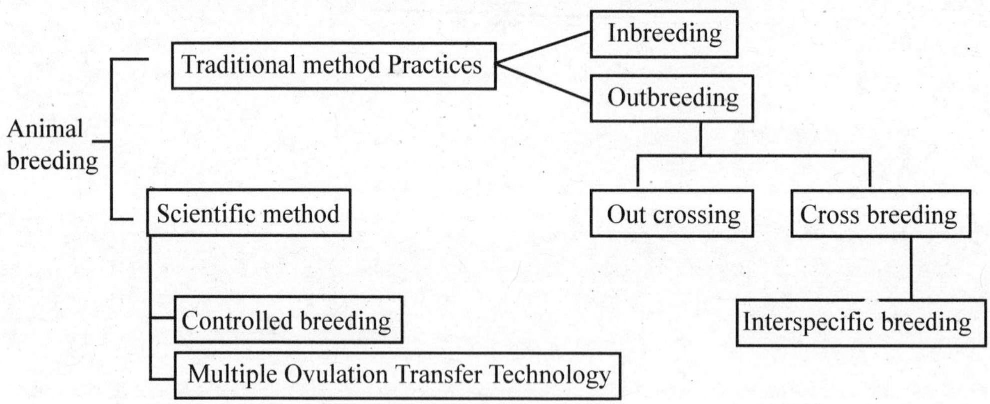

Scientific methods are better in animal breeding.

Specifically MOET method is better because of its:

(*a*) Successful production of hybrids.

(*b*) The egg donor is used again and again and surrogate mothers are used for development of embryos.

(*c*) Successfully increases herd size in a short time.

Q. 5. What is apiculture? How is it important is our lives? (NCERT)

Ans. Beekeeping is called apiculture. It is the maintenance of lives of honeybees for honey production. It is important because:

(*a*) It is the source of honey production.

(*b*) It is the source of beeswax used in various industries.

(*c*) It helps pollinating flowers that is necessary for fruit production, *e.g.* mustard seeds.

Q. 6. Discuss the role of fishery in enhancement of food production.

Ans. Fisheries play an important role in food production. A large number of population is dependent on fish for food. The fishes are of two types—fresh water and marine water. The pisciculture leads to increase in production of fishes and other marine/aquatic animals due to which food production has increased. It is known as Blue Revolution.

Q. 7. Mention any four points important for successful beekeeping.

Ans. 1. Selection of suitable location for keeping bee lives.

2. Management of beehives during different seasons.
3. Knowledge of nature and habits of bees.
4. Handling and collection of products.

Q. 8. Explain what is meant by biofortification?

Ans. Breeding of plants/crops with higher levels of nutrients especially—vitamins, minerals and proteins called biofortification. Plants with enriched nutrients are bred and cultivated to produce rich diet. This is requirement to fulfil the 'hidden hunger' of people who cannot afford to buy enough of fruits and vegetables fish milk and meat. This will 'cure' their deficiency diseases and such population can lead a disease-free life, thereby increases their life span.

Q. 9. Which part of the plant is best suited for making virus-free plants and why?

Ans. Meristem. Because this part is free of virus. After removing it from the plant it can be cultured **in vitro.**

Q. 10. What is the major advantage of producing plants by micro-propagation?

Ans. **Advantages are:**

1. Each plant produced is genetically alive to their parent/original plant. *i.e.* They are same clones.
2. Large number of plants are produced in short duration.

Q. 11. Find out what the various components of the medium used for propagation of an explant *in vitro* are.

Ans. **Components of medium are:**

(1) Sucrose, (2) Inorganic salts, (3) Vitamins, (4) Amino acids, (5) Growth regulators.

Q. 12. Name any five hybrid varieties of crop plants which have been developed in India.

Ans.

Crop	*Variety*
1. *Brassica*	1. Pusa Gaurav 2. Pusa Swarnim
2. Cowpea	1. Pusa Komal
3. Flat bean	1. Pusa Sem 2 2. Pusa Sem 3

Q. 13. What is inbreeding? Why it is done? Give one disadvantage of this type of breeding method.

Ans. When the breeding between animals of the same breed is done then it's called inbreeding. It is done for evolving a pureline of any animal. It leads to inbreeding depression among the breeds.

Q. 14. What is interspecific hybridisation? Give one example.

Ans. The process of mating/crossing animals of two different related species is called interspecific mating. Mule.

Q. 15. How can one do plant breeding for developing resistance to insect pests? Give a few examples to insect resistance characteristics. Also mention the source of pest resistance genes.

Ans. Breeding methods for insect pest resistance involve the same steps as that are needed for other agronomic traits.

Insect resistance characteristics are:

1. Hairy leaves *e.g.* cotton plant has hairy leaves for jassids resistance, in wheat for cereal leaf beetle.
2. Soothed leaf and nectar less cotton varieties do not attract boll worms.
3. Solid stems in wheat are not attacked by stem sawfly.
4. High content of aspartic acid, low nitrogen and sugar content in maize leads to resistance of maize stem bores.

Sources of resistance genes are - cultivated crops, ger plasm of crop/wild varieties.

Q. 16. Briefly write about only two:

(*a*) Out breeding, (*b*) Cross breeding, (*c*) Controlled breeding.

Ans. (*a*) **Out breeding:** It is the process of breeding of the unrelated animals. The animals that are bred are of the same breed but they do not have common ancestors for 4-6 generations. Also animals of different breeds or different species is used for breeding.

(*b*) **Cross breeding:** It is the process of crossing of superior males of one breed with superior females of another breed. By this type of breeding desirable qualities of two different breeds are obtained in the hybrid. The hybrids can be commercially exploited for production. It can also be used for inbreeding. By this method many animal breeds have been produced.

(*c*) **Controlled breeding:** It is the process of artificial insemination. The semen is collected from a male and injected into the reproductive tract of a selected female. The semen may be used immediately at same place or even be frozen transported to distant locations. In this way, the breeding is controlled by the breeder self.

Q. 17. Mention the steps that plant breeds has to undertake to develop a new genetic variety of plant.

Ans. Various steps involved are:

1. **Germ plasm collection**

   The plant breeder has to develop a collection of all varieties of the crop. *i.e.* wild, species and relatives. This is done for exploitation of natural genes available in the population.

2. **Evaluation and selection of parents**

   The germplasm is evaluated and plants are identified for the desirable combination of characters. The selected plants are multiplied for creating purelines of the crops.

3. **Cross hybridisation**

   This step involves the production of hybrids by cross hybridisation/breeding. The hybrid progeny will have the desirable traits of both parents crossed. It is not an easy and one step go as it is not necessary that the hybrid progeny can be produced; as its probability is 1/100 or 1/1000 crosses (one hybrid may developed in 100/1000 crosses clones.)

4. **Selection and testing of superior recombinants**
The selection of desirable hybrids is done from the hybrids available. Some times many hybrids are produced. Then they have to be tested for several generations for developing uniformity by self pollination so that the desired traits do not separate.
5. **Testing, release and commercialisation of new cultivars**
The new selected lines are evaluated for the yield, agronomic traits etc. in research fields under ideal condition of requirements. Then they are cultivated for 3 seasons in a farmer's field in various agroclimatic zones where the crop is usually grown and comparative evaluation is done.

NUTSHELL | MIND MAP

MOET → Hormone to female animal → Super mutation 6-8 eggs → Mating/ Artificial insemination → Blastocysts → Surrogate mother → Progeny

Table 9.1

Crop	Variety	Resistance to diseases
Wheat	Himgiri	Leaf and stripe rust, hill bunt
Brassica	Pusa Swarnim (Karan rai)	White rust
Cauliflower	Pusa Shubhra, Pusa Snowball K-1	Black rot and curl blight black rot
Cowpea	Pusa Komal	Bacterial blight
Chilli	Pusa Sadabahar	Chilly mosaic virus, tobacco mosaic virus and leaf curl

Table 9.2

Crop	Variety	Insect Pests
Brassica (rapeseed mustard)	Pusa Gaurav	Aphids
Flat bean	Pusa Sem 2, Pusa Sem 3	Jassids, aphids and fruit borer
Okra (bhindi)	Pusa Sawani Pusa A-4	Shoot and fruit borer

Table 9.3

Crop	Biofortified products fortified by
1. Rice	Iron
2. Wheat	Protein
3. Carrot, Spinach, Pumpkin	Vitamin A
4. Bitter gourd, bathua, mustard, tomato	Vitamin C
5. **Bathua,** Spinach	Iron, calcium
6. Broad bean, French bean, garden peas	Protein.

HIGHER ORDER THINKING SKILLS (HOTS) QUESTIONS

1. Mention the cause/reason of increase in homozygosity in animal breeds. (*VSA*)
2. What are the disadvantages of inbreeding in animals? (*SA I*)
3. Name the Nobel laureate who introduced dwarf varieties of wheat. How was it useful to India? (*SA I*)
4. *Saccharum barberi* a variety originally grown in North India and *Saccharum officinarum* grown in South India are two varieties of sugar cane. How do they differ from each other? What was done by use of them for cross breeding? (*SA II*)

❑❑❑

CHAPTER 10

MICROBES IN HUMAN WELFARE

Chapter Outline

- Microbes in household products
- Microbes in industrial products
- Microbes in sewage Treatment
- Microbes in production of biogas
- Microbes as biocontrol agents
- Microbes as biofertilisers.

ASSESSMENT QUESTIONS

VERY SHORT ANSWER TYPE QUESTIONS (VSA)

Q. 1. Expand the term LAB.

Ans. **LAB**—Lactic Acid Bacteria.

Q. 2. Mention any two benefits of lactic acid bacteria.

Ans. 1. Helps in formation of curd from milk.

2. Checks disease causing, microbes in our stomach.

Q. 3. How is 'Roquefort cheese' ripened?

Ans. It is ripened by growing a specific fungi.

Q. 4. Bacteria cannot be seen with the naked eyes but these can be seen with the help of a microscope, If you have to carry a sample from your home to your biology laboratory to demonstrate the presence of microbes under a microscope, which sample would you carry and why?

Ans. **Curd.** Because it can be easily viewed under a microscope in school laboratory.

Q. 5. Name the vessels used for growing microbes at industrial level.

Ans. Fermentors.

Q. 6. Name the alcoholic product produced from fermentation of malted cereals and fruit juices by *S. cerevisiae.*

Ans. Ethanol.

Q. 7. What is the name of first antibiotic discovered?

Ans. Penicillin.

Q. 8. Name the enzyme present in detergent formulation, to remove oily stains from the laundry.

Ans. Lipases.

Q. 9. Bottled fruit juices available in market are clear because of which enzymes? Name these.

Ans. (1) Pectinases (2) Proteases.

Q. 10. What are bioactive molecules?

Ans. Bioactive molecules are molecules that are helpful in maintaining human health by developing conditions favourable to the body.

Q. 11. Define the term flocs.

Ans. The mass aerobic bacteria associated with fungal filaments forming a mesh like structure are called flocs.

Q. 12. What is BOD?

Ans. BOD—It is biochemical oxygen demand, *i.e.* the amount of oxygen consumed by aerobic bacteria to oxidise the organic matter in litre of water.

Q. 13. What is the source of biogas during secondary treatment or biological treatment of sewage?

Ans. Flocs.

Q. 14. What are methanogens?

Ans. Methanogens are a group of bacteria that digest cellulose to produce methane.

Q. 15. What does the rising floating cover of biogas plant indicate?

Ans. The production and collection of biogas/gobar gas.

Q. 16. What do you understand by biocontrol?

Ans. The use of biological methods for controlling the plant diseases and pests is called biocontrol.

Q. 17. What are the harmful effects of chemicals such as insecticides and pesticides?

Ans. It pollutes the environment (soil, ground/land, water) and harmiul to living beings-human-animals and plants.

Q. 18. What is Bt?

Ans. It is *Bacillus thuringiensis.*

Q. 19. Define biofertilisers?

Ans. Organisms that enrich the nutrient quality of the soil are called as biofertilisers.

Q. 20. What is the symbiotic association of fungus and plants called as?

Ans. Mycorrhiza.

Q. 21. In which way have microbes played a major role in controlling diseases caused by harmful bacteria?

Ans. By producing chemicals that inhibit the growth of microbes—antibiotics.

Q. 22. Name any two species of fungus, which are used in the production of the antibiotics?

Ans. *Penicillium.*

Q. 23. Mention the name of the microbes from which cyclosporin (an immune suppressive drug) and statins (blood cholesterol lowering agents) are released?

Ans. *Trichoderma polysporum, Monascus purpurens.*

Q. 24. Name some traditional Indian foods made of wheat, rice and bengal gram (or their products) which involve use of microbes?

Ans. (1) Dosa, idli, (2) Dokla.

Q. 25. How do biofertilisers enrich the fertility of the soil?

Ans. They enrich atmospheric nitrogen into organic forms that can be used by plants.

SHORT ANSWER TYPE QUESTIONS (SA-I, II)

Q. 1. Mention the microbes groups and chemical infectious agents that cause diseases to human and other organisms?

Ans. Microbes are—protozoa, bacteria, fungi, microscopic plants.
Chemical agents (proteins) are—viruses, viroids, prions.

Q. 2. Give examples to prove that microbes release gases during metabolism.

Ans. (*i*) Production of CO_2 gas in dough for making foods such as dosa, idli, bread, swiss cheese etc.

(*ii*) Production of CO_2 gas methane and hydrogen from the anaerobic sludge, gobar—the gas is also called biogas/gobar gas.

Q. 3. In which food would you find lactic acid bacteria? Mention some of their useful applications?

Ans. Milk and curd.
They convert the milk into curd. This increases the nutritional quality by increasing the B_{12}. The LAB also checks the disease causing microbes.

Q. 4. Mention a few examples to use of microbes in household products

Ans. 1. *Lactobacillus* in making of curd from milk.
2. Bacteria in making dough or dosa, idli.
3. Microbes in fermentation of palm caps to make toddy.
4. Microbes-in making cheese.

Q. 5. Mention the microbes involved in production of—
(*a*) acetic acid, (*b*) streptokinase, (*c*) cyclosporin & (*d*) statins.

Ans.

Microbial product	Source
(*a*) Acetic acid	*Aectobacter aceti*
(*b*) Streptokinase	*Streptococcus*
(*c*) Cyclosporin A	*Trichoderma polysporum*
(*d*) Statins	*Monascus purpurens*

Q. 6. What is sewage? In which way can sewage be harmful to us?

Ans. The municipal waste water is called as sewage.
It can cause water-borne diseases if the sewage mixes with water resources such as rivers and streams. Hence, sewage treatment before disposal is essential.

Q. 7. What is the key difference between primary and secondary sewage treatment?

Ans.

Primary sewage treatment	Secondary sewage treatment
1. It involves the physical processes filteration and sedimentation.	1. It involves the physical process-aeration of effluent and the biological treatment of effluent with microbes.
2. During this small and large floating debris is filtered out followed by the sedimentation process that allows soil and small pebbles settle as bottom.	2. Sedimentation of bacterial flocs is done to aerobic sludge digesters for digestion.
3. The supernatant water is effluent sent for secondary sewage treatment process.	3. The effluent from secondary treatments is released into natural water bodies such as rivers, streams.

Q. 8. What is activated sludge? How it is different from primary sludge?

Ans. The sediment obtained from the settling of bacterial flocs after reduced BOD of sewage water is called activated sludge. It is formed in secondary treatment process of sewage. It has microbes.

The primary sludge is obtained in primary treatment process by the sedimentation of all solids from the sewage water. It does not have microbes.

Q. 9. Draw the figure of a typical biogas plant.

Ans.

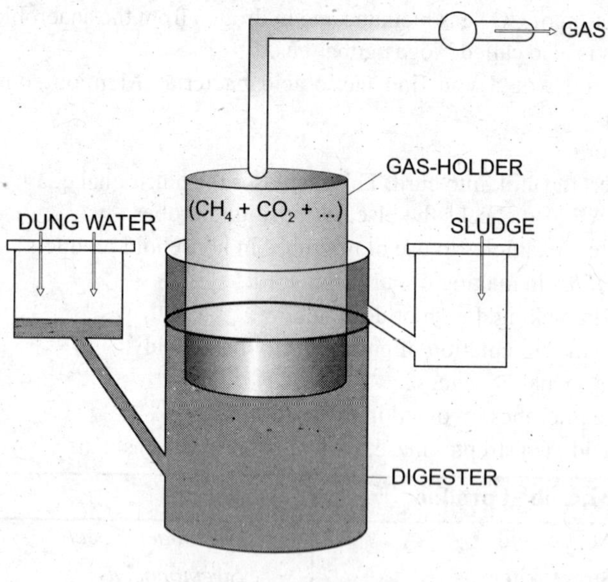

Fig. 10.1. A typical biogas plant.

Q. 10. Do you think microbes can also be the source of energy? If yes, how?

Ans. Yes. Microbes indeed can also be the source of energy. They can be used extensively to produce biogas/gobar gas from animal dung (gobar) that is used as fuel in rural areas.

Q. 11. Microbes can be used to decrease the use of chemical fertilisers and pesticides. Explain how this can be accomplished.

Ans. Chemical fertilisers are the major cause of concern as they cause environmental pollution. The microbes can be of great help in enriching the soil of its nutrients. Such microbes are called biofertilisers. Such as bacteria (Azospirillum, Azotobacter) enrich the soil by adding nitrogen to it. Rhizobium is a symbiotic bacteria that helps the legumes to fix atmospheric nitrogen.

Certain bacteria help is controlling the pests. Such as *Bacillus thuringiensis* (Bt) when consumed by the butterfly larvae it releases toxins that kills the larvae.

Q. 12. How is *Bacillus thuringiensis* (Bt) helpful to farmers?

Ans. This bacteria also called Bt produces toxin in the gut of butterfly larvae. When the larvae feed on the leaves having bacterial spores sprayed by the farmer get infected and later are killed. In brassica and fruit trees, this controls the pest. Bt-cotton has been developed by genetic enginering. It has made the plant resistant to attack by the insect pests.

Q. 13. What is mycorrhiza? How it is useful to plants?

Ans. The association of fungus with its roots is called mycorrhiza. It helps in absorbtion of phosphorous from the soil and passes it to plant. In addition to it, plant with this association becomes

(*a*) resistant to root-borne pathogens, (*b*) tolerant to saline and drought condition.

The result to overall increase in plant growth and development.

Q. 14. Three water samples, namely **river** water, **untreated** sewage water and **secondary** effluent discharged from a sewage treatment plant were subjected to BOD test.

The samples were labelled A, B and C but the laboratory attendant did not note which was which. The BOD values the three samples A, B and C were recovered as 20 mg/L 8 mg/L and 400 mg/L respectively. Which sample of the water is most polluted? Can you assign the correct label to each assuming the river water is relatively clean? (NCERT)

Ans. River water — 8 mg/L Label — A

Secondary effluent — 20mg/L Label — B

Untreated sewage water — 400 mg/L Label — C.

Q. 15. Arrange the following in the decreasing order (most important first) of their importance, for the welfare of human society. Give reasons for your answer. Biogas, citric acid, penicillin and curd.

Ans. 1. **Penicillin**—It is an antibiotic. That helps to kill many bacteria that cause diseases. It helps to maintain health.

2. **Citric acid**—It is a vitamin C. It helps to maintain the health of individual. Such as bleeding gums.
3. **Curd**—It is also a source of protein and keeps the health of the person. It has more nutritional value than milk.
4. **Biogas**—It is the source of energy to rural area. It is obtained from animal dung (gobar). It reduces the environmental pollution.

Q. 16. Explain about microbes as biocontrol agents.

Ans. Biocontrol refers to the use of biological methods for controlling plant diseases and pests. Modern agriculture has become dependent on agro-chemicals such as pesticides, insecticides and chemical fertilisers. These chemicals are not only toxic, harmful to all living beings but are also environmental pollutants. They have caused pollution of all the habitats irrespective of their use in agricultural fields.

A method of controlling the pests by natural predation is one of the best methods that can solve this problem. Therefore, if the population of these pests are kept at a manageable level by a complex system of checks and balance then a vibrant ecosystem can be developed. Bacteria, fungus and viruses can be used as biocontrol agents. For example,

1. **Bacillus thuringiensis** (Bt) produces a toxin in the gut of caterpillars of butterfly that damage the brassicas and fruit trees. Plants sprayed by their spores of this bacteria when consumed by the caterpillars die naturally.
2. **Trichoderma**, a fungus living in root ecosystem controls the plant pathogens.
3. **Nucleopolyhedrovirus**, a baculovirus used to control insects and is ineffective to other insects.

Hence, the use of these microbes helps to control the pests and pathogens thereby it will improve the environment and the ecosystem.

NUTSHELL MIND MAP

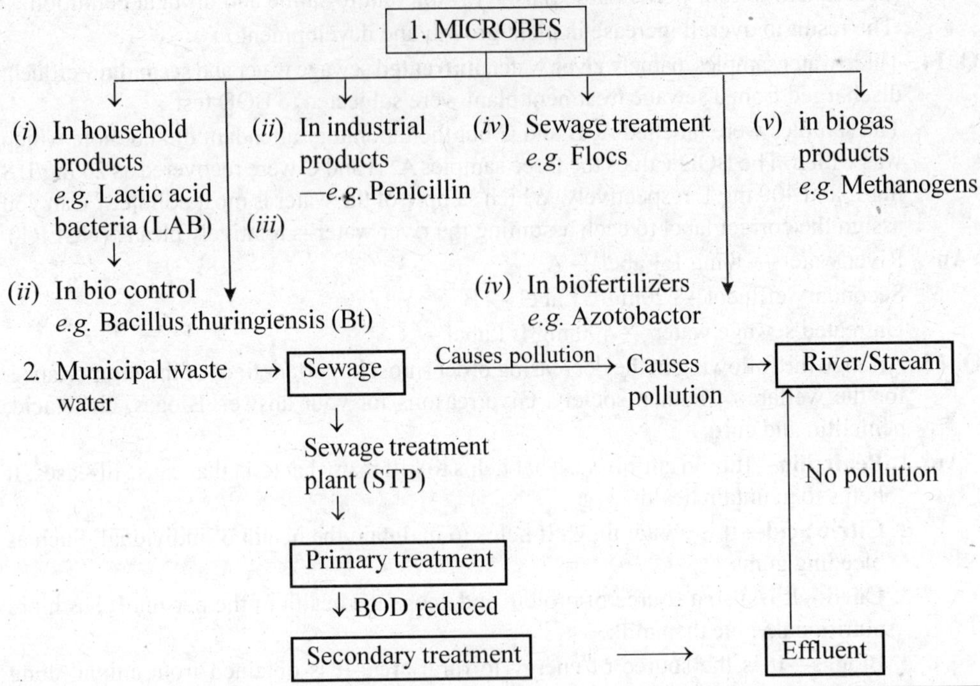

HIGHER ORDER THINKING SKILLS (HOTS) QUESTIONS

1. Mention the use of bacterium - Propionibacterium Sharmanji. (*VSA*)
2. The following are fermented beverages:
   Whisky, brandy, rum, beer, wine
   How are they produced? Name the microbe used. What is the difference among them? (*SA II*)
3. Antibiotics are against 'bio' and 'pro' life. In which context these terms are applicable? (*VSA*)
4. Mention the use of these substances:
   Streptohinase, Cyclosporin A, Statin. (*SA II*)
5. What is activated sludge? (*VSA*)
6. What is inoculum? Give two examples of such a use.
7. What are baculoviruses? What is their use? (*VSA*) (*SAI*)
8. Mention the significance of cyanobacteria with example. (*SAI*)

❑❑❑

CHAPTER 11

BIOTECHNOLOGY : PRINCIPLES AND PROCESSES

Chapter Outline

- Principles of biotechnology
- Tools of recombinant DNA
- Process of recombinant DNA technology

ASSESSMENT QUESTIONS

VERY SHORT ANSWER QUESTIONS (VSA)

Q. 1. Define biotechnology according to European Federation of Biotechnology (EFB).

Ans. According to EFB—biotechnology is the integration of natural science and organisms, cells, parts thereof, and molecular analogues for products and service.

Q. 2. Define genetic engineering.

Ans. The techniques used to alter the chemistry of the genetic material to introduce these into the host organisms in order to change the phenotype of the host is called as genetic engineering.

Q. 3. What is cloning?

Ans. The process of making multiple copies to without the involvement of reproductive process is called cloning.

Q. 4. Name the first restriction endonuclease.

Ans. Hind II.

Q. 5. Give one example to restriction endonuclease.

Ans. Eco R1.

Q. 6. To which class do the restriction enzymes belong? Mention their kinds.

Ans. (1) Nuclease, (2) Exonucleases, Endonucleases.

Q. 7. Name the pathogen of dicot plants that caused tumor and the virus that transformed normal cells into cancer cells in animals.

Ans. (1) *Agrobacterium tumifaciens*, (2) Retro virus.

Q. 8. What is gene gun or biolistics?

Ans. The technique bombarding the plant cells with high velocity micro-particles of gold/tungsten coated with DNA is called biolistics/gene gun.

Q. 9. Define plasmid.

Ans. The circular chromosome of bacterium is called plasmid.

Q. 10. Expand the *Ori.*

Ans. Origin of replication.

Q. 11. Name the enzymes that are used for bacterial cells, plant/animal cells, to break open the cells. For obtaining the genetic material.

Ans. Plant/animal cells—Cellulose (Plant cells)
Bacterial cells — Lysozyme
Fungus — Chitinase.

Q. 12. Which type of bioreactors are used for gene product?

Ans. Stirring type.

Q. 13. What do you understand by downstream processing?

Ans. After the biosynthesis of the gene product, the separation and purification methods are called as downstream processing.

Q. 14. Define recombinant protein.

Ans. The protein formed/produced after the use of recombinant technology is called recombinant protein.

Q. 15. What is the full form of PCR?

Ans. Polymerase Chain Reaction.

SHORT ANSWER TYPE QUESTIONS (SA)

Q. 1. Briefly mention which core techniques have enabled the formation of modern biotechnology?

Ans.

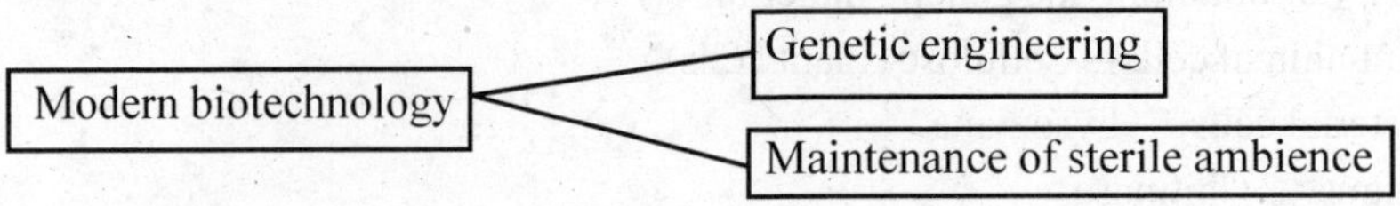

(1) **Genetic engineering:** It involves the techniques to alter the chemistry of genetic material to introduce these into the host organism, in order to change the phenotype of the host.

(2) **Maintenance of sterile** ambience is chemical engineering processes so that the products are produced in large quantities.

Q. 2. How is the technique of genetic engineering advantageous over the traditional hybridization procedures?

Ans. The genetic engineering that includes the creation of recombinant DNA uses gene cloning and gene transfer. It overcomes the limitations and allows to isolate and introduce the desirable genes in the target organism. Where as in the traditional hybridisation procedures the undesirable genes also multiplied with the desirable genes.

Q. 3. What is use of molecular scissors—restriction enzymes? What are vectors?

Ans. These are used to cut the DNA at specific location. The cut DNA when it is linked with the plasmid DNA then the plasmid DNA is called vector.

Q. 4. Mention the role/use of following enzymes in recombinant technology:

(*a*) DNA ligase, (*b*) DNA polymerase, (*c*) Restriction endonuclease.

Ans. (*a*) **DNA ligase:** It is an enzyme used to link the cut DNA (alien, foreign) to the plasmid (native) to produce a DNA recombinant *i.e.* vector.

(*b*) **DNA polymerase:** It is an enzyme in host cell that helps to make multiple copies (clones) of the DNA.

(*c*) **Restriction endonuclease:** It is an enzyme that restricts the growth of bacteriophage in E. Coli.

Q. 5. What is restriction endonuclease? Give one example. How many such enzymes have been identified?

Ans. The enzyme that restricts the growth of bacteriophage in bacteria are called restriction endonuclease. *e.g.* Eco. R1, 900 enzymes.

Q. 6. What is palindromic nucleotide sequence in DNA? What is its significance? Give one example.

Ans. The six base pairs that reads the same on the 2 strands when orientation of reading in kept the same is called palindromic nucleotide sequence.

This sequence is identified by restriction endonuclease enzyme (also called recognisation sequence for Hind II) and it cuts the DNA here.

5′—GAATTC—3′

3′—CTTAAG—5′

Q. 7. Draw the diagram of formation of recombinant DNA by action of Eco R1.

Ans.

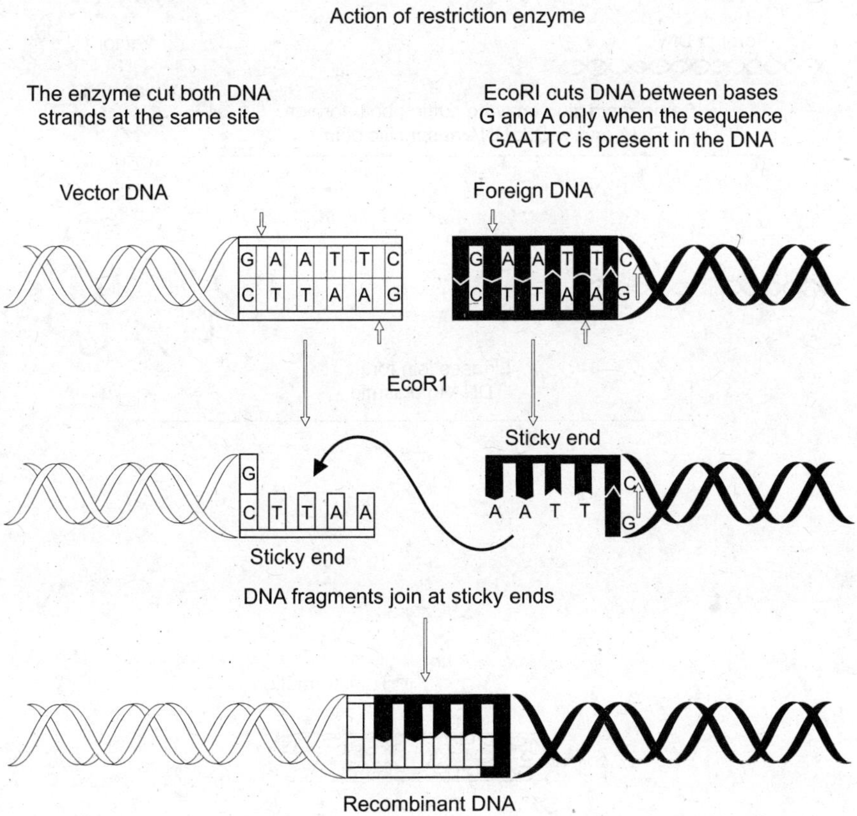

Fig. 11.1. Steps in formation of recombinant DNA by action of restriction endonuclease enzyme-EcoRI.

Q. 8. What are 'sticky-ends'? Name the enzyme responsible for this. Why is it done?

Ans. The cutting of DNA strands at a specific point results in formation of sticky-ends. Restriction enzyme does it. It is done for attaching the foreign DNA strands (cut pieces) to the vector DNA—plasmid of a bacterium.

Q. 9. Do eukaryotic cells have restriction endonucleases? Justify your answer.

Ans. No, they do not have. Because these enzymes are responsible for restricting the growth of bacteriophages attaching bacteria. Hence they are found in bacteria—prokaryotic.

Q. 10. Give the diagrammatic representation of recombinant DNA technology.

Ans.

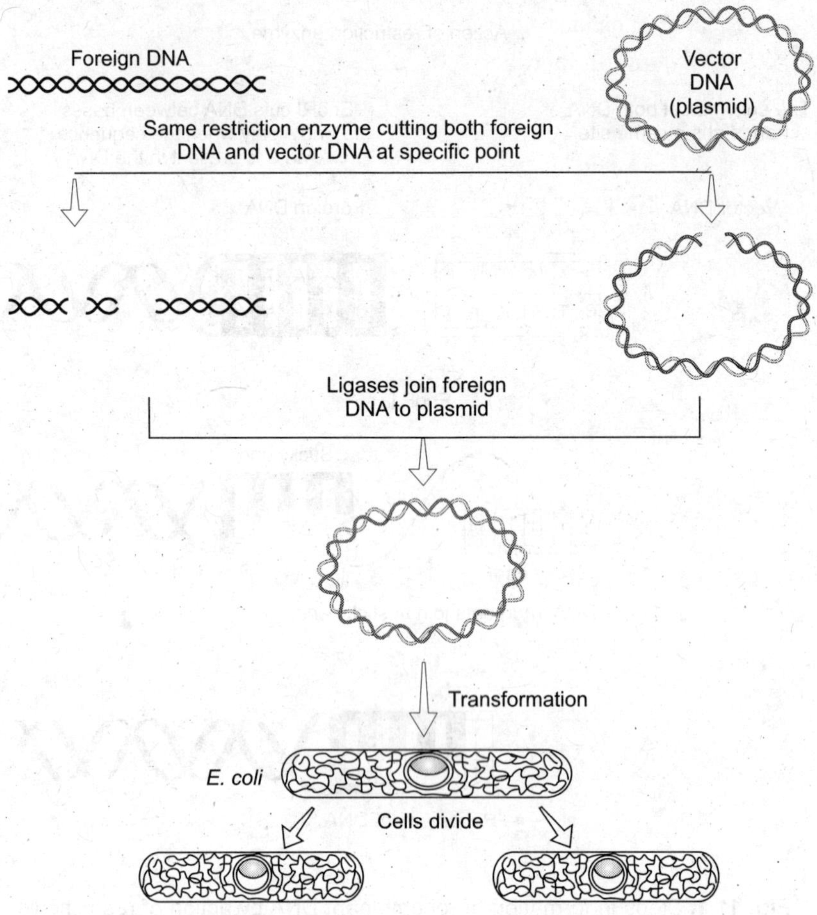

Fig. 11.2. Diagrammatic representation of recombinant DNA technology.

Q. 11. What are the various methods used for making bacterial cells 'competent' to take up DNA?

Ans. The DNA is a hydrophilic molecule. Therefore, it cannot pass through cell membranes. In order to force the bacteria to take the plasmid the bacterial cells must be made competent. This is done by—

(*i*) **Shock treatment method:** Treating the cells with specific concentration a divalent cation such as Ca^{++}, is increases the efficiency with which the DNA enters through the pores of the bacterial cell wall. Then giving shock treatment.

(*ii*) **Micro-injection method:** The recombinant DNA is directly injected into the nucleus of an animal cell.

(*iii*) **Biolistics/gene gun method:** The plant cells are bombarded with high velocity micro particles of gold or tungsten coated with DNA. This is called biolistics/gene gun method.

(iv) **Disarmed pathogen vectors:** In this method the disarmed pathogen vectors are allowed to infect the cell. It transfers the recombinant DNA into the host.

Q. 12. Mention in brief the method used in amplification of 'gene of interest'.

Ans. The method involved for the amplification of 'gene of interest' is called PCR - polymerase chain reaction. It includes three steps—

(*i*) *Denaturation*, (*ii*) Annealing and (*iii*) extension of primers.

The multiple copies of gene (or DNA) are synthesised in **vitro** using two sets of primers (chemically synthesised oligonucleotides that are complementary to the regions of DNA) and enzyme DNA polymerase.

This enzyme extends the primers using the nucleotides provided in the reaction and the genomic DNA as template. If the process of replication is repeated many times, the segment of DNA can be amplified to approximately billion times. *i.e.* 1 billion copies are made.

Q. 13. Give the diagrammatic representation of PCR.

Ans.

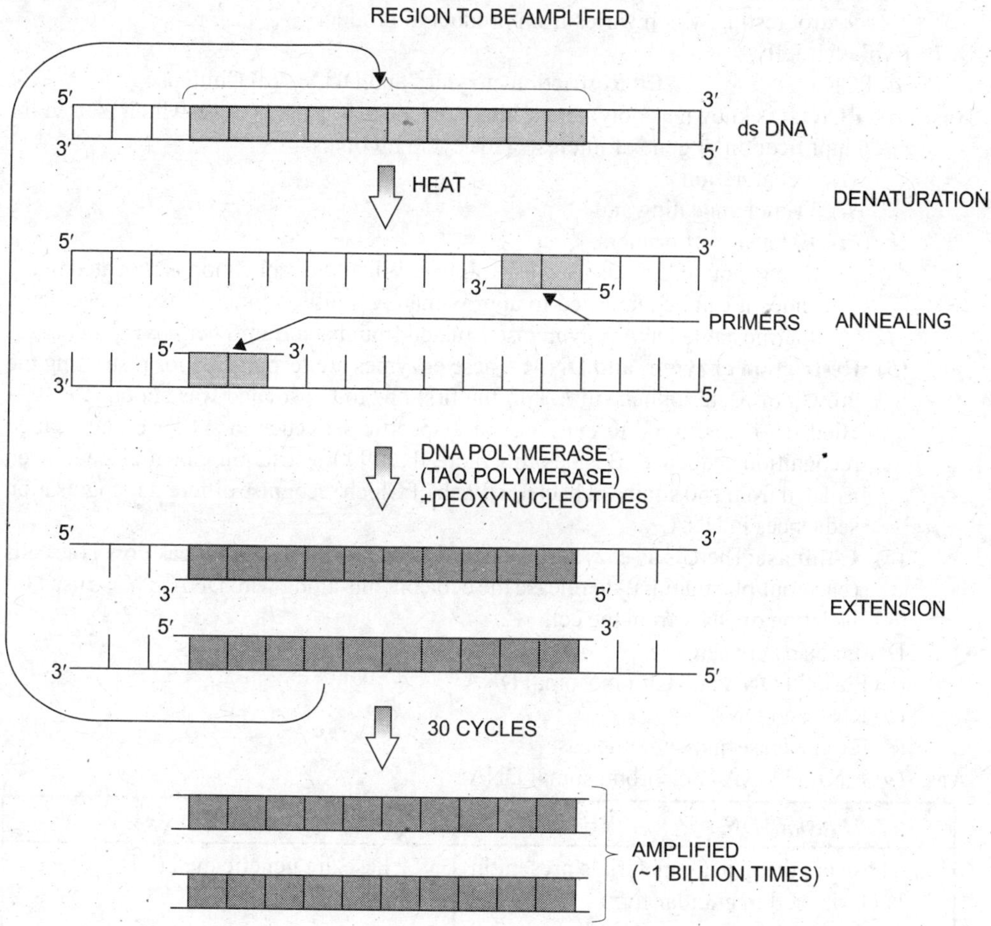

Fig. 11.3. Polymerase chain reaction (PCR) : Each cycle has three steps : (*i*) Denaturation, (*ii*) Primer annealing; and (*iii*) Extension of primers.

LONG ANSWER TYPE QUESTIONS (LA)

Q. 1. Describe briefly the following:
(*a*) Origin of replication, (*b*) Bioreactors, (*c*) Downstream processing

Ans. (*a*) **Origin of replication:** In a chromosome there is a specific DNA sequence called origin of replication. It is responsible for initiation of replication process. If any alien piece of DNA in an organism has to multiply it has to be the part of a chromosome with this - 'origin' Thus, this gives rise to clones of the DNA

(*b*) **Bioreactors:** These are large vessels in which large volumes of biological products such as enzymes are produced from the raw materials using microbial plant, animal or human cells. There are two types is common use - simple stirred-tank type and spragged stirred - tank type.

(*c*) **Down stream processing:** This is the process of making a finished product before marketing. It is collectively called downstream processing. The product has to be formulated with suitable preservatives, then go through clinical trials and quality control testing which varies from product to product.

Q. 2. Explain briefly–
(*a*) PCR (*b*) Restriction enzymes and DNA (*c*) Chitinase

Ans. (*a*) **PCR:** It is known as polymerase chain reaction. It is the process which is used for amplification of gene of interest. This cycle involves.

(*i*) Denaturation,
(*ii*) Primer annealing and
(*iii*) Extension of primers.

The genomic DNA is used as template. When the replication is repeated many times it can be amplified to approximately a billion times. It is achieved by a thermostable DNA polymerase isolated from bacterium *Thermus aquacticus*.

(*b*) **Restriction enzymes and DNA:** These enzymes are responsible for restricting the growth of bacteriophage in *E. coli* the first one to be isolated was endonuclease—Hind II. It was found to cut DNA at a specific sequence in six base pairs called recognition sequence. Besides this more than 900 restriction enzymes have been isolated from 250 strains of bacteria. Each of which recognise different recognisation sequences in DNA.

(*c*) **Chitinase:** There is an enzyme produced by fungus. It is used to break down the cells (bacterial/plant/animal) to release the cell contents along with DNA. This is used for isolation of DNA from the cell.

Q. 3. Distinguish between—
(*a*) Plasmid DNA and Chromosomal DNA
(*b*) RNA and DNA
(*c*) Exonuclease and endonuclease

Ans. (*a*) Plasmid DNA and chromosomal DNA:

Plasmid DNA	***Chromosomal DNA***
1. These are the genetic materials present in bacterial cell in circular form.	1. These are genetic materials present in the bacterial cell.
2. These are for replication of DNA material incorporated in them and thus help in formation of proteins.	2. These are involved with transfer of genetic trails to the progeny by reproduction process.
3. These are used in recombinant DNA technology for formation of desired products.	

(*b*) RNA and DNA

RNA	*DNA*
1. The nucleic acid containing ribulose sugar. 2. It has all the nitrogen bases similar to DNA except one. 3. Uracil n-base is present instead of thymine *n*-base of DNA.	1. The nucleic acid containing sugar. deoxyribose. 2. It has 4 *n*-bases. One is different from that of RNA. 3. Thymine *n*-base is present instead of uracil *n*-base of RNA.

(*c*) Exonuclease and endonuclease

Exonuclease	*Endonuclease*
1. These are one of the kind of restriction enzymes. 2. These function by removing the nucleotides from the DNA molecules.	1. These are the second type of restriction enzymes. 2. These function by cutting the DNA into fragments of specific recognisation sequences.

Q. 4. Describe the features are required to facilitate cloning into a vector.

Ans. The following are the features that are required to facilitate cloning into a vector:

(*i*) **Origin of replication:** This is the sequence from where the process of replication starts and any piece of DNA when it is linked to this **(ori)**, it can be replicated within the host cells. This sequence is also responsible for controlling the number of copies of the linked DNA.

(*ii*) **Selectable marker:** In addition to **(ori)** the vector also needs a selectable marher. It helps in identifying & removing non-transformants and selectively permitting the growth of transformants. The genes encoding resistance to antibiotics such as ampicillin, tetracycline are considered as useful selectable markers for *E. coli* Normally *E. coli* do not carry resistance against any of these antibiotics.

(*iii*) **Cloning sites:** There must be preferably single recognisation site for the restriction enzymes in a vector to link the alien DNA. Presence of more than one recognistion sites within a vector will generate several fragments and it will complicate the gene cloning process.

(*iv*) **Vectors for cloning genes in plants and animals:** The knowledge of understanding how the plant pathogen (such as *Agrobacterium tumifaciens* and *retrovirus*) transfer the genes to plant cells and animal cells respectively to cause tumor and cancer in their hosts has been used to produce desirable products, instead of their original behaviour of causing disease.

NUTSHELL | MIND MAP

Recombinant DNA Technology Steps:

Isolation of DNA → Fragmentation of DNA → Isolation of desired DNA fragment → Ligation of DNA fragment into vector → Transferring recombinant DNA into the host → Culturing the host cells in a medium at large scale → desired product

Antibiotics, vaccines, enzymes etc.

Abbreviations

Ori	:	Origin of Replication.
EFB	:	European Federation of Biotechnology.
Eco R1	:	Escherichia Coli Ry 13.
Ti	:	Tumor inducing
PCR	:	Polymerase chain reaction

HIGHER ORDER THINKING SKILLS (HOTS) QUESTIONS

1. Mention the three basic steps in genetically modifying an organism. (*SAI*)
2. Mention the tools of recombinant DNA technology. (*SAI*)
3. How are the restriction enzymes named? (*SAI*)
4. Draw the figure of a 'stick end' of DNA. (*VSA*)
5. Study the following diagram: (*SA II*)

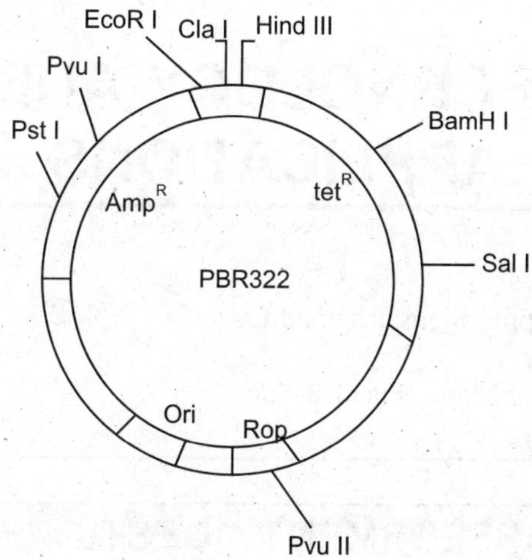

Fig. 11.4. *E. coli* cloning vector pBR322 showing restriction sites.

Expand the terms shown in the figure.

6. What is the colour of iso DNA strands? (*VSA*)
7. Which enzymes are required for cutting of DNA and ligation DNA done to form recombinant DNA? (*SAI*)
8. Explain the process of separation and isolation of DNA fragments. (*LA*)

❑❑❑

CHAPTER 12

BIOTECHNOLOGY AND ITS APPLICATIONS

Chapter Outline

- Biotechnological applications in agriculture
- Transgenic animals
- Biotechnological applications in medicine
- Ethical issues

ASSESSMENT QUESTIONS

VERY SHORT ANSWER TYPE QUESTIONS (VSA)

Q. 1. Expand and define the term GMO.

Ans. **GMO:** Genetically modified organisms.
Organisms whose genes have been altered by manipulation are called GMO.

Q. 2. Mention any two usefulness of GM plants.

Ans. 1. GM plants are more tolerant to abiotic stresses such as temperature, salt etc.
2. GM plants are pest resistant.

Q. 3. Mention the source of Bt gene. What for it is used?

Ans. The source of Bt gene is *bacillus thuringiensis.*
It is used for making bio-pesticide (pest resistant plants)

Q. 4. Give two examples to Bt crops.

Ans. Bt cotton, Bt corn.

Q. 5. What is cry?

Ans. Cry is the gene of Bt that codes for toxin.

Q. 6. What is the number of polypeptide chains in pro insulin in human beings? Name it.

Ans. 3 polypeptide chains. Chain-A, B and C.

Q. 7. Define gene therapy?

Ans. It is the collection of various methods performed that allows the correction of a genetic defect identified/diagnosed in the child/embryo.

Q. 8. Give one example to a gene theory performed.

Ans. Adenosine deaminase (ADA) deficiency.

Q. 9. Define molecular diagnosis?

Ans. It is the process of early diagnosis of a disease yet to show its symptoms.
(**Note:** Usually the purpose of pathological tests is to identify/confirm the presence suspected pathogen in the body. Such a pathogen releases certain chemicals against

which the healthy body releases antibodies to counter it.) Till the time it is done the population of pathogen is very high).

Q. 10. Mention any two molecular diagnosis techniques.

Ans. PCR and ELISA.

Q. 11. What do you understand by transgenic animals? Give one example that has been extensively been used for the purpose.

Ans. Animals that have the DNA manipulated with an extra gene and are used to express it are called transgenic animals. Mice.

Q. 12. Crystals of Bt toxin produced by some bacteria do not kill the bacteria themselves because—

(*a*) bacteria are resistant to the toxin
(*b*) toxin is immature.
(*c*) toxin is inactive
(*d*) bacteria encloses toxin in a special sac.

Ans. (*c*) Toxin is inactive.

Q. 13. Does our blood have proteases and nucleases?

Ans. Yes. They have it during infection to fight or destroy the pathogens.

Q. 14. Define the term biopiracy.

Ans. It stands for the use of bio-resources by MNCs and alter organisations without proper authorisation from the concerned countries and people without compensatory.payment.

Q. 15. Name the rice variety that has been patented by India.

Ans. Basmati rice.

SHORT ANSWER TYPE QUESTIONS (I, II)

Q. 1. What are the three critical research areas of biotechnology?

Ans. The critical research areas of biotechnology are:

Research areas of bio-technology

1. **Providing best catalyst:** To provide best catalyst in the form of a microbe or pure enzyme. e.g. insulin.
2. **Creating optimal conditions:** To create optimal conditions through engineering for a catalyst to act.
3. **Down stream processing:** To provide down stream processing technologies to purify the protein or organic compound produced by the microbe.

Q. 2. Compare and contrast the advantages and disadvantages of production of genetically modified crops.

Ans. The production of the crops for high food production by traditional methods has its own problems. It needs the inputs of agrochemicals such as synthetic chemical fertilisers and pesticides to ensure the productivity. It has its limitations as well. It cannot depend on the agrochemicals throughout. It needs better varieties, which is possible by GM crops.

Advantages of these GM crops are:

1. They are tolerant to abiotic stresses.
2. They are less dependant on chemical pesticides.
3. They have increased efficiency of mineral usage.
4. They have enhanced nutrition value of food.
5. They have reduced post harvest losses.

Disadvantage being that they are not readily acceptable by farmers and people by large as they pose an ecological insecurity of biodiversity.

Q. 3. What are cry proteins? Name an organism that produce it. How has man exploited this protein to his benefit?

Ans. Cry—proteins are toxins produced by the gene by same name in bacteria — *Bacillus thuringiensis*. On introducing this gene into the plant cry protein is produced by the plant. *e.g.* Bt cotton. These proteins have been exploited by human to develop biopesticide. There by controlling the pestillance and increase in crop productivity and reduction on dependance of chemical pesticides.

Q. 4. What are transgenic bacteria? Illustrate using any one example.

Ans. Bacteria that have been manipulated plasmid are called transgenic bacteria. Such bacteria have a forcing gene linked to the plasmid and they are used as vectors to introduce it to the host plant. For example-*Agrobacterium.* It was manipulated and nematode specific genes were introduced through it to the host plant.

The host plant cells produced both sense and antisense RNA. These two RNA's being complementry to each other formed a double stranded (ds RNA) that initiated RNAi. Resulting in RNA interference in silencing the specific mRNA of the nematode. As a consequence of it the nematode could not survive in the transgenic host expressing the specific RNAi. The plant is thus protected from the parasite.

Q. 5. (*i*) What is RNAi?

(*ii*) How does the process work in the cells?

(*iii*) Mention its application in plants?

Ans. (*i*) **RNAi:** RNA interference (RNAi) is the process of cellular defense in all eukaryotic organisms.

(*ii*) The RNA produced by the cell involves the silencing of the specific mRNA due to complementry dsRNA molecule. This molecule binds to the mRNA and prevents the translation (silencing).

(*iii*) This method has been used to develop transgenetic plants that are pest resistant, to a nematode *Meloidegyne incognita.* This pest infects tobacco plant and reduces the yield.

Q. 6. What are the shortcomings of insulin obtained from slaughtered animals? How it has been overcome?

Ans. The insulin obtained from the slaughted animals pancreas were earlier given to diabetic patients. As it was sourced from other animals such as cattle, pigs. The foreign protein' caused allergy to the patients. Now insulin produced by genetic engineering of *E. coli* is used.

Q. 7. Briefly mention the structure of normal insulin. Which technique was used by Eli lilly an American Co. to prepare a mature insulin?

Ans. Mammalian insulin (Human) has three polypetides in the insulin. The insulin is produced in preform as prohormone and it is made functional/Nature by deleting the C peptide chain.

rDNA technique was used by the company. The company prepared two DNA sequences that coded for A and B chains of human insulin. Then it was introduced into the plasmids of *E. coli* to produce these insulin chains. These chains were produced separately, extracted and combined by creating disulphide bonds to give human insulin.

Q. 8. What is gene therapy? Illustrate using the example of adenosine deaminase (ADA) deficiency?

Ans. It is the collection of a genetic defect identified/diagnosed in the child/embryo.

During this process a normal gene into the individual/embryo so that this gene takes over the function of the non-functional gene *e.g.* deficiency. Gene therapy in ADA deficiency follows these steps:

1. **Culture of Lymphocytes:** Lymphocytes from the blood of patient are cultured outside the body.
2. **Introduction of ADA eDNA:** The next step involves the introduction of ADA eDNA (using a retroviral vectors into the lymphocytes.
3. **Lymphocytes return:** The lymphocytes genetically transformed by this method are returned to the patient's body.

   As the lymphocytes live for certain period, patient needs such genetically engineered lymphocytes after some time again.

Q. 9. What is ADA deficiency? How is it cured? It is completely cured? Which method can provide a complete permanent cure?

Ans. Adenosine deaminase enzyme is required for functioning of the immune system in body. It is due to deletion of the gene for adenosine deaminase. In some children it is cured by:

(*a*) Bone marrow transplantation or

(*b*) Enzyme replacement therapy—in which functional ADA is given to the patient by injection. Both are not completely curative. If the gene isolated from marrow cells that produce ADA when introduced into early embryo then it could provide a permanent cure to this.

Q. 10. Mention a few molecular diagnosis techniques. Which one is considered to be very powerful?

Ans.

Molecular diagnosis techniques
1. Recombinant DNA technology.
2. Polymerase chain reaction (PCR)
3. Enzyme linked immunosorbent Assay (ELISA)

PCR has been considered to be very powerful technique because of its amplication of DNA/RNA step. It has been used to early detection of —HIV, gene mutations even in cancer patients.

Q. 11. Diagrammatically represent the experimental steps in cloning and expressing a human gene (Say the gene for growth hormone) into a bacterium like *E. coli.*

Ans.

Fig. 12.1. Host plant-generated dsRNA triggers protection against nematode infestation: (*a*) Roots of a typical control plants; (*b*) transgenic plant roots 5 days after deliberate infection of nematode but protected through novel mechanism.

LONG ANSWER TYPE QUESTIONS (LA)

Q. 1. (*i*) What is the significance of *Bacillus thuringiensis*?

(*ii*) How are the Bt toxins activated?

(*iii*) Mention the insects and toxin categories that are affected by these toxins.

Ans. (*i*) Some strains of bacterium—*Bacillus thuringiensis* (Bt) produces a toxin that are able to kill certain insect pests. Because of this ability these stains of bacteria are used to produce bio-pesticides. *e.g.* Bt cotton, Bt corn etc. thereby reducing the dependence on chemical pesticides. Thus, they have wide applications in agriculture.

(*ii*) Bt toxins are themselves inactive on the bacteria. Because, they need **alkaline ph** of the gut of insect to get activated by dissolving the toxin-protein crystals.

(*iii*) Insect categories that are killed

by Bt toxin	by Cry genes toxin
(*a*) Lepidopterans (tobacco budworm, army worm).	1. Cry AC, Cry Ab-Control bollworms of cotton plants.
(*b*) Caleopterans (bectles)	2. Cry Ab controls corn borer.
(*c*) Dipterans (files, mosquitoes)	

Q. 2. (*i*) What is the significance of transgenic animals for human?

(*ii*) Is this act of producing transgenic animals justified?

Ans. (*i*) The development of transgenic animals is helpful to solve many problems specially health related to human beings. Here are some points that emerge from their use for benefit of human welfare.

(*a*) **Normal physiology and development:** The transgenic animals can be develop to understand the effect of genes in normal function and its development on the body.

(*b*) **Study of disease:** These animals serve as the models for study of disease - development, treatment. Some of the diseases studied by their models are—cancer, cystic fibrosis, rheumatoid arthritis, Alzheimers.

(*c*) **Biological products:** Certain biological products are useful in treating human diseases and health mainetenance. But their production is expensive. Some of such products are— human protein (α-1-antitrypsin) used to treat emphysema.

(*d*) **Vaccine safety:** These models are used to test the safety of vaccine. If successful they could replace monkeys that are used for this purpose *e.g.* polio/vaccine.

(*e*) **Chemical safety testing:** The models with sensitivity to a chemical are developed to study the toxicity in short time.

(*ii*) Though there are several such significant applications and use of transgenic animals for the benefit of human welfare but on other hand if one thinks about manipulation aspects involved, human has used the knowledge in manipulating natural processes. This sounds good but it is unethical and against nature.

NUTSHELL MINDMAP

Applications in agriculture

GMO-Crops → tailor made → starch, fuel, pharmaceuticals

Bt → Bt cotton, Bt corn, rice, tomato, potato → Biopesticides

Agrobacterium → Pest resistant plant soyabean

Applications in medicine: Genetically engineered insulin, gene therapy, molecular diagnosis.
Transgenic animals: For study of disease and its treatment etc.

ABBREVIATIONS

Bt	—	*Bacillus thuringiensis*
Cry	—	gene that codes of toxin - Bt.
ds RNA	—	double stranded RNA.
RNAi	—	RNA interference
ADA	—	Adenosine deaminase
GEAC	—	Genetic Engineering Approval Committee.

HIGHER ORDER THINKING SKILLS (HOTS) QUESTIONS

1. Name any four pesticides developed. (*VSA*)
2. How does the inactive protoxin produced by B-thuringienisis gets active? How does it act on the insect to kill it?
3. Name the nematode that infects the tobacco root? (*SA I*)
4. Study the following figure:

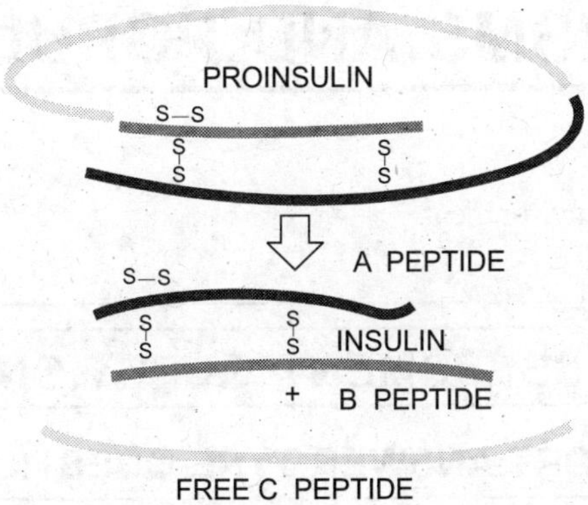

Fig. 12.2

(*a*) What is this process called?

(*b*) How can genetic engineering help in production of insulin? (*SAI*)

5. Consider yourself a genetic engineer. Do you agree that your knowledge must be used for benefit of human kind on the expense of transforming other organisms ethically? (*LA*)

❑❑❑

CHAPTER 13

ORGANISMS AND POPULATIONS

Chapter Outline

- Organism and its Environment
- Populations

ASSESSMENT QUESTIONS

VERY SHORT ANSWER TYPE QUESTIONS (VSA)

Q. 1. Give two examples to biomes.

Ans. (1) Desert (2) Rain forcst

Q. 2. How are the major biomes on earth formed?

Ans. The major biomes are formed due to annual variation in the precipitation in a region.

Q. 3. How are varieties of habitats formed in a biome?

Ans. The variations at regional and local levels within a biome leads to the formation of habitats.

Q. 4. How does the temperature affect the organisms?

Ans. Temperature affects the enzymes kinetics and through this it affects the basal metabolism of the individual.

Q. 5. Mention the four levels of biological organisation ecology is concerned with.

Ans. Ecology is concerned with

1. Organisms
2. Populations
3. Communities
4. Biomes

Q. 6. Mention the four major abiotic factors.

Ans. Major abiotic factor

- Temperature
- Water
- Light
- Soil

Q. 7. How is diapause different from hibernation? (NCERT)

Ans.

Diapause	*Hibernation*
The condition/stage during which zooplanktons suspend their development due to unfavourable environmental condition is called diapause.	The condition during which the animal undergoes to a winter sleep to avoid extreme winter condition/temperature is called hibernation.

Q. 8. If a marine fish is placed in a fresh water aquarium, will the fish be able to survive? Why or why not?

Ans. It will not able to survive because of low salinity of water. It will lead to osmotic problems and keep intaking water inside its body cells.

Q. 9. Define phenotypic adaptation. Give one example.

Ans. The adaptation shown by organism that is restricted to its body only is phenotypic adaptation. It is temporary in nature *e.g.* escaping temperature rises by avoiding it and going to shade.

Q. 10. Most living organisms can not survive at temperature above 45°C. How are some microbes able to live in habitats with temperature exceeding 100°C?

Ans. The microbes living in hydrothermal vents (100°C) have adapted themselves metabolically.

Q. 11. List the attributes that populations but not individuals possess.

Ans. Population attributes are—

(1) Per capita birth and death rates. (2) Sex ratio.

Q. 12. Mention the various growth status of the human population as shown by age pyramids.

Ans. (1) Expanding, (2) Stable, (3) Declining.

Q. 13. Define Darwin fitness (high *r* value).

Ans. When the populations evolve to maximise their reproductive fitness in the habitat in which they live is called Darwin fitness (high r value).

Q. 14. Mention the two values needed to calculate the population size/density at a given time.

Ans. Per capita births, per capita deaths.

Q. 15. If the population density (W) is at time t, then its density at, time t +1 will represented by which equation?

Ans. $N_{t+1} = N_1 + [(B + 1) - (D + E)]$

Q. 16. Mention the equation for representing exponential growth at a given unit time period.

Ans. $rN = \frac{dN}{dt}$.

Q. 17. When the responses are limiting the growth, the growth is represented by which equation? Mention it.

Ans. $\frac{dN}{dt} = rN \frac{K \quad N}{K}$.

Q. 18. When do we get growth curves— J and S shaped, when plotted against population density and unit time?

Ans. J-shaped growth curve is obtained when the responses are not limiting growth.

S-shaped growth curve is obtained when the responses are limiting.

Q. 19. Mention when the growth plot is exponential and logistic?

Ans. The growth plot is exponential when responses are not limiting growth and it is logistic when responses are limiting the growth.

Q. 20. Name important defence mechanisms in plants against herbivores?

Ans. (1) Thorns, (2) Storage of highly poisonous chemicals.

Q. 21. Define competition.

Ans. When the fitness of one species (in terms or '*r*' the intrensic rate of increase) is significantly lower in the presence of another species is called competition.

Q. 22. What is brood parasitism?

Ans. The laying of eggs by a parasitic bird in the nest of its host and lets it to incubate is called brood parasitism.

Q. 23. Define Co-evolution.

Ans. The changes that help one species to evolve against the other is equally balanced by the other species that depends on the first by changes in itself is called co-evolution. *i.e.* both evolve simultaneously.

Q. 24. How are pollinators rewarded by plants/flowers?

Ans. Pollinators get nector or other kind of food in reward of the act of pollination.

Q. 25. Which type of association is—
Sea anemone with down fish.

Ans. Commensalism.

Q. 26. Mention the association type shown by pollinators and plants.

Ans. Mutualism.

Q. 27. What is the ecological principle behind the biological control method of managing the pest insects?

Ans. Predation.

Q. 28. List the various abiotic environmental factors.

Ans. Temperature, Water, Soil, Light.

Q. 29. Select the statement which explains best parasitism.

(*a*) One organism is benefited.

(*b*) Both organisms are benefited.

(*c*) One organism is benefited, other is not affected.

(*d*) One organism is benefited , other is affected.

Ans. (*d*) One organism is benefited, other is affected.

SHORT ANSWER TYPE QUESTIONS (SA-I, II)

Q. 1. Define the terms—eurythermal, stenothermal.

Ans. Organisms that can tolerate a wide range of temperature are called eurythermals. Organisms that can tolerate narrow range of temperatures are called stenothermals.

Q. 2. Why are plants and animals dependent on light?

Ans. **Plants are dependent on light for:**

(1) Photosynthesis.

(2) Photoperiodism—for flowering.

(3) Formation of chlorophyll.

Animals are dependent on light for:

(1) Photoperiodism—for aging, reproductive and migratory activities.

Q. 3. What is adaptation? Why do animals/plants adapt?

Ans. Any change of the organism that enables the organism to survive and reproduce in its habitat is called adaptation.

It is done for reproduction *i.e.* to increase its population (r) and survival.

Q. 4. What are behavioral responses or adaptations? Give one example.

Ans. Responses shown in the behaviour of an organism to cope with the changes in its immediate environment is called as behaviour response. *e.g.* For example, desert lizards bask in day - sun shine to increase their body temperature. When their body temperature falls below the comfort zone. When basking in sun raises the temperature they then move to shade.

Q. 5. Refer the following flow diagram and briefly explain about it.

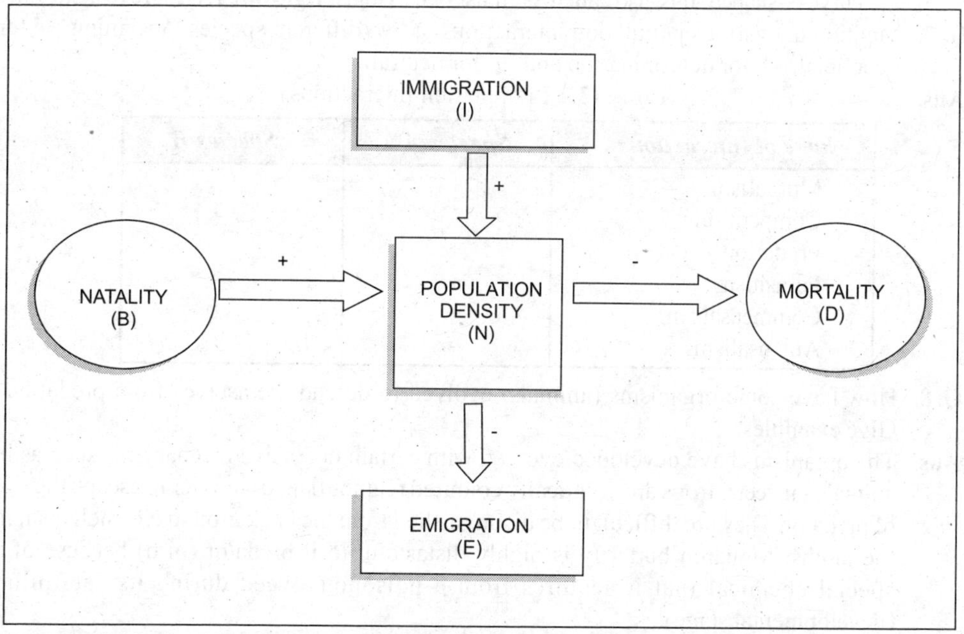

Fig. 13.1.

Ans. The density of a population in a given habitat depends on four basic processes. Two process (natality and immigration) increase the population and other two process (mortality and emigration) decrease the population.

(i) **Natality (B):** It refers to the births during the given time period in that population that are add to the initial density (W).

(ii) **Immigration (I):** It refers to the number of individuals of same species that have been added, they have come from else where during the same time period considered.

(iii) **Mortality (D):** It refers to the death of individuals in population at a given time period.

(iv) **Emigration (E):** It refers to the number of individuals left the habitat and have gone else where during the same time period considered.

Q. 6. What are the two growth models? Mention in brief.

Ans. Growth models: (1) Exponential, (2) Logistic.

1. **Exponential growth model:** The growth of a population is in exponential or geometric fashion. When the resources (food and space) does not pose any limitation. Each species has the ability to realise fully its innate potential to grow in number. The density (W) is represented by dW/dt at a given time period. The plot resulted is J-Shaped. Any species growing exponentially under unlimited resource condition can reach enormous population densities in a short time. However, this does not happen for long, due to other natural reasons.
2. **Logistic growth model:** No population of any species in nature has its disposal unlimited resources to permit the exponential growth. It leads to competition between the individual of the limited resources and eventually the fittest individual survives and reproduces. In nature the given habitat the population can not grow beyond its carrying capacity (K) for that species in a habitat. The population growing in a habitat with limited resources first shows-**lag phase,** then **acceleration** and **deceleration** and finally **asymptote** when it reaches (K). The plot formed is sigmoid curve-S-shaped. It is also called Verhulst - Pearl logistic growth. It is more realistic one.

Q. 7. Mention the various population interactions of two different species. Assigning '+' for beneficial, '–' for determination and '0' for neutral.

Ans.

Table 13.1 : Population Interactions

Name of Interaction	*Species A*	*Species B*
Mutualism	+	+
Competition	–	–
Predation	+	–
Parasitism	+	–
Commensalism	+	0
Amensalism	–	0

Q. 8. How have some organisms (animals) evolved to defend themselves from predation? Give examples.

Ans. The organisms have developed/evolved with certain defensive mechanisms such as in animals - insects, frogs are cryptically coloured (camouflaged) inorder to escape the site of predator. They are difficult to be distinguished from the back ground *e.g.* melanism in the moths; Monarch butterfly is highly distasteful to it predator (bird) because of a special chemical that it acquires from a poisonous weed during its caterpillar (developmental stage).

Q. 9. An orchid plant is growing on the branch of mango tree. How do you describe this interaction between the orchid and the mango tree?

Ans. This is an example of commensalism. This interaction between the orchid and mango tree is beneficial to one species-orchid but the other species-mango tree is neither benefited nor harmed.

Q. 10. Briefly mention of one example to employment of 'sexual deceit'.

Ans. **Ophrys** a mediterranean orchid employs sexual deceit *i.e.* One petal of its flower bears the resemblance of female bee in its colour, size and markings. The male beemistakes it for its partner and 'pseudocopulates' it and thereby gets brushed with pollens. When it repeats the act with other orchid flower of same species the flower gets pollinated.

Q. 11. Distinguish between the following:

(*i*) Hibernation and aestivation.

(*ii*) Ectotherms and Endotherms.

Ans.

(*i*) *Hibernation*	*Aestivation*
The behaviour of organism to escape in time during winter is called hibernation.	The behaviour of organism to escape in time during summer is called aestivation. It is done to escape the summer related problems and dessication.

(*ii*) *Ectotherms*	*Endotherms*
Organisms that can not cope with external environment temperature. changing	Organism that can cope with the changing external environment temperature.

Q. 12. Give an example for:

(*a*) An endothermic animal (*b*) An extothermic animal

(*c*) An organism of benthic zone.

Ans. (*a*) Human, (*b*) Frog, (*c*) Fish.

Q. 13. Define population and community.

Ans. A group of organisms of a particular species, living in an area that share or compete for similar resources and potentially interbreed is called as population. A group of various organism populations that exist in an area and interact in various ways is called a community.

Q. 14. Define the following terms and give one example for each:

(*a*) Commensalism (*b*) Parasitism

(*c*) Camouflage (*d*) Mutualism

(*e*) Interspecific competition.

Ans. (*a*) **Commensalism:** The interaction between two species in which one species is benefited and the other is neither benefited nor harmed is called commensalism *e.g.* barnacles growing on the back of whale.

(*b*) **Parasitism:** The interaction between two species in which one species survives on the expense of other the host. The host is harmed by this association. It is called parasitism *e.g.* malarial parasite causes harm to human host.

(*c*) **Camouflage:** The ability of the prey to escape itself from its predator by its cryptically coloured pattern to make its predator difficult to prey on it is called camouflage *e.g.* moths are camouflaged to escape its predator (bird).

(*d*) **Mutualism:** The association of two species in which both are benefited is called mutualism *e.g.* lichens are the association of fungus and algae where both are benefited.

(*e*) **Interspecific competition:** The competition between different individuals of species/ population for limited sources of food, space, is called interspecific competition *e.g.* flamingoes and resident fishes of south American lake compete for their common food — zooplankton in the lake.

Q. 15. With the help of suitable diagram describe the logistic population growth curve.

Ans.

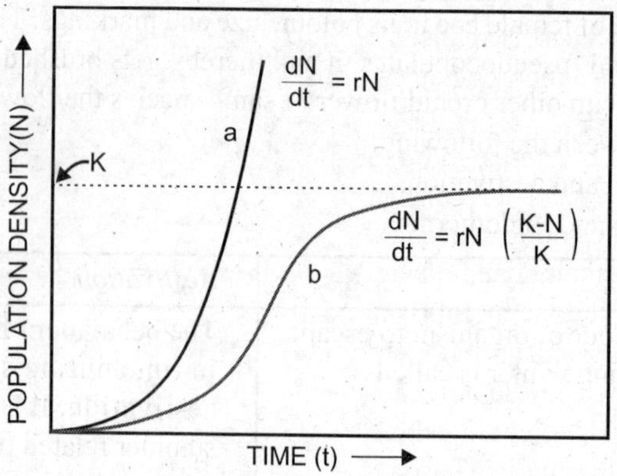

Fig. 13.2. Population growth curve: **a** when responses are not limiting the growth, plot is exponential, **b** when responses are limiting the growth, plot is logistic, **K** is carrying capacity.

Logistic Growth Model: No population of any species in nature has its disposal unlimited resources to permit the exponential growth. It leads to competition between the individual of the limited resources and eventually the fittest individual survives and reproduces. In nature the given habitat the population cannot grow beyond its carrying capacity (K) for that species in a habitat. The population growing in a habitat with limited resources first shows **lag phase,** then **acceleration** and **deceleration** and finally **asymphote** when it reaches (K). The plot formed is sigmoid curve-S-shaped. It is also called Verhulst-Pearl logistic growth. It is more realistic one.

Q. 16. List any three important characteristics of a population and explain.

Ans. (1) **Population density:** The size of a population is the population density. It is represented by N. The total number is the measure of the population. Though in some cases it is difficult. Hence, relative density is sufficient. For example, the number of fish catch per trap is good enough to measure its total population density is the lake.

(2) **Population birth and death rates:** The population birth and death rates are expressed in numbers. The change in numbers is expressed in terms of birth and death in a pond and 5 new plants are added by reproduction then the current population is 25. The birth rate is calculated as 5/20 = 0.2.5/year.

(3) **Age group:** There are different age groups in the population. When the age distribution is plotted for the population, the structure formed is called age pyramid. The shape of the pyramids reflects the growth status of the population: (1) Expanding, (2) Stable, (3) Declining.

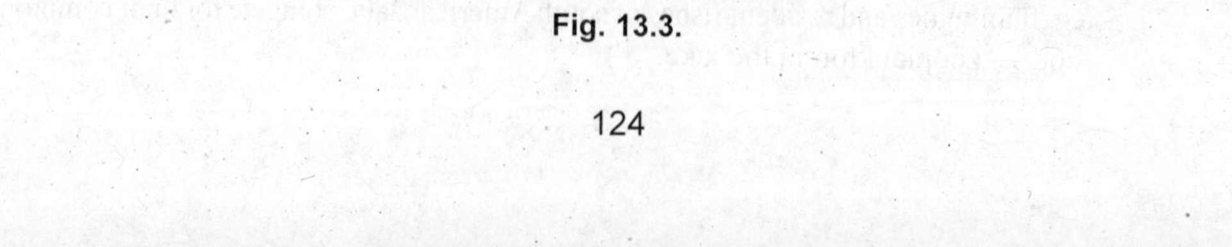

Fig. 13.3.

LONG ANSWER TYPE QUESTIONS (LA)

Q. 1. 'Fitness of a species' is realised/represented by the maximal efficiency of its body functions. How is donor regulated in case of organism when the external environment is not favourable?

Ans. All biochemical reactions and physiological functions inside the body proceed with maximal efficiency and thus enhance the overall fitness' of the species. It requires optimal temperature and osmotic concentration of body fluids. The internal environment has to be consistent/or maintained always. It is done by homeostasis. All organisms do not have this ability it done by following process.

(1) **Regulate:** Organisms have to regulate their body functions in order to maintain the homeostasis. They do it by thermoregulation such as sweating in case of human, or going to shade to cool the body, and osmoregulation such as increasing the water intake or releasing it. These organisms are regulators *e.g.* human can regulate the room temperature by switching on the fan/heater.

(2) **Conform:** 99% of animals and about 100% plants can not maintain a constant internal environment. Their body temperature changes with the ambient temperature. In aquatic animals, the osmotic concentration of the body fluids change with that of osmotic concentrations. These animals and plants are simply as they have the ability to regulate only upto a limited range of environment beyond which they simply conform.

(3) **Migrate:** Some organisms move/migrate temporarily to move hospitable/ comfortable habitat from a stressful habitat due to environmental compulsions. On return of the hospitable condition they go back home. *e.g.* migratory birds.

(4) **Suspend:** Organisms in order to survive adopt various methods/steps. They suspend their active life style, metabolic activities and become dormant. They go for sleep and on return of conductive and comfortable conditions they restore the active metabolic activities. Plants do it by forming thick walled spores, seeds become dormant and germinate in particular season. Animals hibernate, aestivate or diapause (suspend development).

Q. 2. Write a short note on:

(*a*) Adaptations of desert plants and animals.

(*b*) Adaptations of plants and water scarcity.

(*c*) Behavioural adaptations in animals.

(*d*) Importance of light to plants.

(*e*) Effect of temperature or water scarcity and the adaptations of animals.

Ans. (a) **Adaptations of desert plants and animals:** Desert plants and animals live in 'xeric' conditions. The climate is hot and rain fall is scanty. The plants have developed certain processes that help them overcome the xeric conditions such as:

(*i*) They have a special photosynthetic pathway (cpm) that enables them to have stomata closed during the day time.

(*ii*) The plants are succulent and in opuntia the stem does photosynthesis.

Small animals to escape the hot temperature they live in burrow and feel cool. These animals are active at night.

(*b*) **Adaptations of plants and water scarcity:** Desert habitat are water scarce habitat the organisms have to survive in such conditions. They have to depend on what so ever water is available to them. The plants have following adaptations:

(*i*) Stomata are closed during day in some plants. Others have deep seated stomata.

(*ii*) Leaf is modified into small size or spines as in opuntia in order to reduce transpiration.

(*iii*) The stem becomes succulent and stores water *e.g.* opuntia.

Animal like kangaroo rat in North American desert is capable of meeting all its water requirements through its internal fat oxidation. Also the urine is concentrated to minimise the water loss.

(*c*) **Behavioural adaptations in animals:** As the unique feature of mobility is confined to all animals by virtue of it they move from one place to another. They can migrate from one place to another in search of food, shelter and mate. They show many behavioural adaptations in their habitat. Such as desert lizards lack the ability to regulate its body temperature. To keep its body temperature constant it basks in sun in day and on the rise of body temperature it moves to shade.

(*d*) **Importance of light to plants:** Plants need light for (*i*) Photosynthesis and (*ii*) for flowering (photoperiod). Plants of dense forests that lie on lower strata/level and are covered or shadowed by the tall trees, are adapted to photosynthesis in low light conditions. Aquatic plants of deep sea where the light does not penetrate have adapted to other colour of visible spectrum of light for photosynthesis. Such as red and brown algae.

(*e*) **Effect of temperature in water scarcity and the adaptation of animals:** refer to above answers.

NUTSHELL **MIND MAP**

1. Response to abiotic factors. Light, temperature, water, soil. organisms are—conformers, regulators and partial regulators.
2. Adaptations to environment.
3. Population growth—logistic is realistic.
4. Population interaction are '+' '–' or '0'.

HIGHER ORDER THINKING SKILLS (HOTS) QUESTIONS

Q. 1. The following is diagrammatic representation of organismic response. What does it depict? Briefly explain it. *(SA II)*

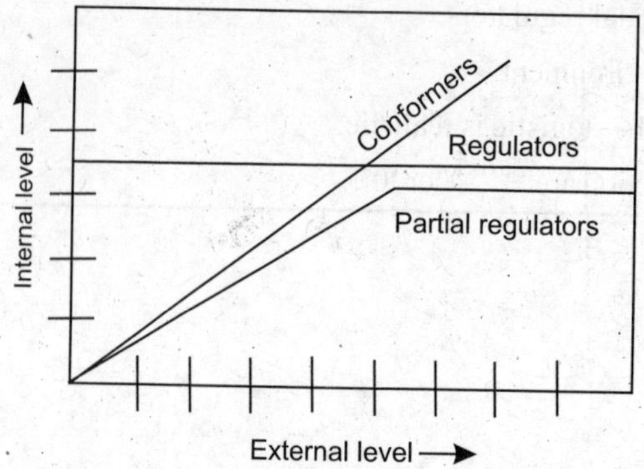

Fig. 13.4. Diagrammatic representation of organismic response.

Q. 2. (*a*) Why do seeds, spores produced by plants undergo dormancy?

(*b*) What is diapause? (SAII)

Q. 3. What do you understand by:

(*a*) Allen's rulé, (*b*) Attitude sickness

Q. 4. Many fishes thrive in Antarctica waters where the temperature is always below 0°C and pressure is >100 times the normal atmospheric pressure. How do they cope with it? (*VSA*)

Q. 5. Briefly explain what does the following equation represents .

$$N_{t+1} = N_t + [(B + I) - (D + E)]$$

where N is the population density, t is time;

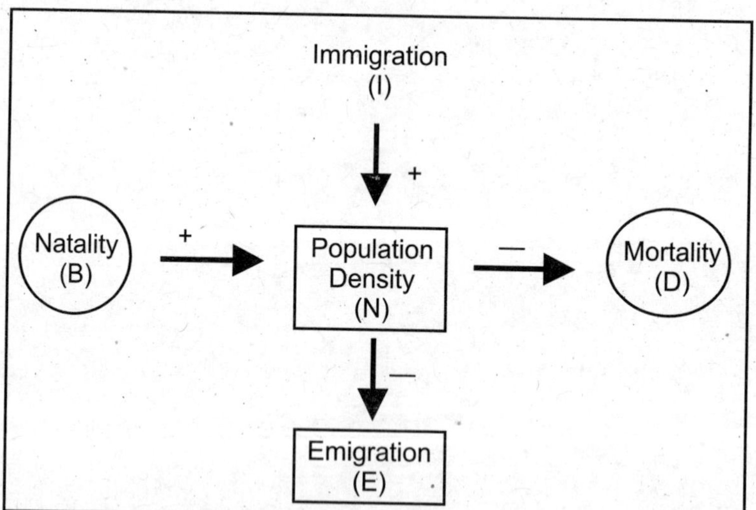

Fig. 13.5.

Q. 6. The following plot represent a population growth curves. Explain about these growth models. What does the equations, K, a, and b denote?

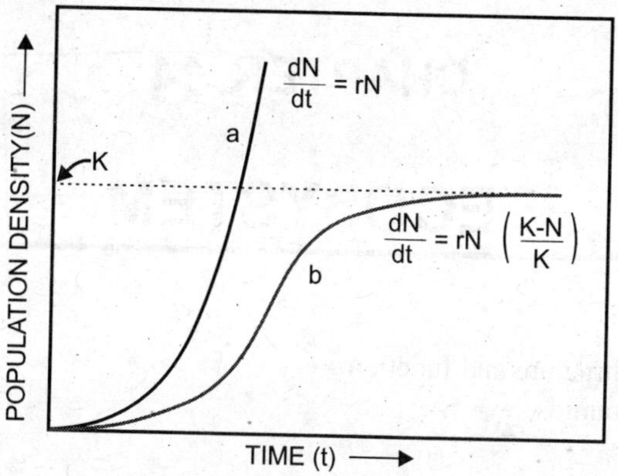

Fig. 13.6.

Q. 7. Mention the phases represented by Verhulst-Pearl logistic growth. *(SA-I)*

Q. 8. Name one example to each population interactions where both interacting species are benefited and determinal. *(VSA)*

Q. 9. Differentiate between commensalism and amensalism assign the appropriate category. *(VSA)*

Q. 10. Categorise the following interactions accordingly:

(*i*) *Prickly* pear cactus was introduced in Australia in early 1920's. It caused havoc by its growth. A moth was introduced in the country to control it. (Which type of interaction it is?)

(*ii*) *Calotropis* produces cardiac glyosides the prevents to grazers to graze on it. (The mechanism).

(*iii*) Host evolves certain special mechanism to reject/resist the parasite. The parasite develops mechanism to counter it to survive. (The phenomenon).

(*iv*) *Anopheles* female mosquito is not considered to be a parasite. (What is its role?) *(VSI)*

❑❑❑

CHAPTER 14

ECOSYSTEM

Chapter Outline

- Ecosystem—Structure and function
- Ecological pyramids
- Productivity
- Ecological succession
- Decomposition
- Nutrient quality
- Energy flow
- Ecosystem services

ASSESSMENT QUESTIONS

VERY SHORT ANSWER TYPE QUESTIONS (VSA)

Q. 1. Mention any two examples of man made ecosystem.

Ans. (1) Crop fields (2) Aquarium

Q. 2. Mention the basic requirement for any ecosystem to function and sustain.

Ans. Solar energy.

Q. 3. Name the types of productivity and the organism responsible?

Ans. **Primary productivity**— plants.

Secondary productivity —consumers.

Q. 4. Mention the raw material of decomposition.

Ans. Detritus.

Q. 5. Select the odd one out:

(*a*) Fecal matter, (*b*) Dead leaves, (*c*) Thermocol, (*d*) Bark.

Ans. (*c*) Thermocol

Q. 6. Give an example to detritivore.

Ans. Earthworm.

Q. 7. Expand the term PAR.

Ans. Photosynthetically Active Radiation.

Q. 8. How much percentage of PAR is captured by the producers to produce food for entire world?

Ans. 2%—10%

Q. 9. Name the herbivores of terrestrial and aquatic ecosystem.

Ans. **Terrestrial herbivore**—Insects, birds, mammals.

Aquatic herbivore—Mollusc.

Q. 10. Define trophic level.

Ans. The position occupied by the organisms in a food chain, due to their food or nutrition is called trophic level.

Q. 11. What is the source of energy to decomposers?

Ans. Detritus or dead biomass.

Q. 12. Expand the terms—GFC, DFC.

Ans. GFC—Grazing Food Chain

DFC—Detritus Food Chain.

Q. 13. Name the ecological pyramid that can never be inverted. Give a suitable explanation for it.

Ans. Pyramid of energy, because when energy flows from one particular trophic level to next trophic level there is always loss of some energy.

Q. 14. Give any two examples of areas where primary succession occurs.

Ans. Bare rock, newly created pond.

Q. 15. What do you understand by standing state of soil?

Ans. The amount of nutrients present in soil at any given time is called standing state.

Q. 16. Give two examples to each type.

(*a*) Gaseous type of nutrient cycle.

(*b*) Sedimentary cycle.

Ans. (*a*) Nitrogen and carbon cycle.

(*b*) Sulphur and phosphorus cycle.

Q. 17. Fill in the blanks:

(*a*) Plants are called as __________ because they fix carbon dioxide.

(*b*) In an ecosystem dominated by trees, the pyramid (of numbers) is__________ type.

(*c*) In aquatic ecosystems, the limiting factor for the productivity is__________ .

(*d*) Common detritivores in our ecosystem are__________ .

(*e*) The major reservoir of carbon on earth is__________ .

Ans. (*a*) Producers (*b*) Upright (*c*) Light

(*d*) Fungi and bacteria (*e*) Ocean

Q. 18. Which one of the following has the largest population in a food chain?

(*a*) Producers (*b*) Primary consumers

(*c*) Secondary consumers (*d*) Decomposers

Ans. (*d*) Decomposers.

Q. 19. The second trophic level in a lake is—

(*a*) Phytoplankton (*b*) Zooplankton

(*c*) Benthos (*d*) Fishes

Ans. (*a*) Zooplankton.

Q. 20. Secondary producers are—

(*a*) Herbivores (*b*) Producers

(*c*) Carnivores (*d*) None of the above.

Ans. (*a*) Herbivores

Q. 21. What is the percentage of photosynthetically active radiation (PAR), in the incident solar radiation:

(*a*) 100% (*b*) 50%

(*c*) 1–5% (*d*) 2–10%

Ans. (*b*) 50%

Q. 22. What happens to humus in soil?

Ans. It is further converted into inorganic nutrients by microbes.

Q. 23. Define standing crop.

Ans. The mass of living material (biomass) at a particular time as a trophic level is called standing crop.

Q. 24. What is climax community?

Ans. The changes that lead finally to a community that is in near equilibrium with the environment where it exists is called climax community.

SHORT ANSWER TYPE QUESTIONS (SA)

Q. 1. What are the two basic categories of ecosystem? Give two examples to each.

Ans.

- Ecosystem
  - Terrestrial
    - Examples
      - Grassland
      - Forest
      - Desert
  - Aquatic
    - Pond, lake
    - Wetland
    - River and estuary

Q. 2. Describe the components of an ecosystem.

Ans. Ecosystem consists of abiotic and biotic components.

Abiotic components: These components are the non-living components. Light, temperature, soil, water are the abiotic factors that make the habitat for living beings. They affect the living organisms behaviour and physiology. The survival of living organisms is directly or indirectly effected by these factors and thus they are dependent on it.

Biotic components: These are the living components. Plants and animals. They live in a habitat and show inter dependance on each other and on the abiotic components. The components of the ecosystem are seem to function as a unit when we consider the following aspects:

Productivity, decomposition, energy flow and nutrient cycling.

Q. 3. Define stratification with an example.

Ans. The vertical distribution of different species occupying different levels is called stratification. It is clearly visible in case of forests.

For example, trees occupy the top vertical strata, shrubs occupy the second and bottom layers/floor are occupied by hurbs and grasses.

Q. 4. What is primary productivity? Give brief description of factors that affect primary productivity.

Ans. The amount of biomass/organic matter produced per unit area over a time period by plants during photosynthesis is called primary productivity (PP). It depends on the plant species, environmental factors, availability of nutrients and photosynthetic capacity of plants. Thus, the PP is variable in different types of ecosystems.

Q. 5. Give an account of energy flow in an ecosystem.

Ans. The energy flow in the ecosystem is unidirectional. It taken place towards higher trophic levels and its dissipation and loss of heat to the environment takes place following both the laws of thermodynamics. The green plants revive solar energy from sun in the form of solar radiation of which 50% of it is photosynthetically active radiation (PAR). Plants absorb on 2-10% of it and use in converting it into their biomass. The consumers depend on the chemical energy source on food. The energy trapped by producer consumers of all levels. Energy amount decreases at successive trophic levels. When any organism dies it is convert to ditritus or dead biomass. This serves the energy source for decomposers.

Q. 6. Give a diagrammatic representation of trophic levels in an example with one example to each.

Ans.

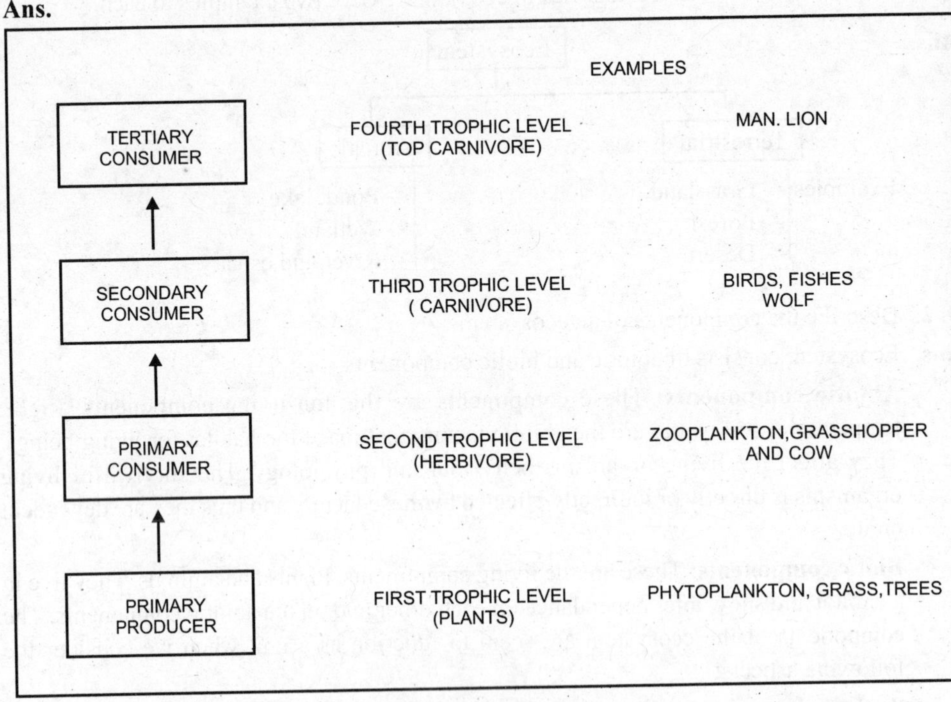

Fig. 14.1. Diagrammatic representation of trophic levels in an ecosystem.

Q. 7. Give a diagrammatic representation of energy flow through different trophic levels.

Ans.

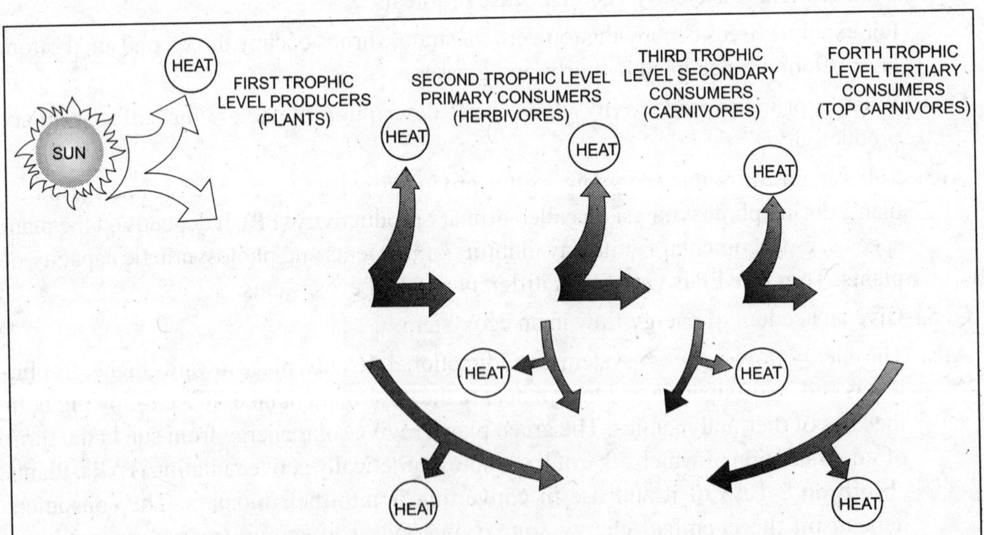

Fig. 14.2. Energy flow through different trophic levels.

Q. 8. What are the limitations of ecological pyramids?

Ans. The limitations of ecological pyramids are:

(*a*) It does not consider the same species belonging to two or more levels.

(*b*) It considers/assumes a simple food chain that does not exist in nature.

(*c*) It does not accommodate a food web in its depiction.

(*d*) It does not give any significance to saprophytes.

Q. 9. (*i*) What is ecological succession?

(*ii*) Define the terms—sere.

Ans. (*i*) The gradual and fairly change in the species composition of an area is called ecological succession.

(*ii*) The sequence of communities that successively change in a given area are called sere.

Q. 10. Arrange the following plant species in the sequential manner of their appearance during a succession. Mention the end product/changes that take place in the habitat.

Bigger plants, stable climax forest, smaller plants, lichen, bryophytes, bare rocks.

Ans. Bare rocks → lichen → bryophytes → smaller plants → bigger plants → stable climax forest.

The xerophytic habitat is converted into a mesophytic habitat as the result of above succession.

Q. 11. What are the various kinds of nutrient cycles? Give it with examples.

Ans.

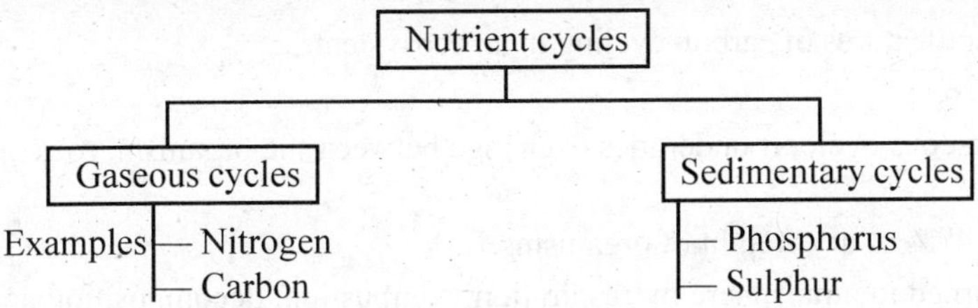

Q. 12. Depict a sedimentary cycle in terrestrial ecosystem.

Ans.

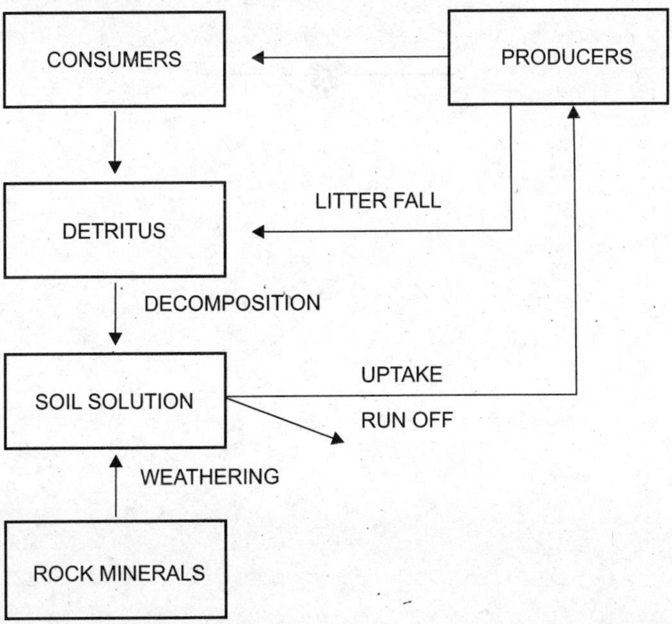

Fig. 14.3. A simplified model of phosphorus cycling in a terrestrial ecosystem.

Q. 13. (1) Mention the various ecosystem services provided to us.

(2) Should these services be priced? If yes, why?

Ans. (1) **Ecosystem services:**

(*i*) Supply of pure air, water.

(*ii*) Mitigation of drought, floods

(*iii*) Nutrient cycling, fertility of soils,

(*iv*) Provision of wild life habitat, biodiversity, storage of a carbon.

(*v*) Pollution of crops—food resources.

(*vi*) Provision for aesthetic, cultural and spiritual values.

Yes, some of the ecosystem services should be priced to put a check on the greed and exploitation of natural resources.

Q. 14. Write important features of a sedimentary cycle in an ecosystem.

Ans. Important features are:

(1) The mineral/nutrient is not released through respiration in the atmosphere.

(2) The atmospheric inputs of (phosphorus) nutrients through rainfall is smaller as in comparison to carbon.

(3) There is no gaseous exchange of the nutrient between the organism and the environment.

Q. 15. Outline salient features of carbon cycling in an ecosystem.

Ans. Salient features:

(1) It is a gaseous cycle. It undergoes exchange between the organism, rocks, air and water.

(2) It forms 49% of dry weight of organisms.

(3) It is returned to atmosphere by respiration, combustion, decomposition and other human activities.

LONG ANSWER TYPE QUESTIONS (LA)

Q. 1. Define decomposition and describe the process and products of decomposition.

Ans. The process of break down of complex organic matter into simple inorganic substances by decomposers is called decomposition.

The processes involved in it are:

1. **Fragmentation:** It involves the breaking down of large particles into smaller particles of detritus by a detritivore.
2. **Leaching:** In this process the water soluble inorganic nutrients go down into the soil horizon and get precipitated as unavailable salts.
3. **Catabolism:** It is the process of enzymatic degradation of detritus into simpler inorganic substances by bacteria and fungus.
4. **Humification:** The formation of dark brown coloured amorphous substance is called humification. The substance is humus. It is rich source of nutrients.
5. **Mineralisation:** During this process the humus further undergoes degradation by microbes and it releases inorganic nutrients. As a overall result of decomposition the soil has carbon dioxide, water, inorganic nutrients.

Q. 2. What are ecological pyramids? Briefly mention about the different types of pyramids.

Ans. The representation of ecological data in a graphical manner results in formation of a pyramid called as ecological pyramids. The commonly studied pyramids are:

Ecological pyramids

1. Pyramid of number
2. Pyramid of biomass
3. Pyramid of energy.

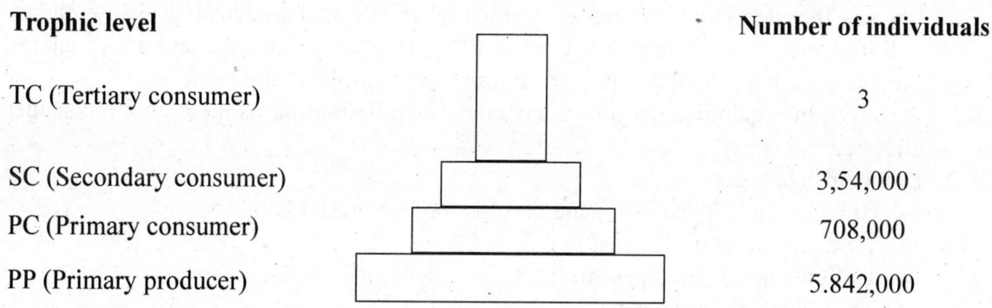

Fig. 14.4(a). Pyramid of numbers in a grassland ecosystem. Only three top-carnivores are supported in an ecosystem based on production of nearly 6 millions plants.

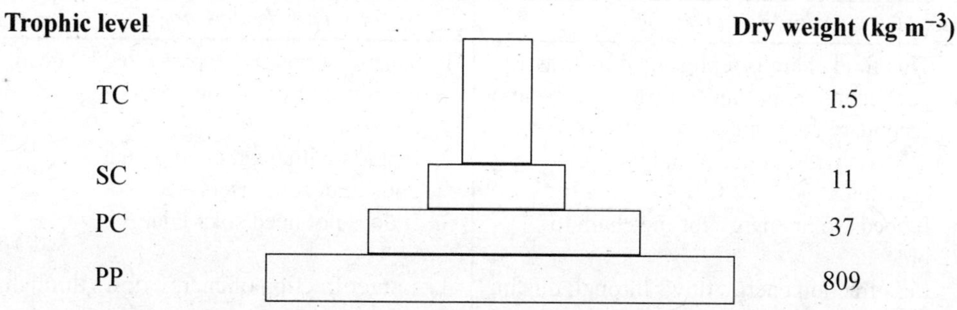

Fig. 14.4(b). Pyramid of biomass shows a sharp decrease in biomass at

higher trophic levels.

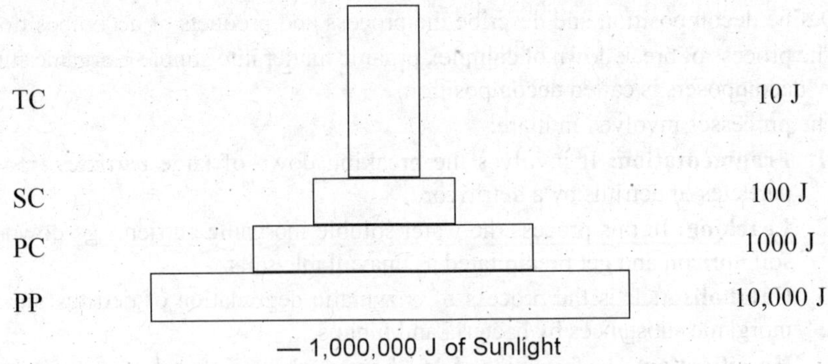

Fig. 14.4(c). An ideal pyramid of energy. Observe that primary producers convert only 10% of the energy in the sunlight available to them into NPP.

1. **Pyramid of number:** The pyramid of number depicts the population in a given ecosystem at a time. Primary producers are the plants that form the base of the pyramid and the consumers occupy the top position. The apex of the pyramid which is small is represented by tertiary consumers the number is usually the least. Pyramid is upright.
2. **Pyramid of biomass:** The pyramid of biomass is upright and represent like the pyramid of number. The data represented is in dry weight (kg m^2) per trophic level. There is a sharp decrease in the biomass if one goes from lower trophic level represented by PP to the TC. In sea the pyramid is generally inverted because the biomass of fishes is far more than that of phytoplankton.
3. **Pyramid of energy:** The pyramid of energy is always upright. It can not be inverted. Because the energy flow is from a lower to higher level and at each level always energy is lost as heat as each step. Each bar of the pyramid indicates the amount of energy present at each trophic level in a given time or annually per unit area.

   However, the ecological pyramids have their own limitations as these do not consider all aspects of ecosystem.

Q. 3. Distinguish between:

(*a*) Grazing food chain (GFC) and detritus food chain (DFC)
(*b*) Production and decomposition
(*c*) Upright and inverted pyramid.
(*d*) Food chain and food web.
(*e*) Litter and detritus
(*f*) Primary and secondary productivity.

Ans. (*a*) *Grazing Food Chain*	*Detritus Food Chain*
1. This food chain is represented by grass, goat, man. *i.e.* producer, primary consumer, secondary consumer.	1. This food chain is represented by dead organic matter, decomposers.
2. It starts with producer and ends in a consumer.	2. It starts with dead organic matter and ends in decomposers.
3. It needs solar energy for the chain to proceed.	3. It does not need solar energy.
4. Less fraction energy flows through this in ecosystem.	4. Larger fraction of energy flows through this system.

(*b*) *Production*	*Decomposition.*
1. It is the first step of the food chain.	1. It is the last step of the food chain.
2. The first trophic level individuals are the autotrophs and the primary consumers the herbivores both are the food producing levels.	2. All level of organisms after death undergo the process of decompositions.
3. It adds to biomass.	3. It degrades the formed biomass after the death of organisms.

(*c*) *Upright pyramid*	*Inverted pyramid*
1. Upright pyramids are of number, energy.	1. Inverted pyramid is formed in case of biomass. The small standing crop of phyto-plankton supports the large standing crop of zooplankton in case of aquatic system.
2. The base is broader than the apex.	2. The base is shorter than the apex.

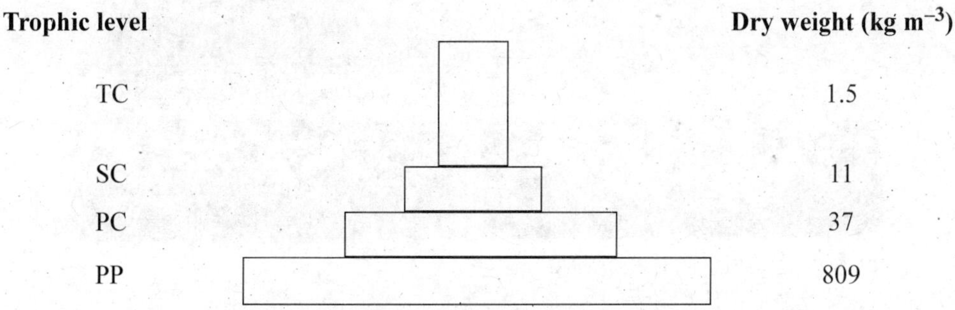

Fig. 14.5 Pyramid of biomass shows a sharp decrease in biomass at higher trophic levels.

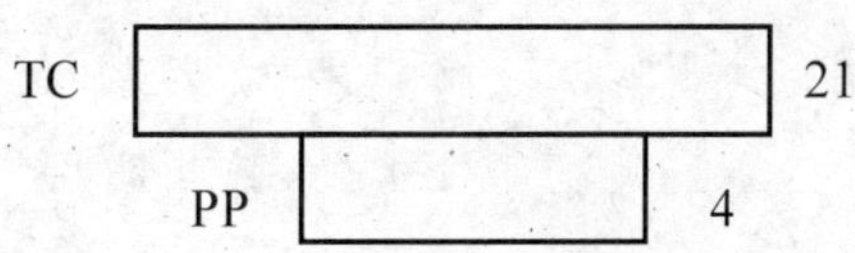

Fig. 14.6. Inverted pyramid of biomass-small standing crop of phytoplankton supports large standing crop of zooplankton.

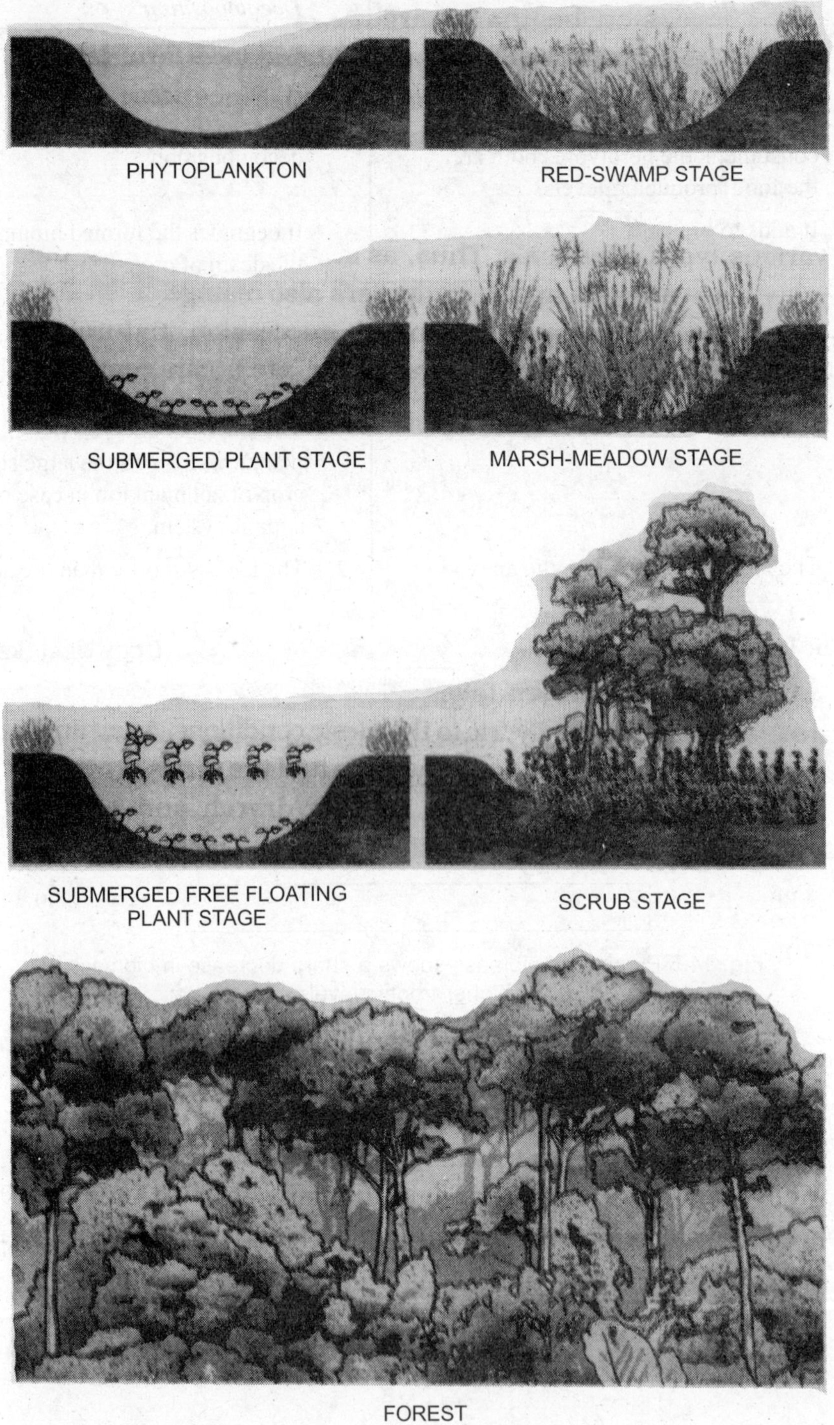

Fig. 14.5. Diagrammatic representation of primary succession.

(*d*) *Food chain*	*Food web*
(*i*) The representation of eat and be eaten principle in the ecosystem. (*ii*) It is a simple representation of producers and consumers of various levels.	(*i*) The representation of inter connected food chains in the ecosystem. (*ii*) The member of a trophic level can be the member of another trophic level.

(*e*) *Litter*	*Detritus*
1. The fresh /recently fallen leaves/ flowers/buds of the plants, tree and their parts are litter. 2. They cover the land surface and can be blown away by wind and water.	1. The dead organic matter on the soil forms detritus. 2. They also cover the land and are affected by decomposers. They can not be blown away because it becomes the part of soil.

(*f*) *Primary productivity*	*Secondary productivity*
1. The production of biomass of plants by the photosynthetic activity is called primary productivity. (PP) 2. It depends on the plant species, solar energy, and environmental factors.	1. The production of new orgánic matter by consumers is called secondary productivity (SP) 2. It depends upon the primary producers.

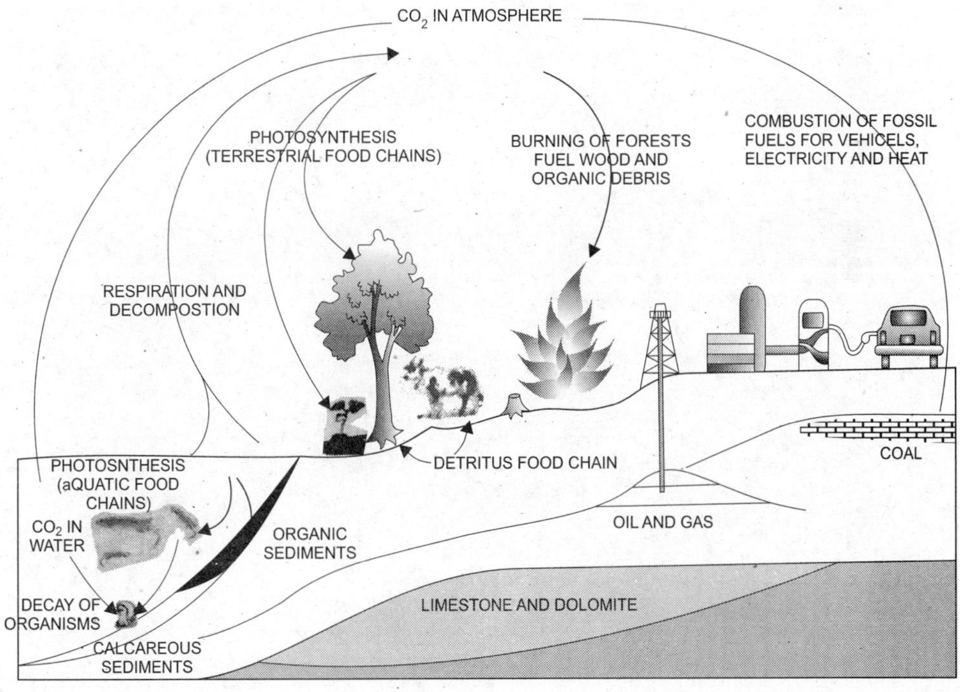

Fig. 14.6. Simplified model of carbon cycle in the biosphere.

HIGHER ORDER THINKING SKILLS (HOTS) QUESTIONS

Q. 1. Briefly mention what does the following equation stand for? (*VSA*)
GPP – R = NPP

Q. 2. What does the following inverted pyramid depict? (*SA I*)

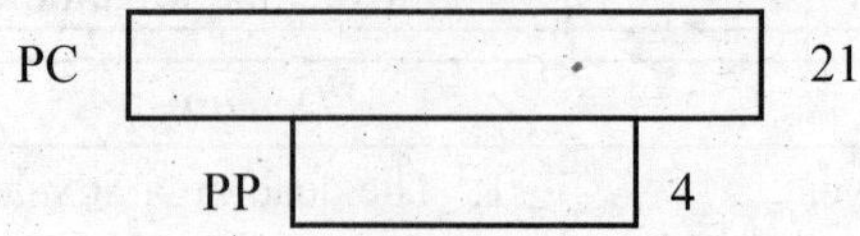

Q. 3. Where does primary and secondary succession start? Mention about both in brief. (*SAI*)

Q. 4. How are hydrarch and research succession different? Both lead to a common condition mention it. (*SA I*)

Q. 5. What is the type of climax community in terms of water needs condition? (*SA I*)

Q. 6. What is the function of reservoir in cycling of materials/nutrients in ecosystem? (*SAI*)

CHAPTER 15

BIODIVERSITY AND CONSERVATION

Chapter Outline

- Biodiversity
- Biodiversity conservation

ASSESSMENT QUESTIONS

VERY SHORT ANSWER TYPE QUESTIONS (VSA)

Q. 1. Name the three components of biodiversity.
Ans. (1) Genetic diversity, (2) Species diversity, (3) Ecological diversity.

Q. 2. How do ecologists estimate the total number of species present in the world?
Ans. A statistical comparison of the temperate-tropical species richness of an exhaustively studied group is made (*e.g.* insects) and extrapolate this ratio other groups to come up with a gross estimate of total number of species on earth.

Q. 3. Mention the patterns of biodiversity.
Ans. (1) Latitudinal gradients, (2) Species-Area relationships.

Q. 4. What is the reason that as we move away from the equator towards the poles the species diversity decreases.
Ans. Latitude.

Q. 5. Which type of plot is obtained for species richness and area in case of taxa?
Ans. Rectangular parabola.

Q. 6. What is the significance of the slope of regression in a species-area relationship?
Ans. The species area relationships among large areas like the entire continent is much steeper.

Q. 7. Name any two recently extinct species, along with the country name.
Ans. (1) Dodo (Mauritius), (2) Quags (Africa).

Q. 8. Which groups of species are more vulnerable to extinction?
Ans. Amphibian.

Q. 9. Which one is the main cause of biodiversity loss?
Ans. Human activities.

Q. 10. Mention the categories that suggest that conservation of biodiversity is necessary.
Ans. (1) Narrowly utilitarian, (2) Broadly utilitarian, (3) Ethical.

Q. 11. Mention the approaches to conserve biodiversity.

Ans.

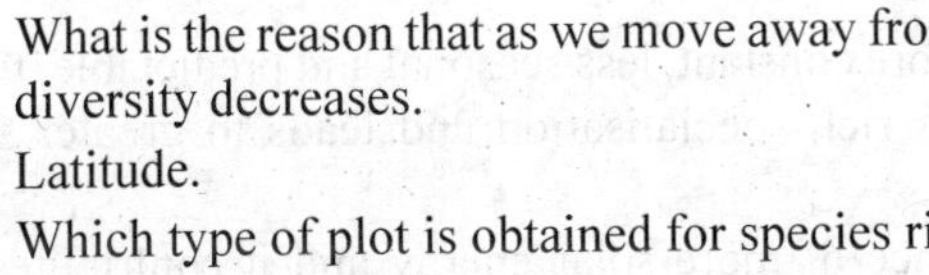

SHORT ANSWER TYPE QUESTIONS (SA-I, II)

Q. 1. Briefly mention about—

(*a*) Genetic diversity, (*b*) Species diversity, (*c*) Ecological diversity.

Ans. (*a*) **Genetic diversity:** The occurrence of single species in high diversity at the genetic level over its distributional range is called as genetic diversity. Such as in *Rauwolfia vomitoria* in Himalaya region, 50,000 varieties of rice, 1,000 varieties of mango in India.

(*b*) **Species diversity:** The occurrence of diversity as the species level in a geographical region is called species diversity. *e.g.* western ghats have more amphibian species diversity than in eastern ghats.

(*c*) **Ecological diversity:** A geographical region having different ecosystems will have more ecologically diverse organisms one having one or two types only. For example, India has more ecological diversity than Norway.

Q. 2. Explain with examples—latitudinal gradients.

Ans. The decrease in the species diversity from equator towards the poles is latitudinal gradient in diversity. This can be justified by following examples:

(*i*) Colombia located near equator has nearly 1,400 species of birds, New York at 41°N has 105 species and Greenland at 71°N has 56 species only. India has 1,200 species.

(*ii*) Equador's forest has upto 10 times more species than mid west of USA for vascular plants.

Q. 3. Give three hypotheses for explaining why tropics show greatest levels of species richness.

Ans. The following three hypothesis for greatest levels of species richness are—

(*a*) **Speciation:** It is the function of time. The tropical latitudes have remained undisturbed for millions of years and had a long time for evolution among species diversification as compared to temperate regions that frequented for glaciations in past.

(*b*) **Tropical environment:** It is more constant, less seasonal and predictable, than the temperate ones. This provides rich specialisation and leads to greater species diversity.

(*c*) **Solar energy:** There is presence of more solar energy and it contributes more productivity and in turn more diversity.

Q. 4. Study the following plot.

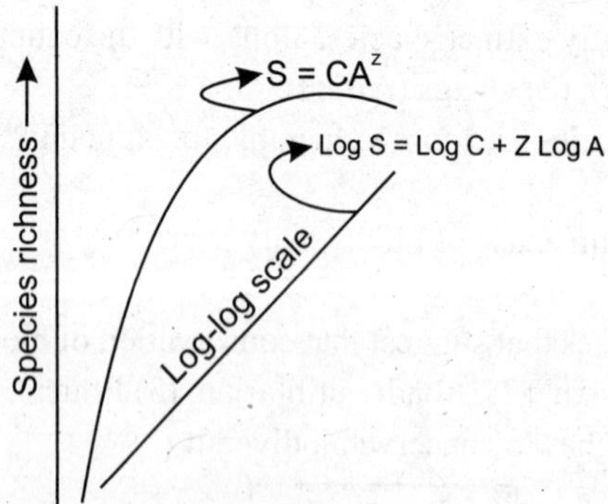

Fig. 15.1. Showing species area relationship. Note that on log scale the relationship becomes linear.

Answer the following:

(*i*) Which line/plot describes the species-area relationship on a logarithmic scale? Give the equation also.

(*ii*) What is the shape of curve for species richness and area for a wide variety of taxa?

(*iii*) What is the value of Z in a region and continent?

(*iv*) What does steeper slope of Z mean?

Ans. (*i*) The straight line represents the relationship. The equation is—Log S = Log C + Z Log A

(*ii*) Rectangular hyperbola.

(*iii*) Z value in a continent lies between - 0.6 to 1.2.
Z value in a continent lies between 0.6 to 1.2.

(*iv*) It means more species richness relationship.

Q. 5. How is biodiversity important for ecosystem functioning?

Ans. Biodiversity is very important for the ecosystem functioning and its stability. It also is responsible for the health of the ecosystem but the very survival of human in the ecosystem on this planet.

Q. 6. How is a stable community identified?

Ans. The following points if observed suggest that the community is stable—

(*a*) It must not show too much variation in the productivity from year-year.

(*b*) It must be resistant or resisetent to occasional disturbances caused by nature and man-made.

(*c*) It must be resistant to invasions by alien species.

Q. 7. How many mass extinction of species are there on records since the origin and diversification of life on earth? How is the present episode different? What is the result of loss of biodiversity in a region?

Ans. There were 5 episodes of mass extinction of species. The present sixth episode is in progress. The current rates of extinction is estimated to be faster than the pre-human times because of our activities. It is estimated to be faster 100–1000 times.
General loss is:

(*a*) Decline to plant production.

(*b*) Lowered resistance to environmental disturbances such as droughts.

(*c*) Increased variability in certain ecosystem processes.

Q. 8. Briefly give the views regarding the reasons for conserving biodiversity.

Ans. There are the following views:

(*a*) **Narrowly utilitarian:** We humans derive countless direct economic benefits from nature. Such as food, medicines and many more utility things. Nations with rich biodiversity can expect to reap enormous benefits from the increasing resources put into bioprospecting.

(*b*) **Broadly utilitarian:** It says that biodiversity plays a major role in many ecosystem services that nature provides. There are many intangible benefits that we derive from nature, including aesthetic pleasures.

(*c*) **Ethical values:** All living beings that share this planet have equal right to live as do humans. We must realise that every species has an intrinsic value, even if we do not have any current economic value. We have to maintain the biological legacy in good order for future generations.

Q. 9. What are sacred groves? What is their role in conservation?

Ans. India has a history of religious and cultural traditions that emphasised protection of nature. In many cultures, tracts of forests are set aside and trees, animals are given total protection. Such forests are called sacred groves. Such forests are called sacred groves which help us to preserve, protect the forests, wildlife and other rare, threatened and vulnerable species.

Q. 10. Among the ecosystem services are control of floods and soil erosion. How is this achieved by the biotic components of the ecosystem?

Ans. Control of floods and soil erosion are done by preserving the forests. There must be a balance between the plants and animals to maintain the biodiversity.

Q. 11. The species diversity of plants (22 per cent) is much less than that of animals (72 per cent). What could be the explanations to how animals achieved greater diversification?

Ans. The animals have higher per cent than the species diversity of plants because they are mobile and move from one place to another. They moved to different habitats/ecosystem and developed species diversity.

Q. 12. Can you think of a situation where we deliberately want to make a species extinct? How would you justify it?

Ans. Human health, followed by health of plants and animals of economic use. The health of human, plants and animal species is always in danger due to pathogens, and vectors, secondary or primary hosts. For the welfare of human, we want to deliberately make such pathogenic species extinct. This will ensure, the pathogenic diseases free human life and animal life.

LONG ANSWER TYPE QUESTIONS (LA)

Q. 1. Explain 'the evil quartet' that causes biodiversity losses

Ans.

Human activities that cause biodiversity losses —
- (i) Habitat loss and fragmentation
- (ii) Over exploitation.
- (iii) Alien species invasions
- (iv) Co-extinctions.

These four are the major causes of loss of biodiversity. It is sobriquet used to describe it.

(*i*) **Habitat loss and fragmentation:** Habitat loss and fragmentation is the most important cause of deriving the plants and animals to extinction. It is evident from the Amazon rain forest. (It is so huge that it is called 'lungs of planet' because it produces 20% of oxygen in the earth's atmosphere.) This forest once covered about 14% of earth's surface is reduced to about 6% only.

(*ii*) **Over-exploitation:** All resources in nature are limited. Man is dependent on nature for every thing. Over-exploitation of natural resources has lead to loss of many things. Such as many species of marine fishes have been endangered mainly because of their economic importance and over harvesting.

(*iii*) **Alien species invasions:**Introduction of alien species in an ecosystem some times turns out to be invasive. It dominates the habitat and causes the decline/extinction of other indigenous species. For example, Threat to our native species by invasive weed species like carrot grass (*Parthenium*), Lantana, water hyacinth (*Eicchornia*).

(*iv*) **Co-extinctions:** When a species becomes extinct, the plant and animal species associated with it in an obligatory way also become extinct. Such as extinction of host species of fish also leads to extinction of assemblage of parasites on it also co-evolved plant and pollinator mutualism show similar effect.

Q. 2. How do we conserve biodiversity?

Ans. We conserve biodiversity by two methods—

(*i*) **in situ (on site) conservation:** Conservation of species at their own habitats is being done world wide by identifying species rich regions. These regions are identified as 'biodiversity hot spots' and there are 34 such hot spots in world. These are regions with very high levels of species richness and high grade of endemism. (species not found elsewhere). Such as western ghats and Sri Lanka, Indo-Burma and Himalaya. Therefore protection extented to the host spots could reduce the ongoing mass extinctions by almost 30%. Similarly, in India due to cultural and religious reasons tracts of forests are set aside. These are called sacred groves. They enjoy the projection and thus the nature is maintained.

(*ii*) **Ex situ (off site) conservation:** This method involves taking care of threatened animals and plants in other specialised places other than their natural habitats. Places such as zoological parks, botanical gardens, wildlife safari. Conservation of gametes, by cryopreservation, fertilised eggs can be obtained *in vitro* tissue culture, seed banks etc. are the other methods of preservation.

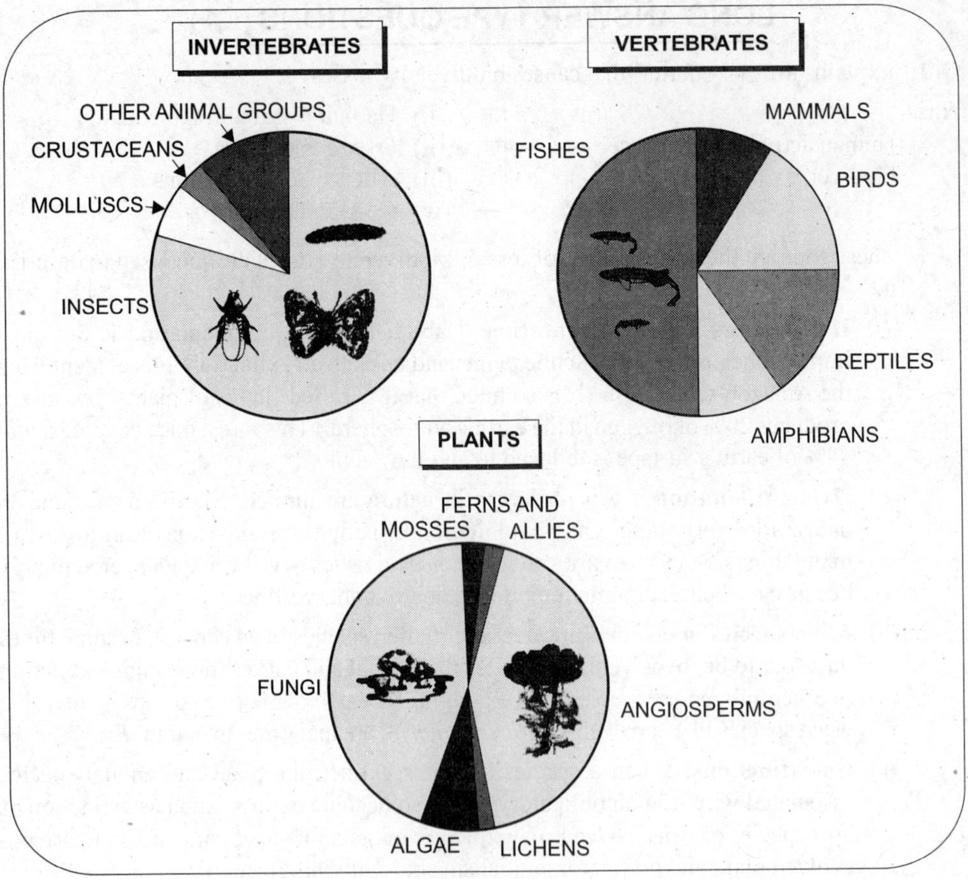

Fig. 15.2. Representation of global biodiversity.

HIGHER ORDER THINKING SKILLS (HOTS) QUESTIONS

1. Give a suitable reason for biodiversity of Amazonian rain forest. (*VSA*)
2. What is bioprospecting? (*VSA*)
3. Give your views regarding loss of biodiversity. (*SA II*)

❑❑❑

CHAPTER 16

ENVIRONMENTAL ISSUES

Chapter Outline

- Air pollution and its control
- Green house effect and global warming
- Water pollution and its control
- Ozone depletion in the stratosphere
- Solid wastes
- Degradation by improper resource utilisation
- Agrochemicals and their effects and maintenance
- Radioactive wastes
- Deforestation

ASSESSMENT QUESTIONS

VERY SHORT ANSWER TYPE QUESTIONS (VSA)

Q. 1. Define the term pollution.

Ans. Any undesirable change in physical, chemical and biological characteristics of air, land, water or soil is called pollution.

Q. 2. What are pollutants?

Ans. Substances that bring about changes in the environment are called pollutants.

Q. 3. Which act has been passed by Government of India to protect and improve the quality of our environment?

Ans. Environment (Protection) Act, 1986.

Q. 4. Name the device used to remove sulphur dioxide from gases?

Ans. Scrubber.

Q. 5. Which size particulate are harmful to human?

Ans. Particulate size 2.5 micrometer or less.

Q. 6. How can the industrial noise be reduced?

Ans. The industrial noise can be reduced by use of sound absorbents and mufflers.

Q. 7. What is the purpose of water Prevention and Control of Pollution Act, 1974?

Ans. This act passed by Govt. of India is to safeguard our water resources.

Q. 8. What is the cause of algal-bloom?

Ans. Presence of large amount of nutrients in water.

Q. 9. Define the term 'Biomagnification'.

Ans. The accumulation of toxic substance in the body of organisms and its increase in concentration in successive trophic levels is called biomagnification.

Q. 10. Name two substances that show biomagnification.

Ans. (1) Mercury, (2) DDT.

Q. 11. Mention two locations where 'Ecosan' is used.

Ans. (1) Kerala (India), (2) Sri Lanka.

Q. 12. Mention one method disposal of hospital waste.

Ans. Incineration.

Q. 13. Mention the methods used to dispose e-waste.

Ans. (1) Burrying in land fills, (2) Incineration.

Q. 14. What are two serious problems for use of nuclear energy?

Ans. (1) Accidental leakage.

(2) Disposal of radioactive wastes.

Q. 15. Which two gases are responsible for green house effect?

Ans. (1) Carbon dioxide, (2) Methane.

Q. 16. Mention the unit used to measure the thickness of ozone in atmosphere.

Ans. Dobson units (DU).

Q. 17. In which months does a ozone hole develop over Antarctica?

Ans. Late August and early October.

Q. 18. Mention the percentage of forest cover for plains and hills by Nation Forest Policy (1988) of India.

Ans. 33% for plains, 67% for Hills.

Q. 19. How is slash and burn agriculture practised in N-E States of India?

Ans. The trees are cut and the plant remains are burnt. Then the cleared land is used for agricultural purpose.

Q. 20. What is Join Forest Management (JFM)?

Ans. It is to work along with local communities for protecting and managing forests.

SHORT ANSWER TYPE QUESTIONS (SA)

Q. 1. Here are figures of two devices. Mention their use in short.

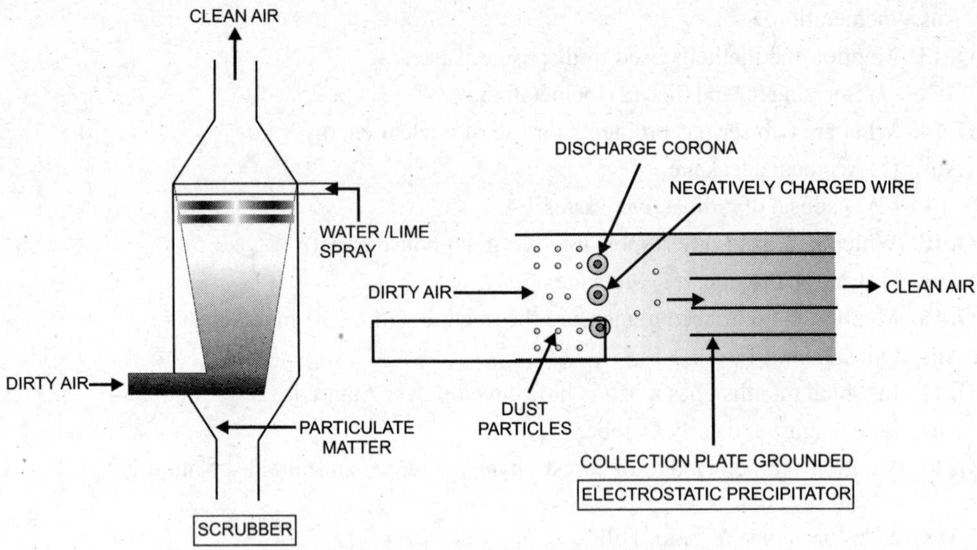

Fig. 16.1. Electrostatic precipitator.

Ans. (1) **Scrubber:** It is a device used for removing sulphur dioxide (SO_2) from the exhaust. The exhaust free of SO_2 is passed through a spray of water/lime. As a result the air becomes clean and it can be released in atmosphere.

(2) **Electrostatic precipitator:** It is a device used to remove particulate matter from the exhaust from a thermal power point. It removes about 99% of the particulate. It has electrode wires that have thousand volts of current. It produces corona that releases electrons. The dust particles attach to the electrons and get negatively charged. These are then collected by collecting plates.

Q. 2. What are the effects on our body of particulates of size 2.5 micrometers?

Ans. These particles are deep inhaled into lungs and cause—

(*i*) breathing and respiratory problems.

(*ii*) irritation, inflammation, damage to lungs.

(*iii*) premature death.

Q. 3. (*i*) Why are auto vehicles filled with catalytic converters?

(*ii*) What do these devices have as catalyst?

(*iii*) How are these converters useful?

Ans. (*i*) Catalytic converters are devices fitted to auto vehicles to reduce atmospheric pollution, due to burning of petrol/diesel.

(*ii*) Rhodium, platinum-palladium are the catalyst fitted to the converters.

(*iii*) These catalyst converters, convert the unburnt hydrocarbons into CO_2, H_2O, and CO and nitric oxide are converted into CO_2, N_2.

Catalytic Converter

Unleaded petrol $\rightarrow$ Hydrocarbons $\longrightarrow$ $CO_2 + H_2O$

CO + Nitric oxide $\longrightarrow$ $CO_2 + N_2$.

Q. 4. Mention any two advantages of CNG as a fuel for autovehicles.

Ans. (1) It can not be adulterated.

(2) It burns completely leaising very little unburnt and also efficiently.

Q. 5. What are the various constituents of domestic sewage? Discuss the effects of sewage discharge in a river?

Ans. The domestic sewage contains—

primarily biodegradable organic matter and many more substances effects of sewage discharge.

The sewage discharged in the river results in consumption of oxygen by micro-organisms for biodegradation, mortality of fish and other aquatic organisms; algal bloom etc. The quality of water deteriorates and gives water a poor quality and makes it unfit for human consumption.

Q. 6. Match the items given in column A and B.

Column A	*Column B*
(*a*) Catalytic converter	(*i*) Particulate matter
(*b*) Electrostatic precipitator	(*ii*) Carbon dioxide and nitrogen oxides
(*c*) Ear muffs	(*iii*) High noise levels
(*d*) Land fills	(*iv*) Solid wastes

Ans. (*a*) (*ii*) (*c*) (*iii*)

(*b*) (*i*) (*d*) (*iv*)

Q. 7. Define eutrophication. What is cultural or accelerated eutrophication?

Ans. The natural aging of lakes due to nutrient enrichment of water is called eutrophication. It may take thousands of years for natural eutrophication.

Human activities, pollutants and other factors accelerate the natural aging process. This is called cultural/accelerated eutrophication.

Q. 8. What is 'sanitary land fill'? Give its one advantage and disadvantage.

Ans. The process of burning the solid wastes in trench or low lying areas and covering it with dust is called sanitary land fill.

The advantage is that wastes are not exposed and breeding of rats and flies cannot take place. Also foul smell emittance is not there. The disadvantage is that the chemicals seepage takes place and it will pollute the underground water resources.

Q. 9. List all the wastes that you generate, at home, school or during your trips to other places, could you very easily reduce? Which could be difficult or rather impossible to reduce?

Ans. List of some wastes generated are—

Polyethenes, aluminium foil, paper, extra food, peels of vegetables, fruits, shells of nuts, egg shells, seeds, rotten food, cartons, bottles, blades, etc.

Yes, some of the above can be easily reduced such as food, wrapping materials etc. Sewage in rather difficult to reduce.

(List of other items can be added to it.)

Q. 10. Why ozone hole forms over Antarctica? How will enhanced ultraviolet radiation affect us?

Ans. Though the depletion of ozone layer is widely in the stratosphere but particularly ozone layer is thin marked between late august and early October over Antarctica. This is called ozone hole. The affects of ultraviolet radiation on human are—

(*a*) skin damage and skin cancer.

(*b*) Inflammation of cornea (snow blindness), cataract.

(*c*) Mutation.

Q. 11. Expand the terms—

Ans. DU, CFC, FOAM, PIL, CNG, CPCB.

(1) Dobson Unit
(2) Chlorofluorocarbon
(3) Friends of the Arcata Marsh
(4) Public Interest Litigation
(5) Compressed Natural gas
(6) Central Pollution Control Board

Q. 12. Discuss the role of women and communities in protection and conservation of forests?

Ans. Women and communities have played a major role in protection and conservation of forests. Two examples are—

Protection of forest trees by Bishnoi Community: In olden days Bishnoi community played a major role in protecting their forest trees in Rajasthan. The women Leader Amrita Devi sacrificed her life for the cause followed by her daughters and her community. Such an example is not witnessed in any part of world except India.

Chipko Movement: Similar movement to protect the trees of hills by Garhwal Himalayas in 1974 was shown. The women of this region hugged the trees and protected them from the axe of timber contractors. People all over the world acclaimed the move.

Q. 13. What measures, as an individual, you would take to reduce environmental pollution?

Ans. Following measures I would undertake to reduce environmental pollution are—

(1) Reduce the use of poly bags, packed materials, autovehicles - car, scooter.
(2) Use recycled materials.
(3) Dump or use dust bin, poly bags for solid wastes dumping.
(4) Minimise the use of substances that cause pollution during production.

Q. 14. Discuss briefly the following:

(*a*) Radioactive wastes
(*b*) Defunct ships and e-wastes
(*c*) Municipal solid wastes.

Ans. (*a*) **Radioactive Wastes:** Radioactive materials are the source of nuclear energy which is used to generate electricity. This source of electrical energy poses a serious problem in the disposal of radioactive wastes and radiation leakage. Already two accidental leakages have taken place in past. It causes damages to organisms because of high mutation rates. It also creates disorders, such as cancer on lower doses. It is extremely potent pollution and it has to be dealt with caution Hence, the wastes are suitably shielded in containers and buried about 500 in deep below the earth.

(*b*) **Defunct Ships and e-wastes:** e-wastes are electronic goods that are irreparable. These wastes are generated in the developed countries and exported to developing countries such as India for dumping. These are either buried in landfills or incinerated. They are also recycled and metals like copper, iron, silicon, nickel and gold are recovered. The recycling of e-wastes in our country involves manual participation. Thus exposing the workers to toxic substances present in e-wastes.

(*c*) **Municipal Solid Wastes:** These are the wastes produced from homes, offices, stores, schools, hospitals etc. These are—plastics, glass, metals, food wastes, plastic, paper, etc. Burning these causes reduction in volume of wastes but produces air pollution, dumping in open serves as breeding ground for rats and flies. Therefore, an alternative method for disposal is sanitary landfills. This also is not cent per cent foolproof as it causes seepage of chemicals to underground water resources.

Q. 15. What initiatives were taken for reducing vehicular air pollution in Delhi? Has air quality improved in Delhi?

Ans. To reduce the vehicular pollution in Delhi following measures were taken:

(*i*) Buses are being run on CNG.
(*ii*) Other private vehicles are also using CNG—the clean fuel.

(*iii*) Use of unleaded, low-sulphur petrol and diesel.
(*iv*) Use of catalytic converters in auto vehicles.
(*v*) All vehicles to meet Bharat stage III norms.
(*vi*) Old vehicles to be replaced by new ones following the prescribed norms.

Q. 16. Discuss briefly the following:
(*a*) Greenhouse gases
(*b*) Catalytic converter
(*c*) Ultraviolet B

Ans. (*a*) **Greenhouse gases:** The increase in the global temperature during the past century by 0.6' is by green house gases. This has been mostly in past three decades. Various greenhouse gases are—CO_2, CH_4, N_2O, CFC. Of these the major contributors are CO_2 (60%) and methane (20%) to total global warming. This rise in temperature due to global warming is leading to deleterious changes in the environment and resulting in odd climatic changes. (*e.g.* El Nino effect).

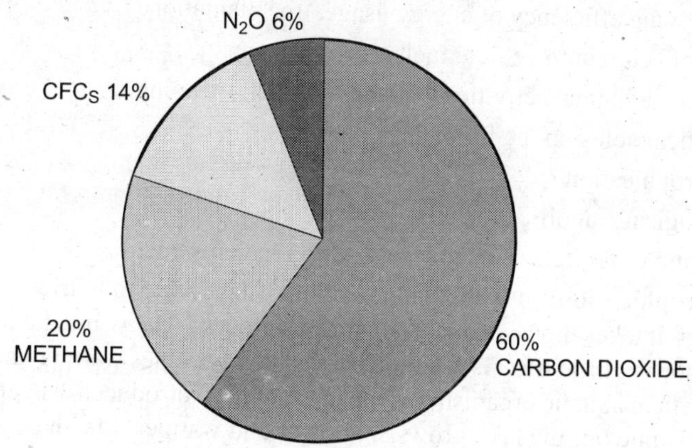

Fig. 16.2. Relative contribution of various greenhouse gases to total global warming.

(*b*) **Catalytic converter:** There are devices fitted to auto vehicles that run on petrol. These work on unleaded petrol (leaded petrol) inactivates the catalyst). The converter has platinum, palladium and rhodium as catalysts. These convert the unburnt hydro carbon into CO_2 and H_2O gas, and carbon monoxide and nitric oxide into CO_2 and N_2 gas. This reduces the atmospheric pollution as the exhaust does not have poisonous gases, unburnt hydrocarbons.

(*c*) **Ultraviolet B:** UV-B radiation is present in the UV radiation. These rays are damaging and cause damages to DNA and mutation. The aging of skin, cancer of skin, damages skin and effects eye. The human eye absorbs it and causes inflammation of cornea called snow blindness, cataract etc. on high dose of UV-B. It can also result in permanent damage to cornea.

LONG ANSWER TYPE QUESTIONS (LA)

Q. 1. Discuss the causes and effects of global warming. What measures need to be taken to control global warming?

Ans. **Causes of global warming:** The global warming is the increase of the earth's temperature. It is because of the natural phenomenon called greenhouse effect. The greenhouse gases—CO_2, CH_4, CFC, N_2O are responsible for the increase in the temperature. These gases are the products of various activities natural and human activities.

Effects of global warming: The main effect of global warming is the rise in atmospheric/earth's temperature. This leads to environmental changes, odd climatic changes, melting of ice caps (Polar and Himalayan) and ultimately rise in sea level.

Control of global warming: Following measures will help in reducing the global warming. These are:

(*i*) Reducing the use of fossil fuel, deforestation, human population growth.

(*ii*) Improving efficiency of energy usage, tree plantation.

(*iii*) Use of better auto vehicle fuels.

(*iv*) Check on human activities that add to global warming.

Q. 2. Write critical notes on the following:

(*a*) Eutrophication

(*b*) Biological magnification

(*c*) Ground water depletion and ways for its replenishment.

Ans. (*a*) **Eutrophication:** It is the natural aging of lakes due to nutrient enrichment of its water. It takes thousands of years for this process. The young lake is cold and clear supporting little life. As the time passes by it becomes warmer and encourages the growth of aquatic organisms as the nutrient gets introduced. The fertility increases, debris pile up, the lake grows shallower and warmer. Marsh plants start growing and fill the original basin. Eventually it converts into a land.

(*b*) **Biological magnification:** It is increase in the concentration of the toxic substance of successive trophic levels. A few toxic substances present in industrial waste waters accumulate in organisms. Such as DDT and mercury. It takes place in aquatic ecosystem. The water with 0.003 pph DDT is the starting point and it gradually increases in organisms of successive levels upto 25 pph. This concentration disturbs the calcium metabolism in birds and causes thinning of egg shell which breaks prematurely and causes decline in bird population.

(*c*) **Ground water depletion and ways for replenishment:** Ground water is the source of water for most of the human activities. Regions that are having less annual rainfall depend on underground water for agricultural purposes-irrigation. Over exploitation of ground water for irrigation, construction, domestic use, industrial use has depleted it in many areas. The water level has gone down. This causing water crisis specially in summer and drought hit regions. Its replenishment can be done by judiciously using the water at our disposal. Water must not be wasted at any shape/activities. Rain water harvesting must be practised by an large by every one so that the ground water can be recharged annually. Also, reforestation, less deforestation must be in practice.

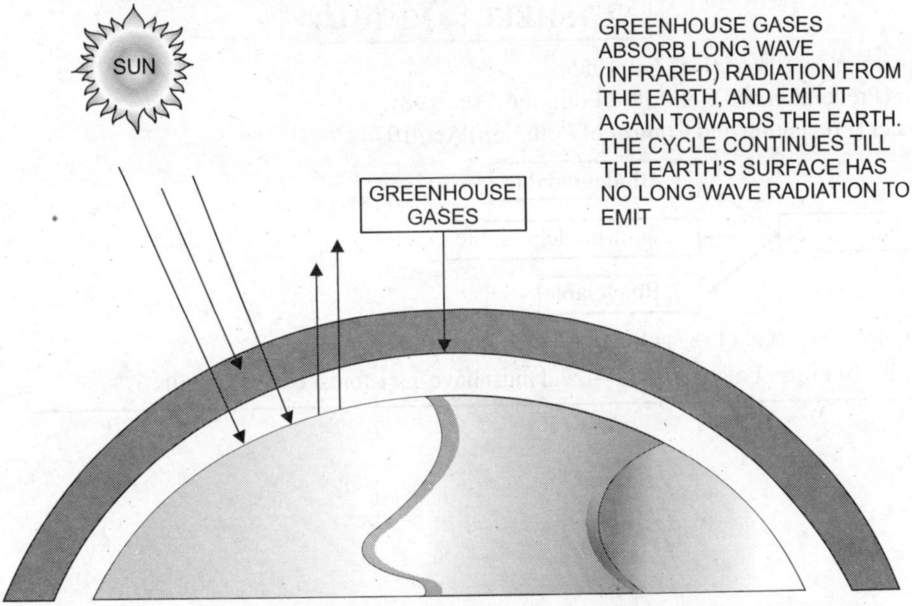

Fig. 16.3a. Sunlight energy at the outermost atmosphere.

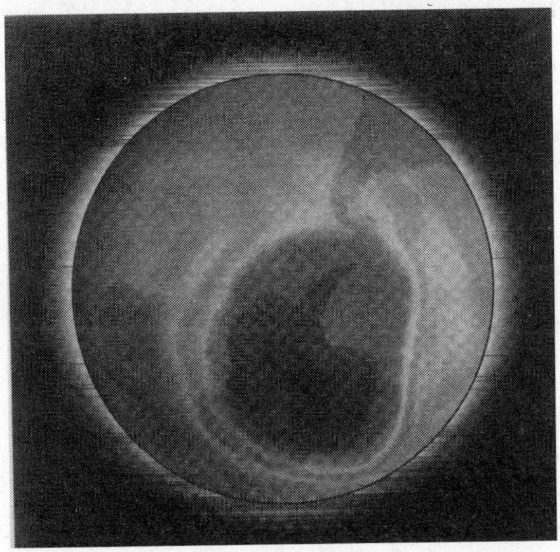

Fig. 16.3b. Ozone hole is the area above Antarctica, shown in purple colour, where the ozone layer is the thinnest. Ozone thickness is given in Dobson unit (see carefully the scale shown in colour violet to red). The ozone hole over Antarctica develops each year between late August and early October.

NUTSHELL | MIND MAP

Environment (Protection) Act, 1986.
Air (Prevention and Control of Pollution) Act, 1981.
Water (Prevention and Control of Pollution) Act, 1974

Solid wastes
- 1. Biodegradable
- 2. Non-biodegradable
- 3. Recyclable

Montreal Protocol (1987) effective 1989. For ozone depletion.
Nation of Forest Policy (1988)—Land must have 33% forest cover and hills 67%

HIGHER ORDER THINKING SKILLS (HOTS) QUESTIONS

1. Following is the plot on effect of sewage discharge on some important characteristics of a river. *(SA II)*

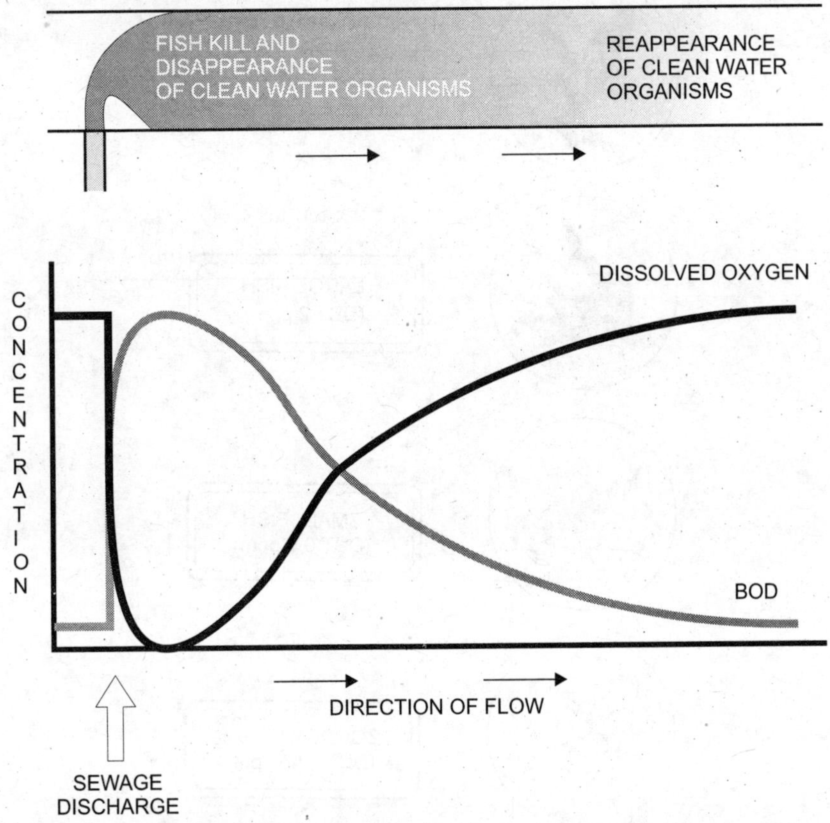

Fig. 16.4.

(*i*) What does this plot indicate?

(*ii*) Why is BOD high first than reduced later?

(*iii*) Why the dissolved oxygen (DO) is less first and high later?

(*iv*) When there is fish mortality and reappearance?

2. This is the figure of aquatic food chain. What does this figure depict? What is this process called as?

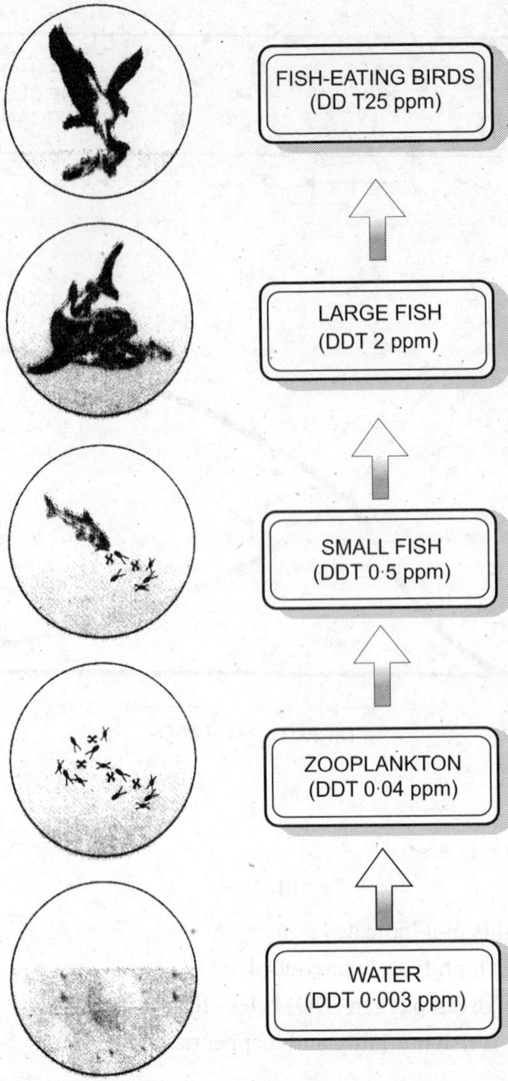

Fig. 16.5

3. You might have heard of thermal power plants. How does the waste water, eliminated from such plants, effect the aquatic organisms? *(SA-I)*
4. Greenhouse effect is a naturally occurring phenomenon. Mention its benefit and harmful effects. *(SA-II)*
5. (*i*) How is ozone formed in stratosphere?
   (*ii*) What is 'good ozone' and 'bad ozone', and where are they present? *(SA-II)*
   (*iii*) How is the balance of ozone affected in stratosphere?
6. Mention a few consequences of deforestation. *(SA-I)*

❑❑❑

VALUE BASED QUESTIONS (Solved)

(courtesy:ziet bhubaneswar)

Q. 1. Tarun was one of the best boys in the class. Somehow, he was not doing well in class XI. He got frustrated with his results and resorted to drugs. He started misbehaving with parents and friends. The school authorities counseled Tarun but to no effect. His parents were upset and took him to a Psychologist. After a few months he recovered.

(*a*) What values did the Principal reflect through his initiative?

(*b*) What is drug abuse?

(*c*) Name some commonly abused drugs and their source.

(*d*) What should be the attitude of his parents after his recovery?

Ans. (*a*) The Principal showed his social liability and responsibility.

(*b*) Intake of drugs for a non-medical purpose in the dose, strength, frequency and the way of taking which impairs mental and physical functions of the user is drug abuse.

(*c*) (*i*) **Opium :** from plant Papaver somniferm— its derivatives includes **morphine, codeine, heroin, smack** i.e. brown sugar etc.

(*ii*) **Cocaine :** from Erythroxylon coca, **crack** - a cocaine derivative, **caffeine** from Thea sinensis, Coffea Arabica, Theobroma cacao

(*iii*) LSD : from fungus Claviceps purpurea

(*iv*) **Any other may be included**

(*d*) Parents should be compassionate and more caring towards the child and behave normally as they had been doing prior to drug abuse incident.

Q. 2. Joy was selected as captain of the school football team for the district level tournament. He attended a blood donation camp to donate blood and came to know that he was HIV positive. He lost interest in games and refused to play or study. He started counting his days. He remained absent from school for a long time. The Biology teacher visited his house and counselled him. Joy was back at school and also played the tournament.

(*a*) What sense of responsibility did the Biology teacher exhibit?

(*b*) Should a person detected to be HIV positive be isolated from the society? Do you agree?

(*c*) How could AIDS spread be prevented?

Ans. (*a*) The teacher shows social and moral responsibility along with his commitment to service as a professional teacher.

(*b*) No. AIDS is not a contagious disease and not spread until a blood/body fluid contact is established.

(*c*) AIDS is not spread by: body contact in crowded place, hand shaking, sharing telephone, meal, utensil or clothings, light kissing, using same toilet seat or even swimming pool. It is not transmitted by blood sucking vectors or by coughing and sneezing. HIV spread can be prevented by avoiding : 1. Unprotected sex with an infected person; 2. Transfusion of infected blood/blood products; 3. Sharing of contaminated syringes/needles; 4. Infected mother to child.

Q. 3. Ratan lives in a remote village. His father has arranged the marriage of his younger sister, who is only 14 years old, to a well to do middle aged man. Ratan objected to his father's act. Ratan was not convinced by his father's idea that a better groom might not be available later. Ratan complained to the vaillae head and got the problem solved.

(*a*) Did Ratan act properly by approaching the village head? Why/Why not?

(*b*) What biological considerations made Ratan object to his father's decision?

(*c*) What values and responsibilities did Ratan show?

Ans. (*a*) Yes, it was necessary to stop the act since as per the government order, the minimum marriaeable age of girl is 18 years.

(*b*) Ratan thought of the following Disadvantages of ealy marriage :

Reproductive health problems; Teenage pregnancy; Child birth associated trauma; High postnatal mortality

(*c*) Sense of responsibility and consciousness for his family and respect for government laws. He expressed his views boldly for the right cause.

Q. 4. Mohun came across a young couple staying in the adjacent room in the hotel. He learnt that the couple had been visiting different temples and performing rituals to get a child. Mohun was astonished and explained to them about ART which he had recently studied in Biology. The couple were happy and understood their wrong approach and thanked Mohun.

(*a*) Identify the values which Mohun has shown.

(*b*) What is ART? What are the various method included in ART?

(*c*) What are the limitations for which ART is not commonly accepted?

Ans. (*a*) Sympathetic attitude with alertness and practical approach.

(*b*) Assisted Reproductive Technology

Methods are : (i) test tube baby programme which includes IVF and Zygote or embryo transfer (ii) gamete intra fallopian transfer (iii) Intra cytoplasmic sperm injection (iv) artificial insemination methods.

(*c*) (*i*) These techniques require extremely high precision handling by specialized professionals and expensive instrumentation. Therefore, these facilities are at present available only in a very few centres in the country.

(*ii*) Emotional, religious and social factors are also deterrents in the adoption of these methods. Limited knowledge about ART is also a negative factor.

Q. 5. A teenage girl accidently became pregnant. She stopped coming to college and also preferred to remain isolated. She was scared to inform her parents. One of her friends Sweta met her and came to know about the problem. She took her to a doctor and got her aborted. She convinced the parents and kept the matter concealed.

(*a*) Did Sweta take the correct decision? What values did she show?

(*b*) What is the medical term for abortion? What is the period which is considered safe for abortion?

(*c*) What prevention may be taken to avoid pregnancy?

Ans. (*a*) Yes. Sweta expressed her helpful attitude and true friendship. She had social commitment and sensitivity to act as per the situation.

(*b*) Medical termination of pregnancy (MTP) or induced abortion. It is safe up to the first trimester of pregnancy (12 weeks).

(*c*) (*i*) Abstinence

(*ii*) Contraceptive methods

Q. 6. On World Population Day Rohit and his friends arranged an awareness campaign about family planning programme in their locality. Some elderly people rebuked the children and asked them not to talk on such things in public. The children convinced the elders about the need for the programme and on understanding their point of view, they (elders) also joined the campaign.

(*a*) What values did the elderly people and Rohit show on the occasion?

(*b*) Why is such awareness programme necessary?

(*c*) What role has the government played in controlling population exposion?

Ans. (*a*) Rohit and his friends showed understanding of population explosion, team work and motivational capacity.

(*b*) To overcome the problems faced by the family and the nation due to increasing population and simultaneously to disseminate the message of deriving the benefits of having a small family.

(*c*) (*i*) Public awareness through mass media

(*ii*) Education at all levels

(*iii*) Family planning

(*iv*) Increasing marriageable age (18 for girls, 21 for boys)

Q. 7. Some parents wrote a complaint letter to the local municipality to remove all hoardings in the city advertising the use of condoms and matters relating to AIDS prevention. The children of these parents came to know about the matter and raised their voice against removal of those hoardings. The parents were convinced by the awareness level of their children and withdrew the complaint.

(*a*) Parents considered the hoarding as sight pollution. Do you agree?

(*b*) What value is promoted by the children protesting against their parents?

(*c*) What are the methods by which AIDS spreads?

Ans. (*a*) No. The awareness among our people about AIDS not reached to that extent; and forceful and constant reminding is required. Our country is overpopulated and number of AIDS patients is growing very fast.

(*b*) Sense of understanding AIDS and application in life, National responsibility and commitment towards society.

(*c*) (*i*) Unprotected sexual contact

(*ii*) Use of contaminated needles and syringes

(*iii*) Use of contaminated razors or other instruments used for piercing body parts e.g. pinna

(*iv*) Transfusion of infected blood or blood products

(*v*) Organ transplant

Q. 8. Rita and her parents were watching a TV serial in the evening. During a commercial break, an advertisement flashed on the screen which was promoting use of sanitary napkins. Rita was still watching the TV. The parents got embarrassed and changed the channel. Rita objected to her parents' behavior and explained the need for these advertisements.

(*a*) What values did the parents show?

(*b*) Briefly describe the phases of a menstrual cycle.

Ans. (*a*) The parents were traditional but showed maturity and openness later and understood the need for such advertisements.

(*b*) (*i*) Menstrual phase

(*ii*) Proliferative phase

(*iii*) Secretory phase

Q. 9. Anita was happy when she gave birth to her first child. Her in-laws were dissatisfied at her not giving birth to a male child and blamed Anita. Anita tried to convince her in laws that she had no role in the child's gender. They understood the biological reason but were yet to be satisfied. Anita's husband took up the matter and convinced the parents.

(*a*) What values did Anita's husband show in the above situation?

(*b*) What governs sex determination in humans? How is it different from birds?

(*c*) Why can't Anita be blamed for not giving birth to a male child?

Ans. (*a*) Strong and determined personality with responsibility towards the family and respect for the wife.

(*b*) Sex chromosomes. In human males it is XY and in females it is XX in birds, male is ZZ while female is ZW.

(*c*) Human females are homogametic i.e. produces only one type of gametes containing 22+X chromosomes only. Males are heterogametic and produce two types of gametes 22+X and 22+Y. It is the type of male gamete which determines the sex of the foetus. If X chromosome containing sperm fuses with the egg, it produces a female child whereas if Y chromosome containing sperm fuses with the egg, it produces a male child.

Q. 10. Mrs. Kavita was eager to know the sex of the foetus which her daughter-in-law was carrying. She was so anxious that she could pay any amount for that. The doctor refused to disclose the result of the test.

(*a*) What value do you learn from the doctor's act?

(*b*) How can one know the sex of the foetus? How is it done?

(*c*) Why is disclosing the sex of the foetus banned in our country?

Ans. (*a*) The doctor is devoted to his duties and has professional ethics.

(*b*) (*i*) By amniocentesis and genetic studies on amniotic fluid.

(*ii*) By ultrasonography

(*c*) There have been numerous cases where the female fetuses have been aborted. This anti-feeling for the girl child is a crime against humanity. This is symptomatic of the fact that the male members in the society have antipathy towards, and bias against, the females. In addition, the number of females to males has also come down significantly, Thereby adversely affecting the country's demographic dividend.

Q. 11. Ravi was rushed to a nearby hospital after an accident which caused a lot of blood loss. The hospital failed to supply O negative blood for transfusion. Rahman who was attending a patient learned about the situation and agreed to donate blood being of the same blood group. Ravi's mother initially refused but was latter convinced by her daughter.

(*a*) What values do you find in Ravi's sister and Rahman?

(*b*) Why can't O positive blood be transfused into Ravi'body?

(*c*) What is the genetic basis of blood group inheritance?

Ans. (*a*) Humanity is above all religion. Ravi's sister shows understanding of science. Rahman believes in helping a person in need without thinking about which religion or caste he belongs to.

(*b*) O+ blood group contains antigen for Rh factor. Rh negative blood lacks the antigen. So if the two blood are allowed to mix, the inevitable result is that it should cause reaction and clotting, and further consequence is serious complications.

(*c*) Human blood groups are A, B, AB and O The four phenotypes are expressed by paired combination of three alleles (I^A, I^B and i). I^A and I^B are dominant alleles for blood groups A and B respectively. O blood grop is due to lack of any dominant gene. Its genotype is ii. Alleles I^A I^B expresses both dominant traits and the blood group is AB.

Q. 12. While finalising an alliance between his son and Rita, Mr. Ram was curious to know what was Rita's blood group. Nobody was interested in their blood groups since their horoscopes matched. Mr. Ram was adamant in wanting to know the blood groups before finalizing. The senior people got annoyed. Then Rita stood up and gave the reasons. Mr. Ram was happy and the marriage date was finalized.

(*a*) Mr. Ram's refusal to accept only horoscopes shows certain values. What are they?

(*b*) What effect on the foetus may be expected if the father has A+ and the mother O+ blood groups?

(*c*) What is the possible remedy in case of an Rh factor incompatibility between the foetus and mother's blood?

Ans. (*a*) Mr. Ram was not orthodox, he had a modern and scientific outlook.

(*b*) If the mother carries a foetus having A blood group, it acts as antigen to mother's blood. The mother accordingly develops antibodies against the foetus. Severity is observed in the subsequent issue where the child may be born with anaemia and jaundice.

(*c*) Today, when a woman with the potential to develop Rh incompatibility is pregnant, doctors administer a series of two Rh immune-globulin shots during her first pregnancy. The first shot is given around the 28th week of pregnancy and the second within 72 hours after giving birth. Rh immune-globulin acts like a vaccine, preventing the mother's body from producing any potentially dangerous Rh antibodies that can cause serious complications in the newborn or complicate any pregnancies.

Q. 13. Sonam is a bright, fair girl. Her parents are dark complexioned. Her friends in college regularly passed remarks asking her how she was so fair or what treatment she had undergone to become fair. Sonam got irritated at their repeated embarrassing questions. Her friend Srijita came to her support and invited the friends to the Biology lab where she explained the inheritance of body colour. The friends realized their mistake and stopped teasing Sonam.

(*a*) What good values did Srijita reflect from her deeds?

(*b*) What is the name of the inheritance pattern discussed?

(*c*) Which other characters in human follow the same pattern?

(*d*) Explain how Sonam could be fairer than her parents.

Ans. (*a*) Humanity and responsibility towards a friend. She also used her knowledge to educate her friends.

(*b*) Polygenic inheritance or quantitative inheritance.

(*c*) Height, weight, skin colour, size of some organs, face form, intelligence etc. of human beings are examples of quantitative inheritance.

(*d*) Since each dominant allele synthesizes equivalent amount of melanin pigment (to give skin colour), the skin colour is in direct proportion to the number of dominant alleles inherited. If the sum of recessive alleles inherited by the offspring be more than or equal to that of the parents, the child is expected to be fairer than the parents; e.g. if the parents are heterozygous for all alleles (3 dominant and 3 recessive), then they are intermediate in colour. If the child inherits 4 recessive alleles from the parents, the expression shall be fairer than the parents.

Q. 14. During Primary art classes the teacher asked Parthiv to mix green and yellow paint and report on the combined colour formed. Parthiv could not find green colour in his box and was scolded by the teacher who found it lying right in front. Suddenly, Vijay realized that Parthiv was not able to identify red colour and reported the matter to the teacher who was of the opinon that he lacked colour concept. After school was over, Vijay reported this matter to Parthiv's parents.

(*a*) What values did Vijay possess?

(*b*) Did Parthiv lack knowledge of colours? If not give the biological reason for the same.

(*c*) Give the technical term for this type of inheritance. Explain with a typical example.

Ans. (*a*) Vijay was alert, curious, clever and a responsible child.

(*b*) According to the teacher, Parthiv lacks the concept of colours. But when he could not identify red colour, it proved to be a case of colour blindness. It is a sex linked inherited disorder congenital defect.

(*c*) This is a human disease which causes the loss of ability to differentiate between red colour and green colour. The gene for this red-green colour blindness is present on X chromosome itself. Colour blindness is recessive to normal vision.

If a colour blind man (XCY) marries a girl with normal vision (XX), the daughters would have normal vision but would be carrier, while sons would also be normal Cross (a)

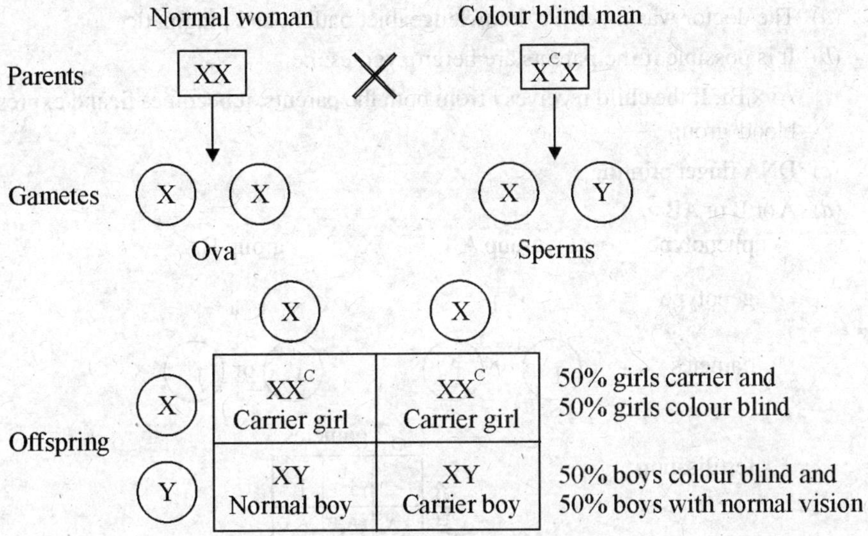

If the carrier girl (heterozygous for colour blindness, XCX) now marries a colour blind man XCY the offspring would show 50% females and 50% males. Of the females, 50% would be carrier for colour blindness and the rest 50% would be colour blind. Of the males, 50% would have normal vision and the 50% would be colour blind.

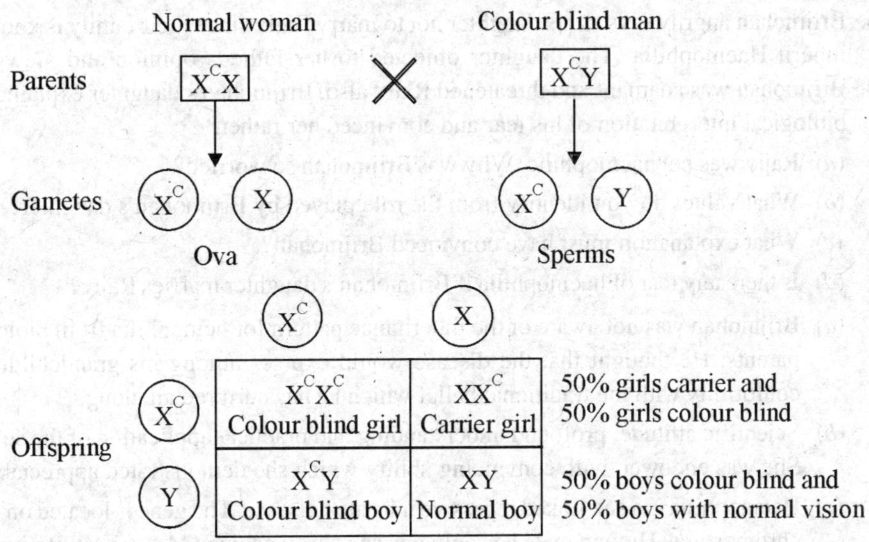

Q. 15. A Couple quarreled with the hospital authority on suspicion that their child had been exchanged after birth. The couple based their argument on the fact that their child is O blood group whereas they are A and B blood groups respectively. The doctor smiled and explained.

(*a*) What values of the doctor is reflected here?

(*b*) How can the child be O blood group as explained by the doctor?

(*c*) Which test method can be considered authentic to identify the biological parents of the child?

(*d*) Name the other blood group (s) which the child could have inherited.

Ans. (*a*) The doctor was assertive, knowledgeable, patient and pragmatic.

(*b*) It is possible if the parents are hererozygotes, i.e.
Ai × Bi. If the child receives i from both the parents, it becomes ii, and expresses O blood group.

(*c*) DNA finger printing

(*d*) A or B or AB

phenotype	group A	X	group B
genotype	$I^A I^O$		$I^B I^O$
gametes	I^A or I^O		I^A or I^O

fertilisation

♀ gametes \ ♂ gametes	I^B	I^O
I^A	$I^A I^B$	$I^A I^O$
I^O	$I^B I^O$	$I^O I^O$

genotype	$I^A I^B$	$I^A I^O$	$I^B I^O$	$I^O I^O$
phenotype	group AB	group A	group B	group O

Q. 16. Brijmohan angrily says to his daughter not to marry Rajiv since their family is known to inherit Haemophilia. The daughter objected to her father's opinion and viewpoint. Brijmohan was adamant and threatened Rajiv also. Brijmohan's daughter explained the biological interpretation of his fear and convinced her father.

(*a*) Rajiv was not haemophilic. Why was Brijmohan so worried?

(*b*) What values do you identify from the role played by Brijmohan's daughter?

(*c*) What explanation must have convinced Brijmohan?

(*d*) Is there any fear of haemophilia if Brijmohan's daughter marries Rajiv?

Ans. (*a*) Brijmohan was not aware of the inheritance pattern for hemophilia from biological parents. He thought that the disease would express among his grandchildren in conformity with the traditional belief which he has nurtured all along.

(*b*) Scientific attitude, profound understanding and practical application of the subject. She was endowed with convincing ability which she demonstrated appreciably.

(*c*) Haemophilia is a sex linked recessive inherited disease. The gene is located on the X chromosome. Human male has only one sex chromosome (44A + XY). Rajiv is not haemophilic, since he does not have the gene on his X chromosome. There remains no chance for him to pass on any haemophilic gene to the next generation.

(*d*) No, there remains no fear if they are married, provided the girl is not a carrier of haemophilia. If the girl is a carrier, then the chance for the son to be haemophilic is 50%.

Q. 17. Ratan was a known sportsman in his school. While returning home, he found some unknown miscreants beating a young boy. He tried to drive them off but by that time the boy died of injury. The police arrested Ratan and he was put on trial. The judge being convinced by Ratan's plea, ordered for DNA finger printing reports.

(*a*) Ratan's fingerprints on the dead body were sufficient to convict him but the judge asked for authentic proof? What values can be observed?

(*b*) What is the basis of DNA finger printing?

(*c*) Explain the steps in DNA finger printing.

Ans. (*a*) The judge showed wisdom, and signified his intention to search for the truth.

(*b*) (*i*) DNA fingerprinting involves identifying differences in some specific regions in DNA sequence called as **repetitive DNA**.

(*ii*) Depending on base composition (A: T rich or G : C rich), length of segment, and number of repetitive units, the satellite DNA is classified into many categories, (Micro-satellites, mini-satellites etc.).

(*iii*) These sequences normally do not code for any proteins, but they form a large portion of human genome. These sequences show high degree of polymorphism and form the essential basis of DNA fingerprinting.

(*c*) (*i*) isolation of DNA,

(*ii*) digestion of DNA by restriction endonucleases,

(*iii*) separation of DNA fragments by electrophoresis,

(*iv*) transferring (blotting) of separated DNA fragments to synthetic membranes, such as nitrocellulose or nylon,

(*v*) hybridisation using labelled VNTR probe, and

(*vi*) detection of hybridised DNA fragments by autoradiography.

Q. 18. During an excursion to a botanical garden, the teacher shows an old tree which was on the verge of extinction. As soon as the teacher advanced with the students, some enthusiastic students climbed up the tree and started cutting the branches, collecting its leaves as precious collection. Rajesh instead took photographs of the tree from various angles. The boys mocked at Rajesh while the teacher appreciated him.

(*a*) What values did Rajesh possess?

(*b*) Why should we conserve biodiversity?

(*c*) How can biodiversity be conserved?

Ans. (*a*) Respect for nature, scientific attitude with a vision of the future

(*b*) We should conserve Biodiversity, since it provides us—

- main source of food
- source of economically important natural fibres (cotton, flax, hemp, jute etc.)
- Plant products (gum, resin, dye, fragrance, waxes, wool, leather, honey, lac, pearl from underwater sea, silk, Ivory from elephant, horns from elephant, rhino, cow, buffalo)
- Drugs and medicine
- Sports and recreation
- Aesthetic value
- Cultural value

• Scientific research

• Eco system services

(More points may be added)

(*c*) **In situ conservation :** Sacred grove, Biosphere reserve (Terrestrial and Marine), National parks and Wild life sanctuaries etc.)

Ex situ conservation : (*i*) Sacred plants, home gardens; (*ii*) Seed banks, gene bank, cryopreservation; (*iii*) Botanical garden, Zoological garden, Aquaria etc.

Q. 19. Seeing a crowd of students in one corner of the school, the Principal rushed to see the matter and found some children beating and chasing a small monitor lizard. On seeing the Principal, all the children fied to their classes except Alok who requested the Principal to arrange for some medical assistance for the injured animal. The Principal rewarded the student.

(*a*) Was Alok an indisciplined boy who did not run to the class on seeing the Principal? What values does the act promote?

(*b*) How do endangered species differ from vulnerable species?

(*c*) Mention the factors resulting in loss of biodiversity/extinction.

Ans. (*a*) No. Alok was a brave and courteous boy. He expressed his love for animals, commitment towards natural resource conservation.

(*b*) **Endangered species** (when population of a species reduces to a level which poses immediate danger of extinction, e.g. one horn rhinoceros, great Indian bustard, musk deer etc.).

Vulnerable species (species whose population has greatly reduced and, may be endangered species in future if the causative factors continue to operate; e.g. Asiatic wild ass, black buck, spotted deer, golden langur etc.)

(*c*) (*i*) abitat loss and fragmentation

(*ii*) Over exploitation

(*iii*) Alien species invasion

(*iv*) Co-extinction

Q. 20. During a visit to a government ofice with his father, young Pratap saw dirty spittoons in every corner of the building. Some people were spitting paan and gutka through the window grills. As soon as he objected to their action, Pratap was scolded by some perons and the quarrel between the two parties became a matter of concern. The very next week, Pratap was amazed to see the walls cleaned, no spittoons and a notification hung to maintain cleanliness and hygiene inside the office. The officer appreciated Pratap.

(*a*) What values are promoted through the incident?

(*b*) Which diseases are transmitted through droplets and air?

(*c*) How does chewing paan or gutka cause health hazard?

Ans. (*a*) Self Awareness, boldness, initiative and commitment towards community health.

(*b*) Diphtheria, scarlet fever, influenza, common cold, measles, mumps, tuberculosis.

(*c*) Gutka contains heavy amounts of magnesium as well as calcium carbonate which body can cause respiratory and cardiac depression, while calcium carbonate or lime damages the mucosa, causing chronic mucosal injuries, blisters and ulcers in the mouth. Apart from this, gutka can also cause hypertension, oral cancer and reproductive health dysfunction.

Possible problems : Hypertension and cardiovascular diseases, nervous system disorders, liver and kidney diseases, reproductive health dysfunctions, oro-dental problems, oral cancer metabolic disorders including diabetes and obesity, and psychological disorders including addiction; can be caused by excessive consumption of gutka.

Q. 21. Raj's mother wondered why the mosquitos were not responding to the mosquito repellent which she had been using for several years. Raj asked his mother to change the brand they were using. When it worked, she opined that the quality of the brand she had been using all along might have degraded over the time. Raj objected and explained to his mother the reality.

(*a*) What values are reflected in the above case?

(*b*) Why did the mosquitoes not respond to the repellent? Explain on the basis of Natural Selection.

(*c*) Cite any two examples of natural selection which we often come across.

Ans. (*a*) Raj's mother was too judgemental while Raj had a Scientific attitude, approach and sense of exploration.

(*b*) Sensitive ones died leaving behind the resistant strains which multiplied to increase their population.

(*c*) (*i*) Bacteria developing resistance towards antibiotics

(*ii*) Pesticide resistance (DDT resistant mosquitoes)

Q. 22. One Sunday morning Ratan and his friend emptied all the overhead tanks belonging to flat owners who were not residing in their apartments for the last few months. On their return, the owners complained about their empty tanks and created unrest in the campus. Some elderly people spoke against Ratan and his friends. Ratan humbly apologized for the inconvenience caused but explained why they had done so. The people were happy and appreciated the boys.

(*a*) What was the objective behind Ratan's act?

(*b*) What values did he promote?

Ans. (*a*) The water in the tanks had become stagnant and become a breeding ground for mosquitoes.

(*b*) Social responsibility, commitment towards community health and respect towards elders.

Q. 23. Samir planned to introduce MOET in his farm. He purchased one high milk yielding exotic breed of cow. Within a few years he earned lot of money by selling calves but the mother cow met with a premature death. Raghavan objected to Samir earning money by this way.

(*a*) What values in life did Raghavan possess?

(*b*) Expand MOET.

(*c*) Briefly describe the process.

Ans. (*a*) Raghavan was bold, having love for animals. He had ethics and prudence.

(*b*) Multiple Ovulation Embryo Transfer echnology.

(*c*)
- The cow is administered hormones, with FSH-like activity, to induce follicular maturation and super ovulation (*instead of one egg, which they normally yield per cycle, they produce 6-8 eggs*).
- The animal is either mated with an elite bull or artificially inseminated.
- The fertilised eggs at 8-32 cells stages, are recovered non-surgically and transferred to surrogate mothers.
- The genetic mother is available for another round of super ovulation.
- This technology has been demonstrated for cattle, sheep, rabbits, buffaloes, mares etc. High milk-yielding breeds of females and high quality (lean meat with less lipid) meat-yielding bulls have been bred sucessfully to increase the herd size within a short span of time.

Q. 24. Jeevan was waiting at a bus stop. Many passengers along with their kids were on their way to school. A bus came and painted the children with black smoke ejected from the exhaust pipe. Jeevan immediately stopped the bus and called the conductor and driver to show what they had done. Passengers waiting in the bus-stop supported Jeevan while those on board became restless for being delayed.

(*a*) What values did Jeevan promote through his action?

(*b*) Why are children more affected by vehicle exhausts?

(*c*) Cars are seen with Bharat stage IV stickers. What does it imply?

(*d*) How do catalytic convertors reduce vehicular gas emission?

Ans. (*a*) Jeevan shows alertness, responsibility and firmness in tacking a problem. He expresses boldness towards environment consciousness.

(*b*) Height of the exhaust pipe emitting smoke is closer to the height of the children.

(*c*) It indicates that the vehicles comply with the new auto fuel policy. At present vehicles conforming to Euro-IV or equivalent BS-IV norms are to ply in the identified 11 cities, rest of the country is amenable to compliance with Euro III/BS-III norms.

(*d*) In these devices, platinum - palladium and Rhodium are used as catalysts. As the exhaust passes through the convertor, unburnt hydrocarbons are converted into CO_2 and H_2O. Carbon monoxide and nitric oxide are changed into CO_2 and N_2 gas respectively. Vehicles fitted with such equipment should run on unleaded petrol only since lead in petrol inactivates the catalysts.

Q. 25. Saptarshi entered into a quarrel with some farmers who were spraying DDT in their field. Many people gathered at the spot to see and enjoy the incident. The angry mob demanded that Saptarshi should not interfere in the farmers' job. Saptarshi tried to explain his point and finally succeeded. The farmers gave up spraying DDT.

(*a*) What did Saptarshi explain to the farmers?

(*b*) What is Biomagnification? Explain with an example.

(*c*) What values did Saptarshi promote?

Ans. (*a*) Saptarshi explained the health hazard on self and others due to DDT spraying.

- That DDT was a Non Biodegradable substance

- That DDT could enter into the food chain and in course of time everyone associated would be affected due to its accumulation in the blood.

(b) • Biomagnification refers to increase in concentration of the toxicant at successive trophic levels.

- This happens because a toxic substance accumulated by an organism cannot be metabolised or excreted, and is thus passed on to the next higher trophic level.

(c) Health awareness, eco frienly nature, sympathy and boldness for the right cause.

Q. 26. Sanjeev lives in a remote village where electricity has not reached every home. He discovered that people keep their kerosene oil lamp lit in their rooms while sleeping. Next day he called a meeting of all the residents and explained the ill effects of the smoke. They met the village head and requested for electrification of their village at the earliest.

(a) What values did Sanjeev show here?

(b) What could be the ill effect of the oil lamp?

Ans. (a) Health Consciousness, Responsibility toward humanity, and leadership quality.

(b) **Carbon monoxide** is produced by burning of kerosene oil. When rooms are not properly ventilated, carbon monoxide emitted by these appliances is accumulated. Carbon monoxide being an odovrless, tasteless, and colorless gas is known as the **"silent killer"**.

Early symptoms of carbon monoxide poisoning are headaches, fatigue, Dizziness, Weakness, Nausea, Vomiting, Chest pain. Prolonged exposure can lead to brain damage and even death.

Q. 27. Durng her tour to a renowned forest, Sakshi saw a highway being constructed which passes through the middle of the forest. She was unhappy. On return she contacted the local eco club and approached the concerned department to stop the work.

(a) What values did Sakshi reflect here?

(b) What would be the effect on Biodiversity if the highway is constructed?

Ans. (a) Love for nature and environmental consciousness. She was brave and focussed having vision to see the disaster in the future.

(b) Continuity of the habitat (here forest) is disrupted. Animals get confined to smaller area.

Fragmentation characteristically reduces species richness, and may reduce the efficacy of ecosystem functioning. Fragmentation not only reduces the amount of functional habitat, but it may isolate a species population into subpopulations, that may be sufficiently near the minimum viable population size to risk local extinction from successive demographic processes or catastrophic events.

Q. 28. Richa was walking through a village. She saw a group of women quarrelling near a well. She moved forward to know what was going on and came to know that the quarrel was on fetching water. She immediately solved the problem by telling them a story on how birds solved their similar problem.

(a) What values of Richa can be observed here?

(b) Give a scientific interpretation of sharing a common resource by animals.

(c) Provide an example from your text.

Ans. (*a*) Richa shows brilliance and cheerfulness through her Problem solving ability. She has a helping attitude.

(*b*) Resource Partitioning

(*c*) Simialar Species Compete for Limiting Resources

Complete Competitors Cannot Coexist

Dividing the Resource : Species can divide up a limiting resource, such as food, water, or habitat, by using different slices or even using the same "slice" but at different times.

Q. 29. Aditya participated in a group discussion in his school on "The ill effects of Tobacco on Human Health". In the evening he goes with his family for dinner and insists upon sitting in the "Non-Smoking Area" to which his father (who is a heavy smoker) objects.

(*a*) In this situation, who wins your support - Aditya's concern for health & environment or his father's objection? Justify giving two reasons.

(*b*) Suggest any three effective propaganda campaigns for anti-tobacco awareness.

Ans. (*a*) I will support Aditya's concern for the health of his family. Both Active as well as Passive smoking is injurious to health as smoking is associated with increased incidence of cancers of lungs, urinary bladder, throat and oral cavity, bronchitis, emphysema/coronary heart disease/gastric ulcer etc.

(*b*) (*i*) By printing statutory warning about ill effects on cigarette packets.

(*ii*) Campaigns in mass media such as Television, Newspaper, Internet etc.

(*iii*) Prohibiting smoking in public places except in designated smoking zones.

Q. 30. Mrs. R. Mohanty found Mohan a very brilliant student of the class, score less marks in SA-1 Examination. She noticed that he was not submitting his asignments in time and was remaining isolated. She called him, talked in a friendly manner and found that he resorted to drugs due to constants quarrels between parents. The class teacher called the parents and counselled them.

(*a*) What values did Mrs. R. Mohanty reflect through her intiative?

(*b*) Why is it not easy to leave drugs?

(*c*) What advise Mrs. R. Mohanty might have given to the parents?

Ans. (*a*) Through her initiative, she showed social responsibility.

(*b*) Drugs taken for non-medical purpose makes the individual dependant physiologically and psychologically on them.

(*c*) She might have advised them to get away with the differences; to deal in a very compassionate and caring way with the child and help him to get away from drugs, if required may seek medical help.

Q. 31. In India horoscopes of girl and boy are matched before fixing mariage. But Smita was against this, rather wanted future grooms blood to be tested for HIV. When asked for HIV test, the groom and his parents disagreed and left immediately.

(*a*) Was Smita wrong in wanting the future grooms HIV blood test done? What type of responsibility did she show?

(*b*) Why did Smita wanted to get the boy's HIV test done?

Ans. (*a*) No, Smita was not wrong. She showed her family and social responsibility.

(*b*) HIV causes AIDS. It can spread through sexual contact. If the boy is HIV positive, she may get the virus, and Human Immunodeficiency Virus (HIV), being transmitted transplacental, her future baby may also suffer from AIDS.

Q. 32. Mallika was working with a multinational company and doing very well. But her mother was very much worried about her marriage as she was already 32 years. She made her understand the consequences of late marriage and motherhood, and convinced Mallika to get married. Though her boss was reluctant to give leave.

(*a*) Did Mallika take the correct decision of getting married? What values did she show?

(*b*) What are the consequences of late motherhood?

(*c*) Name some disorders which may result due to late motherhood?

Ans. (*a*) Yes, social and family responsibility.

(*b*) Chances of formation of abnormal gametes which becomes more after the age of 35 years in women and, thereby. Can cause abnormal children.

(*c*) Down Syndrome – 45 + XX / 45 + XY

Turner's Syndrome – 44 + XO

Klinefelter's Syndrome – 44 + XXY

Q. 33. Mr. R. K. Sharma, an English teacher of the school was discussing about the heavy work pressure and increase in the school timings. He was feeling very exhausted and weak after going back from school. Mr. Saha, a biology teacher who was listening to the conversation interrupted and asked Mr. Sharma to get his blood tested for blood sugar. Mr. Sharma got annoyed and said that till date at the age of 80 also their parents are hale and hearty, so how can he get high blood sugar. Mr. Saha made him understand about the disorder and got him convinced to get his blood tested.

(*a*) What sense of responsibility did the biology teacher exhibit?

(*b*) How did he convince Mr. Sharma to get his blood tested?

(*c*) Name the disorder Mr. Saha is talking about? Is it genetic?

(*d*) Is it curable? What are the precautions to be taken?

Ans. (*a*) Humanity and social responsibility.

(*b*) The disorder may occur due to stress, modern life style, untimely food intake and poor exercise.

(*c*) Mr. Saha was talking about Diabetes. No, it may not necessarily be genetic.

(*d*) It is not curable, but can be contolled by keeping oneself stress free, taking food timely, taking balanced diet, doing mild exercises daily; and, if required, by taking medicines on regular basis under supervision of a qualified practising medical doctor.

❑❑❑

SAMPLE QUESTION PAPER - I

SECTION-A

1. The turkey usually produces females for several generations. How is this possible?

2. The meiocyte of an onion plant contains 32 chromosomes. Workout the number of chromosomes found in its endosperm.

3. The gene I that controls the ABO blood grouping in human beings has three alleles IA, IB and i.

   (a) How many different genotypes are likely to be present in the human population ?

   (b) Also, how many phenotypes are possibly present ?

4. Pick out the ancestral line of Cycads from the list given below—

   Ferns, herbaceous lycopods, seed ferns, and horsetails

5. Name the source of smack. Mention one way in which it affects the human body.

6. In plants, how is alien DNA introduced into the host cell ?

7. Mr. Galgotia eats curd / yoghurt. In this case, which trophic level will he occupy?

8. In the absence of the predators, which curve, a) or (b) would appropriately depict the prey population ?

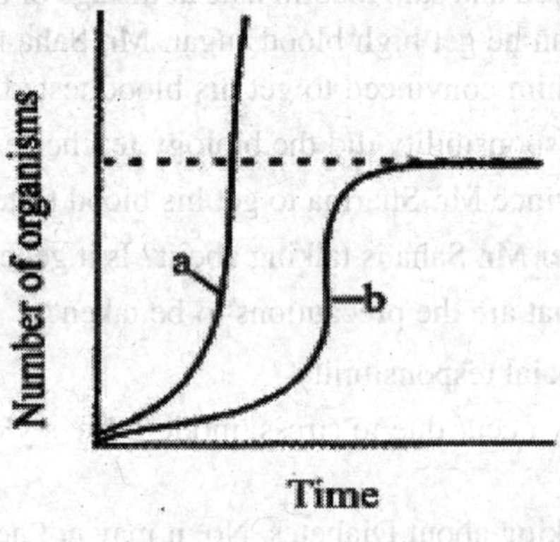

SECTION - B

9. Identify the type of flower shown in A and B. Which out of the two will produce an assured seed set.

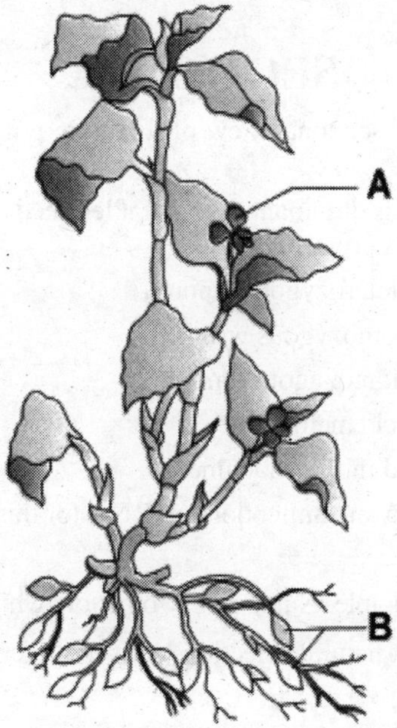

10. Fed up of a large family, a couple wanted to adopt a terminal method of contraception. Describe the process conducted by the doctor in either of the cases (male / female partner)

OR

A mother of a one-year-old daughter wanted to space her second child. Her doctor suggested CuT. Explain its contraceptive actions.

11. The human male and female birds are heterogametic while the human female and male birds are homogametic. Why are they called so?

12. What are interferons? Explain its role in providing immunity. Also name the kind of immunity provided by it.

13. What is allergy? Name the antibody responsible for it. Also mention two chemicals released from the mast cells during an allergic reaction.

14. Give reason—

(a) Bottled fruit juices bought from the market are clearer as compared to those made at home.

(b) Large holes are found in "Swiss cheese".

15. In which parts of the body of the hosts do the following events in the life cycle of *Plasmodium* take place. Along with the body parts name the hosts too—

(i) Fertilisation

(ii) Development of gametocytes

(iii) Release of sporozoites

(iv) Asexual reproduction

16. What are the latest methods of detection of cancer?

17. State two important defence mechanisms in plants against herbivory, with an example each.

18. Compare the grazing food chain and detritus food chain in the aspect of their (a) origin and (b) energy status.

SECTION - C

19. Draw a labelled diagram of the sectional view of a mature pollen grain of angiosperms. Explain the function of any two of its parts.

20. In a pea plant, smooth seed coat is dominant over wrinkled seed coat. What will be the expected ratio of phenotypes of the offspring in a cross between

(i) Heterozygous smooth × Heterozygous smooth

(ii) Heterozygous smooth × Homozygous wrinkled

(iii) Heterozygous smooth × Homozygous smooth

21. A tRNA is charged with aminoacid methionine

(i) Name the process involved in the attachment

(ii) Point out the mRNA codon and anticodon on tRNA for this aminoacid.

(iii) What is heterochromatin?

22. (a) State Hardy Weinberg principle. Name any two factors which affect it.

(b) Draw a graph to show that natural selection leads to directional change.

23.

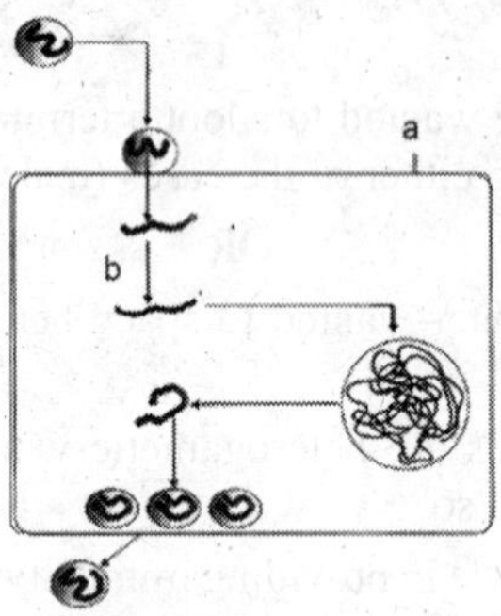

(i) What does this diagrammatic sketch depict ?

(ii) Identify 'a' and 'b'.

(iii) Name the widely used diagnostic test when a person gets this disease.

OR

Fill in the blanks in the different column of the table given below:

Disease	Casual organisms	Medium of transfer	Symptoms
Amoebiasis	Entamoeba histolytica	a	Diarrhoea
Typhoid	b	Contaminated food	Sustained high fever
c	Plasmodium	Bite of infected female Anopheles mosquito	Chill and high fever
Pneumonia	Steptococcus	d	Fever and cough

24. A crane had DDT level as 5 ppm in its body. What would happen to the population of such birds ? Explain giving reasons.

25.

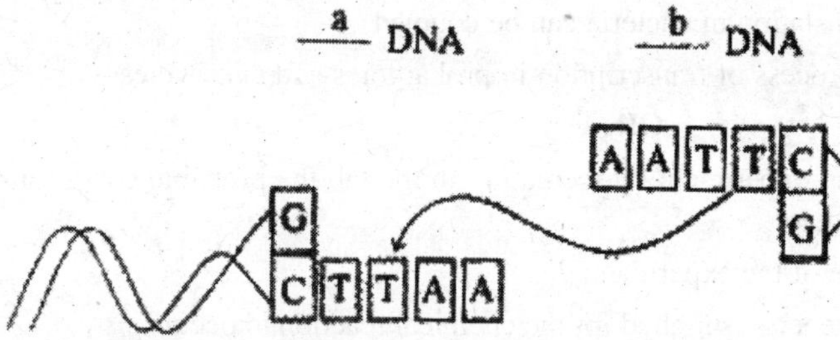

Study the linking of DNA fragments shown above.

(i) Name 'a' DNA and 'b' DNA

(ii) Name the restriction enzyme that recognises this palindrome

(iii) Name the enzyme that can link these two DNA fragements.

26.

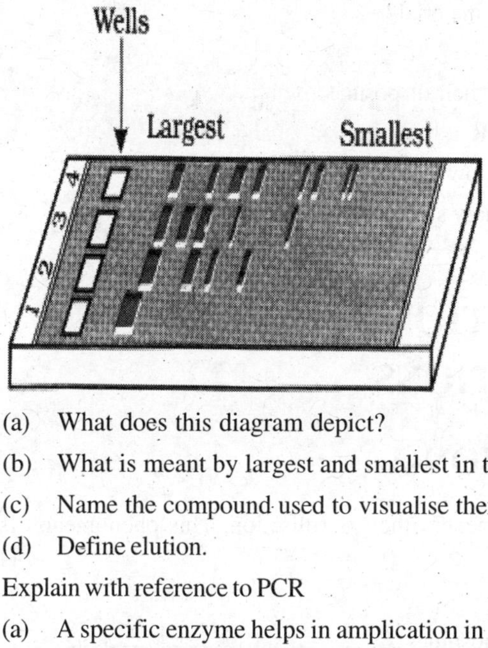

(a) What does this diagram depict?

(b) What is meant by largest and smallest in the picture?

(c) Name the compound used to visualise them.

(d) Define elution.

27. Explain with reference to PCR

(a) A specific enzyme helps in amplication in PCR. Name the bacterium from which it is isolated and state how its thermostable nature is helpful.

(b) Explain its use in molecular diagnosis.

SECTION - D

28. A woman has conceived and implantation has occurred in her uterus. Explain the sequence of changes upto parturition which take place within her body.

OR

"Incompatibility is a natural barrier in the fusion of gametes." Justify the statement.

29. (a) Give reasons for—

(i) Both strands of DNA are not copied during transcription.

(ii) Transcription and translation in bacteria can be coupled.

(b) Differentiate between the process of transcription in prokaryotes and eukaryotes.

OR

Stanley Miller performed an experiment by recreating in the lab the probable conditions of the atmosphere of the primitive earth.

(i) What was the purpose of the experiment ?

(ii) In what form was the energy supplied for the chemical reaction to occur?

(iii) What is biogenesis?

(iv) Give a diagrammatic representation of Miller's experiment.

30. (a) On seeing the bad state of roads in your locality, as a student, you have recommended to the Municipal Corporation to use polyblend.

(i) What is polyblend? Point out its raw material?

(ii) How will it be advantageous?

(b) What are e-wastes? Explain the method of their disposal.

OR

(a) What is meant by ecological succession? How does it occur? Explain.

(b) Differentiate between Primary and Secondary succession.

SAMPLE QUESTION PAPER - I SOLUTIONS

SECTION-A

A1 In a turkey, female gametes undergo development without fertilisation. This phenomenon is called parthenogenesis. [1 Mark]

A2
- meiocyte has 32 chromosomes (2n)
- hence its gamete will have 32/2 = 16 chromosomes
- therefore endosperm will have 16 × 3 = 48 chromosomes (3n) [1 Mark]

A3 (a) 6 , (b) 4 [1 Mark]

A4 Seed ferns [1 Mark]

A5 Source - latex of poppy plant (*Papaver somniferum*) = ½

Effect - Acts as a depressant. = ½ [1 Mark]

A6 The plant cells are bombarded with high velocity micro - particles of gold or tungsten coated with DNA in a method known as biolistics or gene gun. [1 Mark]

A7 Third trophic level [1 Mark]

A8 Curve 'a' [1 Mark]

SECTION - B

A9 A - Chasmogamous flower = ½

B -Cleistogamous flower = ½

Cleistogamous flower produces an assured seed set. [1 Mark]

A10 **Male Partner :** Vasectomy—a small part of the vas deferens is removed or tied up through a small incision in the scrotum.

Female Partner : Tubectomy—a small part of the fallopian tube is removed or tied up through a small incision in the abdomen or through vagina. [1 Mark]

OR

CuT release Cu^+ ions, increases phagocytosis of sperms, suppresses sperm motility, reduces fertilising capacity. = ½ × 4 = 2 [2 Marks]

A11 Genotype of human male is—XY

Genotype of female bird is—ZW = ½

The sex chromosomes are dissimilar and hence are called heterogametic. = ½

Genotype of human female is XX

Genotype of male bird is ZZ = ½

The sex chromosomes are similar, hence homogametic = ½

[½ + ½ + ½ + ½ = 2 Marks]

A12 Interferons are proteins secreted by virus-infected cells. = ½

Role : It protects non - infected cells from further viral infection = 1 Innate Immunity = ½

[½ + 1 + ½ = 2 Marks]

A13 The exaggerated response of the immune system to certain antigens present in the environment = ½ IgE = ½

Histamine and serotonin = ½ + ½ = 1 [½ + ½ + 1 = 2 Marks]

A14 (a) Bottled juices are clarified by the use of pectinases and proteases = ½ + ½ = 1

(b) Large holes are due to production of large amount of CO_2, by a bacterium named *Propioni-bacterium sharmanii* = ½ + ½ = 1 [1 + 1 = 2 Marks]

A15 (i) Inside stomach / intestine of Mosquito host

(ii) In the blood of human host

(iii) Into the blood of human host

(iv) Inside liver cells and RBCs of human host.

A16 Surgery, radiation therapy, chemotherapy and immunotherapy [½ × 4 = 2 Marks]

A17 (a) Thorns are the most common morphological means of defence eg. Acacia and Cactus = 1

(b) Many plants produce and store toxic chemicals such as cardiac glycosides to discourage browsing animals. eg. Calotropis = 1 [1 + 1 = 2 Marks]

A18 (a) Grazing food chain starts from producers while detritus food chain starts from organic matter = 1

(b) Grazing food chain is the major conduit of energy flow in an ecosystem = 1

[1 + 1 = 2 Marks]

SECTION - C

A19

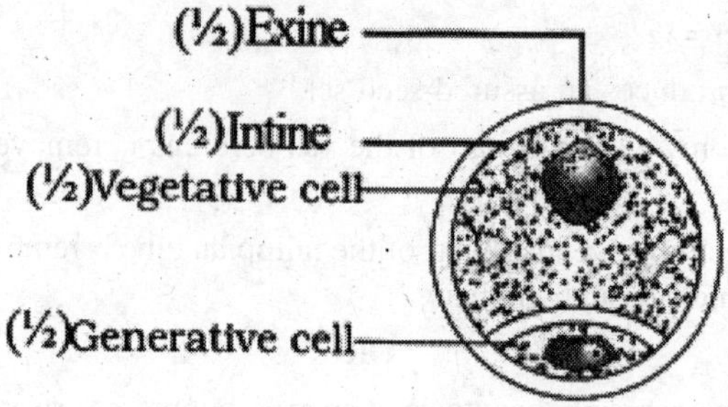

= ½ × 4 = 2

Exine—	It can withstand high temperature / strong acids / alkali
Intine—	It is a thin and continuous layer made up of cellulose and pectin
Vegetative Cell—	It is bigger, has abundant food reserve.
Generative Cell—	It divides mitotically to give rise to two male gametes.

(any two = ½ × 2 = 1)

[2 + 1 = 3 Marks]

A20 Smooth seed coat (dominant) = S

Wrinkled seed coat (recessive) = s

(i) Heterozygous smooth × Heterozygous smooth

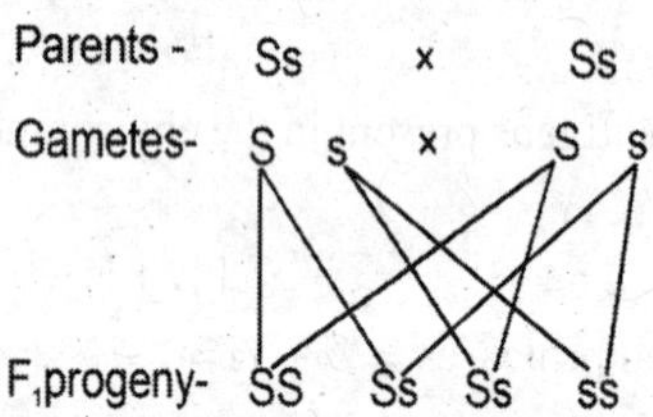

3 smooth : 1 wrinkled = 3 : 1 ratio

(ii) Heterozygous smooth × Homozygous wrinkled

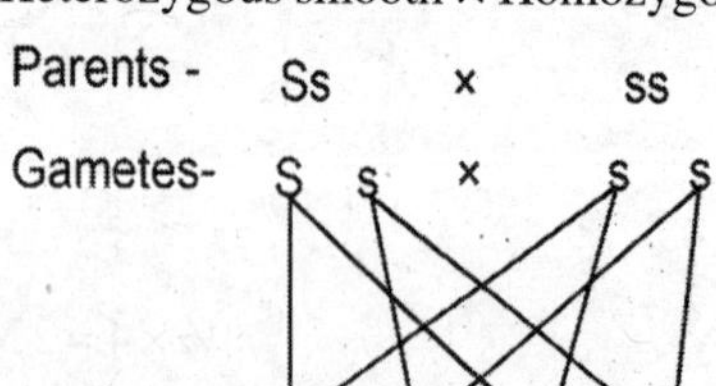

Phenotype—2 smooth : 2 wrinkled = 1 : 1

(iii) Heterozygous smooth × Homozygous smooth

Parents - Ss × SS

Gametes- S s × S S

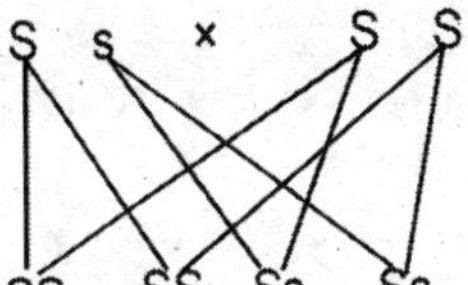

F_1 gen. - SS SS Ss Ss

Phenotype—All smooth = 1 : 0 [1+1+1 = 3 Marks]

A21 (i) Initiation = 1

(ii) mRNA codon = AUG = 1

(iii) The densely packed and dark stained / transcriptionally inactive chromatin is called as heterochromatin = 1 [1+1 + 1 = 3 Marks]

A22 (a) Allelic frequencies in a population are stable and constant from generation to generation. = 1

Gene flow, genetic drift, mutation, genetic recombination, natural selection (any two = ½ × 2 = 1)

(b)

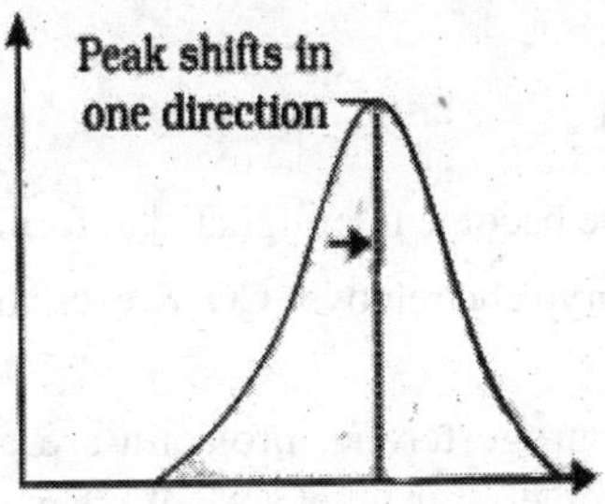

[1 + 1 +1 = 3 Marks]

A23 (i) Replication of retrovirus = 1

(ii) a -Plasmamembrane

b- formation of viral DNA by reverse transcriptase ½ × 2 = 1

(iii) ELISA (Enzyme linked immunosurbent assay) = 1

[1 + 1 + 1 = 3 Marks]

OR

(a) Water, vegetables, fruits etc. contaminated with the eggs of the parasite.

(b) Salmonella typhi

(c) Malaria

(d) Pneumonia spreads by cough and sneezes by sharing drinking glasses and eating utensils with an infected person and contact with used tissues or handkerchief.

[1 + 1 + 1 = 3 Marks]

A24 Population of birds will decrease. High concentration of DDT disturbs calcium metabolism in birds which causes thinning of eggshell and their premature breaking, eventually causing decline in bird populations.

[3 Marks]

A25 (i) 'a' – Vector DNA; 'b' – Foreign DNA = ½

(ii) EcoRI

(iii) DNA ligase

[½ + 1 + 1½ = 3 Marks]

A26 (a) Gel electrophoresis = ½

(b) DNA fragments / bands = ½

(c) Ethidium bromide = 1

(d) The separated bands of DNA are cut out from agarose gel and DNA extracted from gel piece = 1
[½ + ½ + 1 + 1= 3 Marks]

A27 (a) *Thermus aquaticus* = 1
It remains active during the high temperature induced denaturation = 1

(b) Very low concentration of a bacteria or virus can be detected by amplification of their nucleic acid by PCR = 1

[1 + 1 + 1 =3 Marks]

SECTION - D

A28

- After implantation the chorionic villi and uterine tissue become interdigitated to form placenta.
- Placenta facilitates supply of O_2 & nutrients to the embryo and removes CO_2 & excretory materials produced by the embryo.
- Increased production of hormones like estrogens, progesterone, prolactin are essential for supporting foetal growth, metabolic changes in the mother & maintenance of pregnancy.
- The inner cell mass differentiates into three distinct germ layers (mesoderm, ectoderm & endoderm) which gives rise tô all tissues (organs) in adults.
- After one month of pregnancy the embryo's heart is formed.
- By the end of the second month of pregnancy the foetus develops limbs & digits.
- By the end of 12 weeks (first trimester) most of the major organ systems are formed.
- By the end of 24 weeks (second trimester) the body is covered with fine hair, eyelids separate and eyelashes are formed.
- The signals for parturition originate from the fully developed foetus and the placenta which induce mild uterine contractions called foetal ejection reflex.
- This triggers release of oxytocin from maternal pituitary along with stimulatory reflex resulting in stronger contractions leads to parturition. = ½ × 10 = 5 [5 Marks]

OR

- Incompatibility is considered as the most widespread & effective device to prevent inbreeding and outbreeding.
- Pollen pistil interaction is a dynamic process involving pollen recognition followed by promotion or inhibition of the pollen.

- It acts as a natural barrier by the interaction of chemical substances produced by the style.
- Normally the pollen belonging to right mating type germinate on stigma, develop pollen tube & bring about fertilization.
- The pollen grains belonging to other mating type are discarded = $1 \times 5 = 5$

[5 Marks]

A30. (a) (i) It is a fine powder of recycled modified plastic. This mixture is mixed with bitumen used to lay roads = 1

Raw material - Plastic film waste = 1

(ii) Blends of polyblend & bitumen, when used to lay roads, enhances the bitumen's water repellant properties and helps to increase road life by a factor of three = 1

(b) Irreparable computers and other electronic goods are known as e-wastes = 1

Burried in landfills or incinerated = 1 [1+1+1+1+1 = 5 Marks]

OR

(a) The gradual and fairly predictable change in the species composition of a given area = 1

During succession some species colonise an area & their populations become more numerous, where as populations of other species decline and even disappear = 1 + 1 = 2

(b)

Primary Succession	**Secondary Succession**
It occurs in an area which has been bare from the beginning.	It occurs in an area which has been denuded recently.
Soil is absent at the time of beginning of primary succession.	Soil is present in the area where secondary succession begins.
Takes a long time for completion.	Takes less time for completion

(any two differences $1 \times 2 = 2$)

[1 + 2 + 2 = 5 Marks]

SAMPLE QUESTION PAPER II

SECTION-A

1. In the whiptail lizards only females are born generation after generation. There are no males: How is this possible? 1

2. In the following figure of a fruit, label the part which is protective in function and that which is responsible for producing new plants. 1

3. Which Mendel's law of inheritance is universally acceptable and without any exception? State the law. 1

4. In the following pedigree chart, state if the trait is autosomal dominant, autosomal recessive or sex linked. Give a reason for your answer.

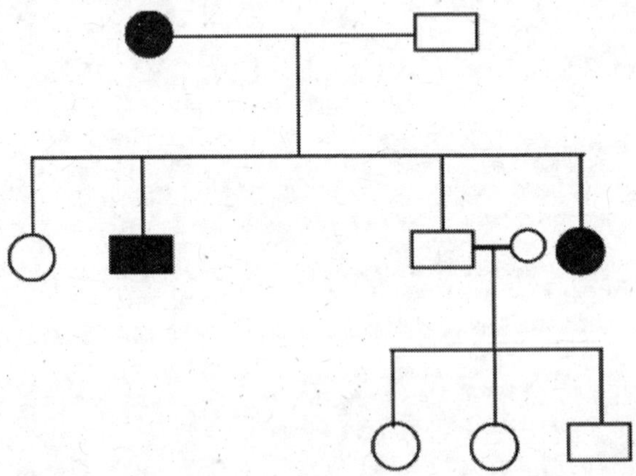

(195)

5. Given below are pairs of disease and causative organism. Which out of these is not a matching pair and why?

2 Filariasis :	*Wuchereria*
Ringworm :	*Ascaris*
AIDS :	Human immuno virus
Malaria :	*Plasmodium*

6. In the picture provided, what is the relationship between (1) and (2) with respect to population interaction and between (3) and (4) with respect to trophic levels?

7. Provide one word or one sentence information about 'plasmid' with respect to its (i) chemical nature and (ii) its duplication.

8. Expand the following (i) PCR (ii) Bt

SECTION -B

9. In the adjacent population growth curve, (i) What is the status of food and space in the curves (a) and (b)? (ii) In the absence of the predators, which curve (a) or (b) would appropriately depict the prey population?

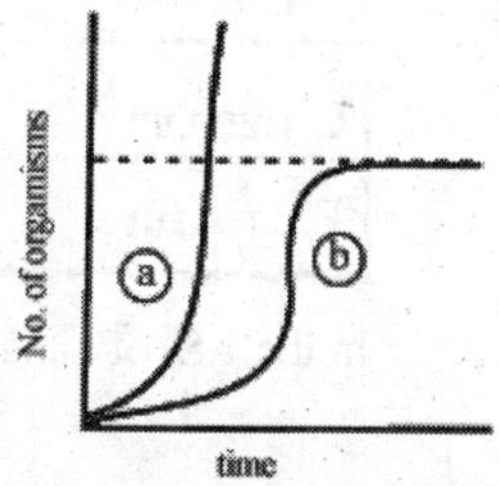

10. Given below is a sequence of steps of transcription in a eukaryotic cell. Fill up the blanks (1, 2, 3, 4) left in the sequence.

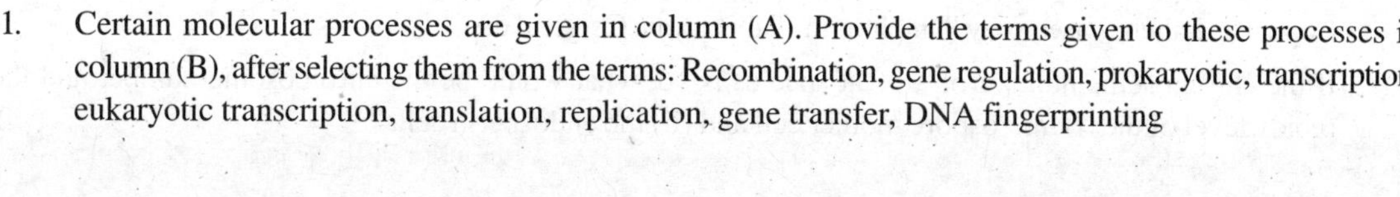

OR

11. Certain molecular processes are given in column (A). Provide the terms given to these processes in column (B), after selecting them from the terms: Recombination, gene regulation, prokaryotic, transcription, eukaryotic transcription, translation, replication, gene transfer, DNA fingerprinting

Column A		Column B
(i) DNA	DNA	____________
(ii) DNA	hnRNA	____________
(iii) mRNA	Protein	____________
(iv) Repressor Protein + Operator	No transcription	____________

$\frac{1}{2} \times 4 = 2$

12. In the following table the ecological units are mentioned in the first column vertically and their attributes are mentioned horizontally. Match the ecological units and its attribute and put a tick in the blanks within the table: 2

Attribute Ecological → Unit ↓	Age	Flow of Energy	Natality	Predator-prey relationship
Individual organism				
Population				
Community				
Ecosystem				

13. In the T.S. of a mature anther given below identify "A" and "B" and mention their function.

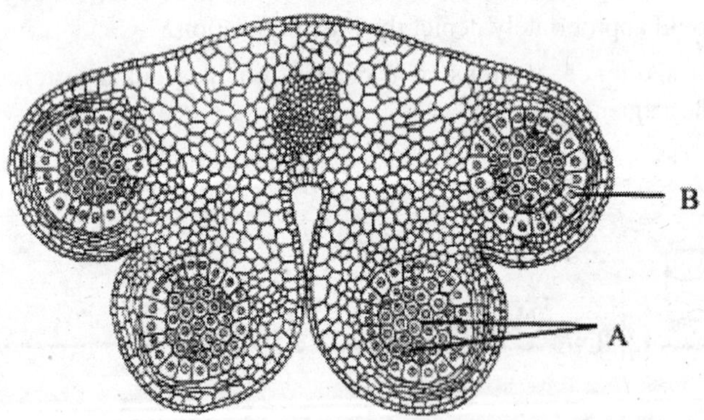

14. In the table given below, select and enter one correct device out of the following : Oral pill, condom, Copper T, Saheli, Vasectomy, Diaphragm, Tubectomy, Cervical cap

15. If the chromosome number of a plant species is 16, what would be the chromosome number and the ploidy level of the (i) microspore mother cell and (ii) the endosperm cells? 2

Method of birth control	Device
Barrier	
IUD	
Surgical Technique	
Administering Hormones	

16. In the pie charts (A) and (B) drawn below to show the global animal diversity, which groups of animals would you name and write on the areas shaded black in (A) and (B). In which kind of habitat would you find these groups of animals? 2

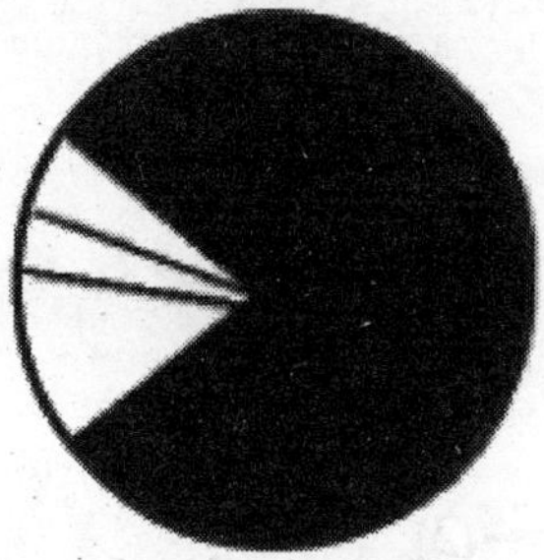

(A) INVERTERBRATES

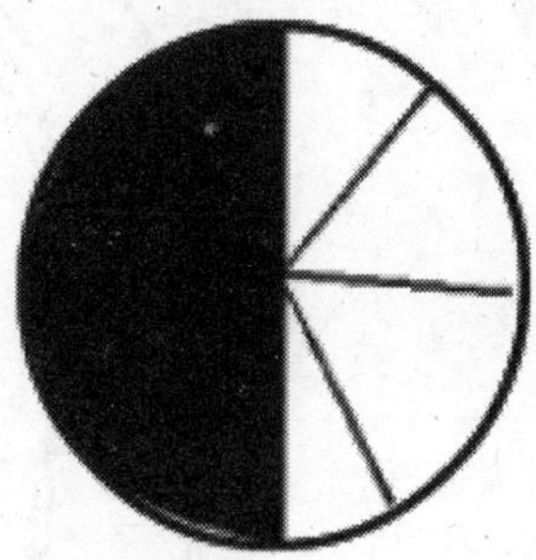

(B) VERTEBRATES

17. In the pyramid of biomass drawn below name the two crops : (i) one which is supported and (ii) the one which supports. In which ecosystem is such a pyramid found?

(½ + ½ + 1) = 2

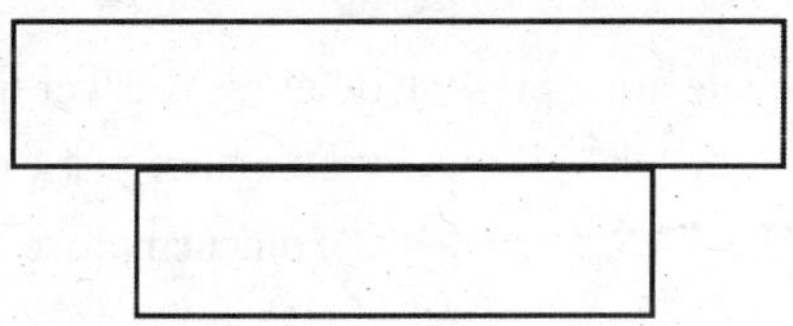

18. The steps in a programme are:

- Collection of germplasm
- Crossbreeding the selected parents
- Selecting superior recombinant progeny
- Testing, releasing and marketing new cultivars.

(i) What is this programmme related to?

(ii) Name two special qualities as basis of selection of the progeny.

(iii) What was the outcome of the programme?

(iv) What is the popular term given to this outcome? Also name the Indian scientist who is credited with chalking out of this programme.

19. What is measured in BOD test ? BOD level of three samples of water labelled as A, B and C are 30 mg/ l, 10 mg / l and 500 mg/l respectively. Which sample of water is most polluted ?

SECTION - C

20. How are biofertilisers different from fertilisers such as NPK that we buy in the market? Justify the role of *Rhizobium* as a biofertiliser.

21. In the adjacent figure of a typical dicot embryo, label the parts (1), (2) and (3). State the function of each of the labelled part.

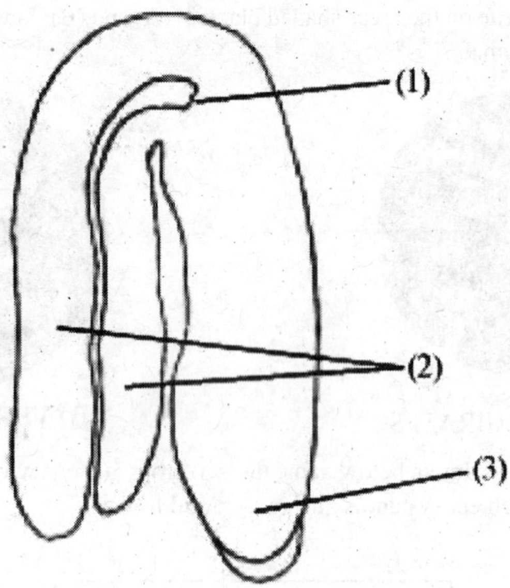

22. The events of the menstrual cycle are represented below. Answer the questions following the diagram.

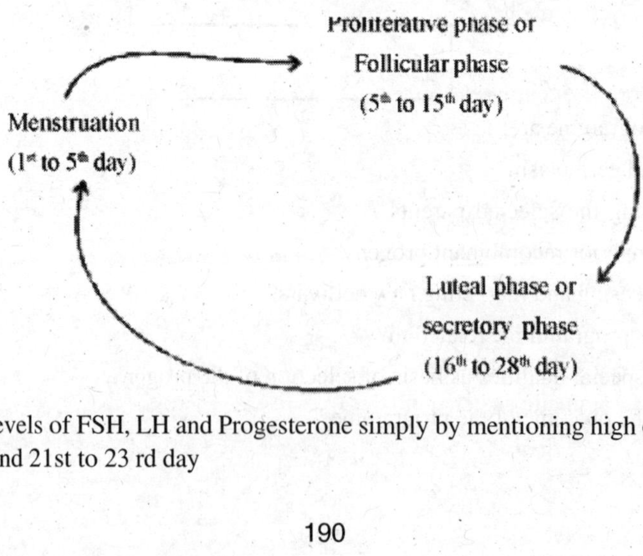

(i) State the levels of FSH, LH and Progesterone simply by mentioning high or low, around 13th and 14th day and 21st to 23 rd day

(ii) In which of the above mentioned phases does the egg travel to the fallopian tube?

(iii) Why is there no menstruation upon fertilisation?

23. Few gaps have been left in the following table showing certain terms and their meanings. Fill up the gaps. 3

Terms	Meanings
(i) -	Non coding sequence in eukaryotic DNA
(ii) -	Technique used in solving paternity disputes
(iii) Restriction endonuclease	________________
(iv) Plasmid	________________
(v) Transgenics	________________
(vi) -	Nucleotide sequences with single base differences

24. $A_{3'}$ ———————— $_{5'}B$ 3

$C_{5'}$ ———————— $_{3'}D$

AB and CD represent two strands of a DNA molecule.

When this molecule undergoes replication, forming a replication fork between A and C in the above.

(i) Name the template stands for replication.

(ii) Using which strand as the template, will there be continuous synthesis of a complementary DNA strand?

(iii) Complementary to which strand will okazaki segments get synthesised discontinuous snthesis will occur.

(iv) What are template strands and Okazaki pieces?

(v) In which direction is a new strand synthesised?

25. "A population has been exhibiting genetic equilibrium." 3

Answer the following with regard to the above statement.

(i) Explain the above statement.

(ii) Name the underlying principle.

(iii) List any two factors which would upset the genetic equilibruim of the population.

(iv) Take up any one such factor and explain how the gene pool will change due to that factor

OR

In the 1950s, there were hardly any mosquitoes in Delhi. The use of the pesticide DDT on standing water killed their larve. It is believed that now there are mosquitoes because they evolved DDT resistance through the interaction of mutation and Natural Selection. Pointwise, state in a sequence how that could have happened. 3

26. A thallasemic child needed repeated blood transfusions got infected by HIV. 3

(i) Use a rough diagrammatic sketch and arrows to show how the virus increased in number.

(ii) Why did the increased number of the HIV virus deteriorate the child's immunity?

(iii) Which diagnostic test showed that the infective virus was HIV?

27. Microbes play a dual role when used for sewage treatment as they not only help to retrieve usable water but also generate fuel. Write in points how this happens? 3

28. Name the particular technique in Biotechnology whose steps are shown in the figure. Use the figure to summmarise the technique in three steps.

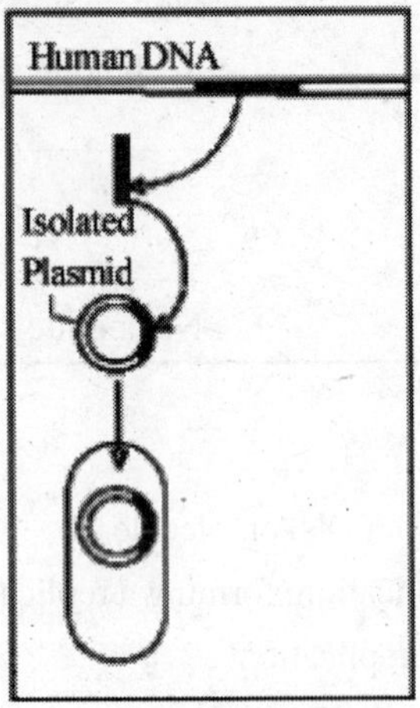

SECTION - D

29. With an example, explain how biotechnology has been applied in each of the following:

(i) In curing Diabetes mellitus

(ii) In raising pest resistant plants

(iii) In producing more nutritionally balanced milk.

Do you think it is ethical to manipulate organisms for human benefits? Justify your answer.

OR

Name any two cloning vectors. Describe the features required to facilitate cloning into a vector. 5

30.

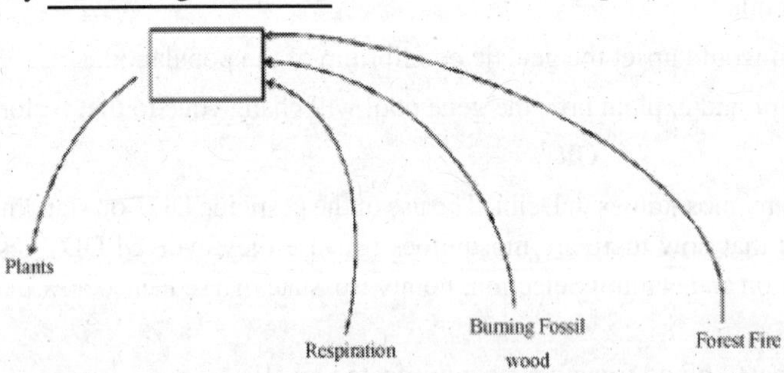

The above diagram shows a simplified biogeochemical cycle

(i) Name the compound whose cycle is depicted.

(ii) In what way do vehicles add this compound to the atmosphere?

(iii) What adverse effect does its excess have on the environment?

(iv) Cite an event which depicts this effect in the modern times.

(v) Suggest two ways of reducing this effect.

OR

Create an aquatic food chain in a water body into which effluents flow from a pesticide factory. Diagrammatically represent biomagnification in this food chain. Explain why a decline in the predator-bird population is expected, when it feeds on the tertiary consumers of this food chain. 5

30. Study the following carefully and explain why mutation (A) did not cause any sickle cell anemia in spite of change in the molecular structure of the gene which codes for Haemoglobin, when as a similar mutation (B) did. (The question is based on properties of the genetic code. c = codon, a = amino acid, Hb = Hoemoglobin)

Codons for Hb : C_1-C_2-C_3-C_4-C_5-GAA-GAA-C_8 ....

Amino acids in Hb : a_1-a_2-a_3-a_4-a_5-Glutamic acid -Glutamicacid-a_8 ....

(Normal Haemoglobin)

Mutation (A) : C_1-C_2-C_3-C_4-C_5-GAA-GAA-C_8 ....

a_1-a_2-a_3-a_4-a_5-Glutamic acid-Glutamic acid-a_8 ....

(Normal Haemoglobin)

Mutation (B) : C_1-C_2-C_3-C_4-C_5-GUG-GAA-C_8 ....

a_1-a_2-a_3-a_4-a_5-Valine-Glutamic acid -a_8 ....

(Sickle cell Haemoglobin) 5

OR

One chromosome contains one molecule of DNA. In eukaryotes the length of the DNA molecule is enormously large. Explain how such a long molecule fits into the tiny chromosomes seen at Metaphase. 5

SAMPLE QUESTION PAPER - II
SOLUTIONS
SECTION-A

	Value Points	Marks
1.	Through asexual reproduction/ parthenogenesis.	1
2.	Correctly labelled pericarp and seed.	(½ x 2) = 1
3.	The law of segregation; The factors or alleles present in pairs segregate during gamete formation/ or similary worded.	1

4. Autosomal dominant; defective trait in both male and female progeny/unaffected child did not pass down trait. 1

5. Ringworm: *Ascaris* ; Because ringworm is a disease caused by a fungus (or named fungus) Ascaris causes Ascariasis. 1

6. Predator-prey/Predation between level (1) and (2); Producer-consumer between levels (3) and (4) (½ x 2) = 1

7. Plasmid made of DNA/Deoxy ribonucleic acid; Replicates/duplicates along with host bacterial DNA (½ x 2) = 1

8. Polymerase chain reaction; *Bacillus thuringiensis* (no mark if specific name written with capital T) (½ x 2) = 1

SECTION-B

9. (i) a = Unlimited food and space, B = limited food and space

(ii) curve a, K/carrying capacity ½ x 4 = 2

10. (1) RNA polymerase; (2) hn; (3) m; (4) poly A tail ½x4=2

11. Replication; Eukaryotic transcription; translation; gene regulation (½ x 4) = 2

12. Individual = age; population = Natality; community= predator-prey relation; ecosystem = energy flow (½ x 4) = 2

13. A - Sporogenous tissue; form microspores or pollen grains.

B - Tapetum; nourishes the developing pollen grains.

14. Barrier = Diaphragm/ condom/cervical cap 1UD = Copper T

Surgical technique = Vasectomy / Tubectomy

Hormonal administrations = Oral pill/saheli (½ x 4) = 2

15. (*i*) Microspore mother cell = 16; diploid/ 2n

(*ii*) Endosperm cell = Triploid / 3n (½ x 4) = 2

16. (A) Insects/arthropods; aerial/air/ground/ soil/ water etc.

(B) = fishes/pisces; aquatic/ water/ sea/river etc.

17. Phytoplankton; zooplankton; aquatic/water ecosystem showing pyramid of biomass

(½ + ½ + 1) =2

18. Plant breeding; high yield and pest resistant/drought resistant etc. (any two) for increase in food production; green revolution; M.S. Swaminathan (½ x 4) = 2

19. BOD test measures rate of uptake of O_2 microorganisms in a a sample of water. Greater the BOD of water, more is pollution =1

Sample 'C' is most polluted because it has highest BOD level among the three samples of water = 1 1 + 1 = 2

SECTION-C

20. Biofertilisers = organisims enriching nutrient quality of soil; fertilisers = chemical synthesised in factory; Rhizobium has symbiotic association with leguminous roots and fixes nitrogen

1 x3 =3

21. Label 1 : Origin of plumule; plumule grows into shoot Label 2 : Cotyledons; food storage Label 3 : Origin of radicle ; radicle grows into root (½ x 6) = 3

22. (i) FSH and LH : high and progesterone low; FSH and LH : Low and Progesterone high;

(ii) Luteal phase (iii) uterine wall and blood vessels help maintain implanted embryo;

½ + ½ +1+1 = 3

23. Intron; DNA finger printing; cuts specific nucleotide sequence; extrachromosomal DNA in bacteria/ vector; modified organisms/ organisms with foreign gene; SNP (½ x 6) = 3

24. (i) AB, CD (ii) AB (iii) CD;

Template strands : parental DNA strands complementary to which new strands of DNA are synthesised; 5' - 3' ; small pieces of DNA complementany to template. (½ x 6) = 3

25. (i) Allelic frequencies in the gene pool of a population remains unchanged for generations;

(ii) Hardy-Weinberg equilibrium

(iii) Any two factors - mutation/Natural selection : gene flow/genetic drift/ migration

(iv) Mutation : changes alleles/ Natural selection : brings about grater reproduction of certain/ alleles gene flow. migration genetic drift : alleles move out of gene pool

(½ x 6 = 3)

OR

Certain larvae born with mutation; which conferred resistance to DDT; DDT sensitive larvae died; DDT resistant larvae completed life history and became adult mosquitoes; natural selection caused greater reproduction of DDT resistant mosquitioes; which soon replaced DDT sensitive mosquitoes. (½ × 6) = 3

26. (i) simplified (virus replicated in host cell, many viruses , infect new cell)

(ii) Viral DNA enters helper T-lymphocytes, which are responsible for immunity; virus replicates and attacks other T- lymphocytes whose number decreases.

(iii) ELISAtest /Enzyme linked immunosorbent assay. (1 + 1 + 1) = 3

27. Heterotrophhic microbes naturally present in sewage are used; vigorous growth of aerobic microbes as flocs use up organic matter in effluent and reduce BOD of waste water; other kinds of bacteria grow in it anaerobically; and digest the bacteria and fungi called flocs (masses of bacteria associated with fungal filaments); as they digest flocs a mixture of CH_4, H_2S, and CO_2 or biogas are evoloved; which can be used as fuel. (½x6)=3

28. Genetic engineering/Recombinant DNA technology; segment of DNA removed from human cell and DNA segmant incorporated into bacterial plasmid ; Plasmid taken up into bacterial cell which makes protein directed by human DNA. (1 + 1 + 1) = 3

29. (i) Page 211 production of insulin to cure diabetes mellitus or gene therapy for cure of ADA

(ii) Page 209 - using *Agrobacterium* vectors to introduce nematode specific genes or RNAi

(iii) Page 213- generating transgenic cow such as Rosie. (1 x 5) = 5

Ethical standards required as genetically manipulated organisms may harm other organisms/results unpredictable.

OR

Cloning vectors - (i) plasmids, (ii) bacteriophages (iii) YACS, (iv) BACS (any two) 1

Features required to facilitate cloning into a vector are (1 x 4) = 4

(a) Origin of replication (ori) - Sequence where replication starts and any piece of DNA when linked to this sequence can be made to replicate within host cells.

(b) Selectable marker - Helps in identifying and eliminating non-transformants and selectively permitting the growth of the transformants.

(c) Cloning sites : Few or single recognition sites are preferable

(d) Vectors for cloning genes in plants and animals, e.g. genetically modified *Agrobacterium tumifaciens* and retroviruses.

30. (i) CO_2

(ii) Fuels burnt in vehicles emit CO_2 which goes into atmosphere

(iii) Causes global warming

(iv) Long summer/ Himalayan caps melting/floods etc.

(v) Plant more trees/Afforestation/ car pool/ any other (any two) 1 x 4 + ½ x 2 = 5

31.
- Genetic code degenerate i.e more than one code for one amino acid.
- Both GAG, GAA code for glutamic acid.
- Mutation of third base/ nucleotide—no change in phenotype in mutation A/Wobble hypothesis
- In case of change on 2nd codon of triplet code as in Mutation B, codon stands for a different amino acid valine.
- Hb becomes different / normal Hb becomes Hbs/Structure of protein changed.

(1 x 5) = 5

OR

DNA is packaged in the cell in the following manner:

(a) As Nucleosomes consist of Histone octamer around which the positively charged DNA is wrapped around to form a nucleosome. A typical nucleosome contains 200bp of DNA helix.

(b) Repeated units of nucleosomes then form chromatin (in a nucleus). The nuceleosomes represent the "Beads on String" structure as seen in electron microscopic picture.

(c) These are then further coiled and condensed at metaphase stage to form chromosomes.

(d) For packaging of chromatin at higher level, non-histone proteins are required. 5

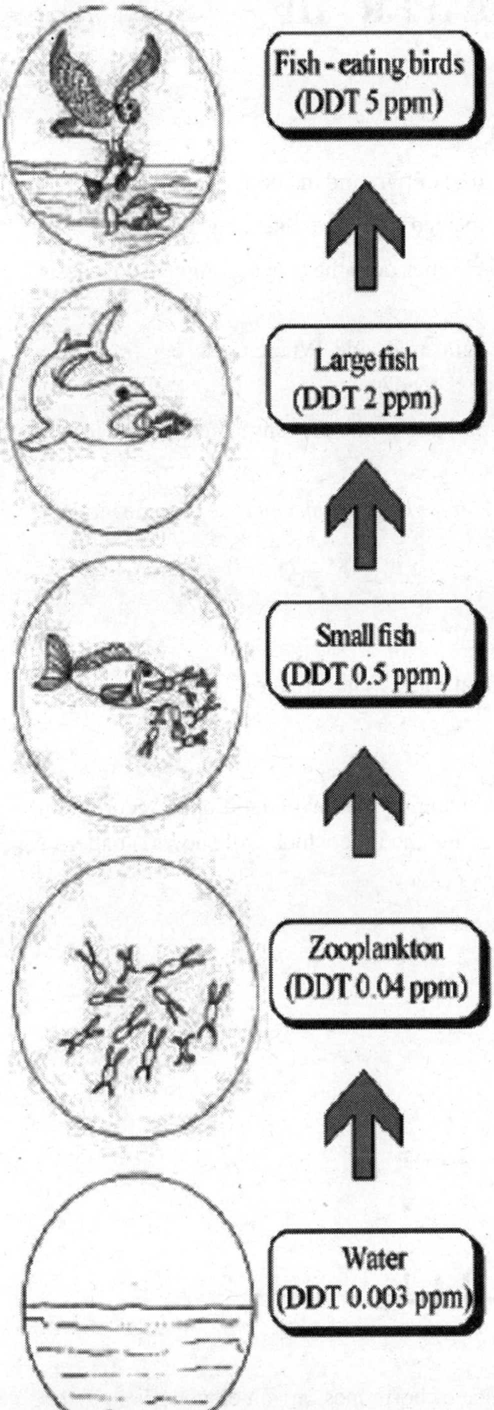

Correct food chain - 1

correct doses of DDT - 1

High conc. of DDT disturbs
Ca (Calcium) metabolism in birds - 1

Thinning of egg shell - 1

Premature breaking of egg shell eventnaly leads
to decline in bird population - 1

(*Note :* Food chain may be depicted in writing or through pictures)

SAMPLE QUESTION PAPER - III

SECTION-A

1. Cite an example of an inverted ecological pyramid. What kind of pyramid of energy would it have? 1
2. When is the structure and composition of a community expected to remain unchanged? 1
3. At what stage of life is oogenesis initiated in a human female? When does the oocyte complete oogenesis? 1
4. After a successful in-vitro fertilisation, the fertilised egg begins to divide. Where is this egg transferred before it reaches the 8-cell stage and what is this technique named? 1
5. AaBb was crossed with aabb. What would be the phenotypic ratio of the progeny? Mention the term to denote this kind of cross. 1
6. In F. Griffith's experiment, how did the nonvirulent strain of *Streptococcus Pneumoniae* become virulent?
7. State the use of :

   (*i*) *Trichoderma* with respect to organ transplant, and

   (*ii*) Nucleopolyhedrovirus with respect to pest management 1
8. Bacteria that convert milk into curd play two other beneficial roles. What are they?

SECTION B

9. Given below is a graph depicting organismic response to changing external conditions. According to their response the organisms are grouped into two types. Name the type which will show (i) pattern A and (ii) pattern B. 2

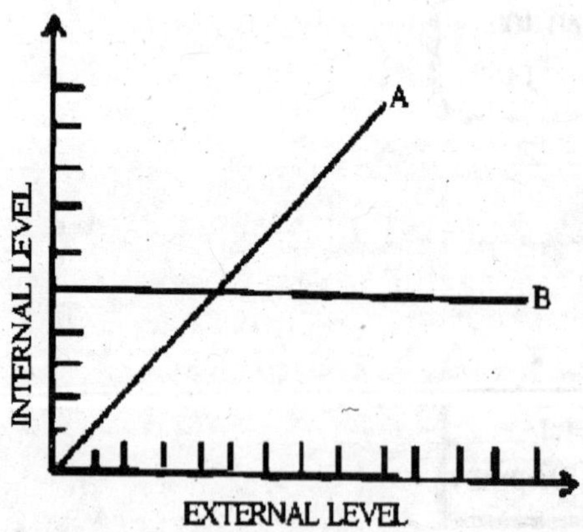

10. Given below is an incomplete flow chart showing influence of hormones on gametogenesis in males. Observe the flow chart carefully and fill in the blanks A, B, C, and D 2

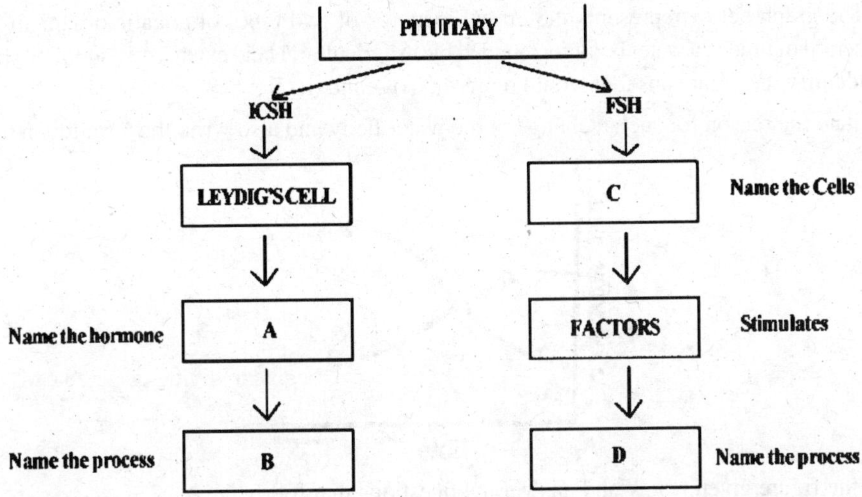

11. Read the sequence of the nucleotides in the given segment of mRNA and the respective amino acid sequence in the polypeptide chain.

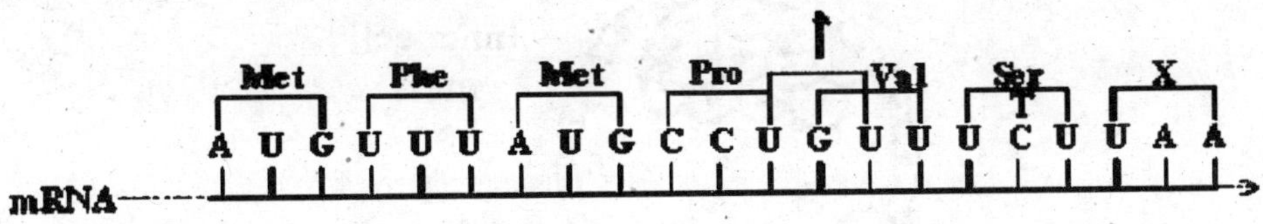

Polypeptide : met-phe-met-proline-valine-serine

(i) Provide the triplet of bases (codon) for (a) valine (b) proline

(ii) Write the nucleotide sequence of the DNA strand from which this mRNA was transcribed.

(iii) What does the last codon of this RNA stand for? 2

OR

11. The following table shows the genotypes for ABO blood grouping and their phenotypes. Fill in the gaps left in the table

S.No.	Genotype	Blood Group
1	$I^A I^A$	A
2		A
3	$I^B I^B$	B
4		B
5	$I^A I^B$	
6		O

12. (a) The graph below represents the growth patterns of two types of aquatic organisms over a brief period of time in a water body surrounded by an agricultural land extensively supplied with fertilisers. Identify the organisms that would represent (i) A and (ii) B.

(b) State the reason for such a change in the water body and also write the term given to it.

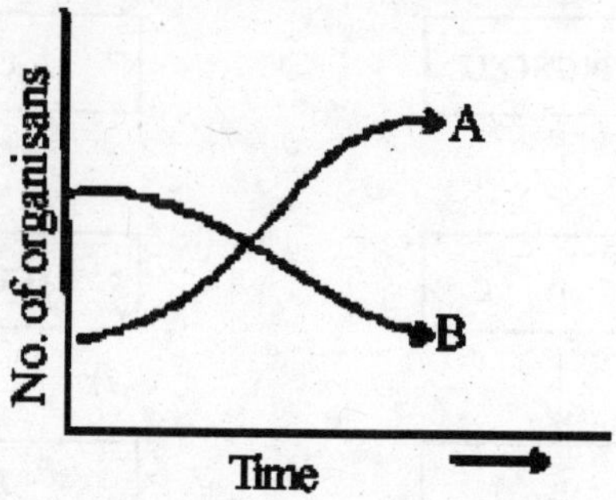

13. Study the figure given below and answer the questions that follow:

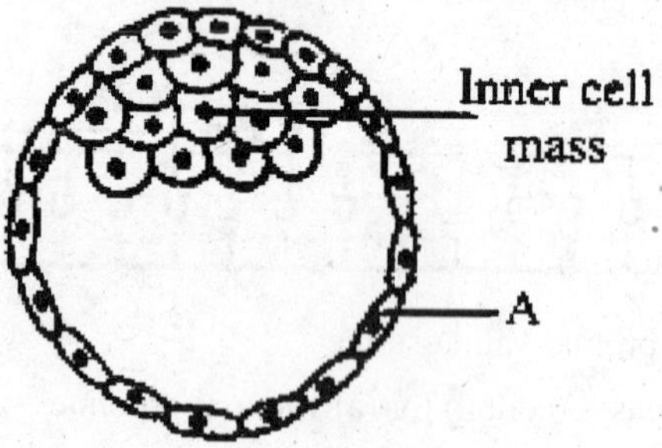

(a) Name the stage of human embryo the figure represents.

(b) Identify 'A' in the figure and mention its function.

(c) Mention the fate of the inner cell mass after implantation in the uterus.

(d) Where are the stem cells located in this embryo?

14. Following are the steps in MOET programmme for herd improvement in which a cow has been administered hormones with FSH like activity. Arrange steps A to D in their correct sequence.

A. Transferred to a surrogate mother.

B. It is either mated with an elite bull or artificially inseminated.

C. Fertilised eggs at 32 cell stage are recovered non-surgically.

D. It produces 6-8 eggs instead of one egg which they normally yield per cycle. 2

15. (i) In which disease is there an uncontrolled division of cells resulting in formation of tumours? How is this disease detected?

(ii) How do interferons help in controlling the disease?

16. State the principle underlying 'gel electrophoresis' and mention two applications of this technique in biotechnology. 2

17. You have developed a GM organism. Which government organisation will you approach to obtain clearance for its mass production? Why is such a body necessary? Give two reasons. 2

18. A person shows a strong immunogenic reactions while exposed to certain substances. Name this condition and common term for such substances. Mention the cell and its chemical which causes this condition.

SECTION C

19. Amazonian rain forest has the greatest biodiversity on earth. List any two hypotheses that are proposed by the biologists to account for the greater biological diversity. 3

20. (a) In which part of the human female reproductive system do the following events take place?

I - Release of 1st polar body. II - Release of 2nd polar body.

III - Fertilisation IV - Implantation

(b) From where do signals for parturition originate and what does maternal pituitary release for stimulating uterine contractions for child birth? 3

21. A true breeding tall plant is crossed with a true breeding dwarf plant. F_1 progeny is 100% tall and F_2 has tall : dwarf in the ratio 3:1 (i) Explain why F_1 shows only one type of parental phenotype; (ii) Name the patterns of inheritance in which the ratio deviates from above. Also mention the deviated phenotypic ratio. 3

22. In the following diagram the two DNA strands represented are ready for transcription

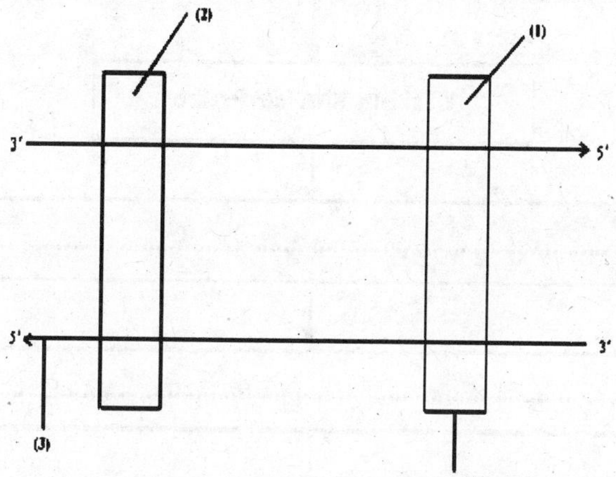

(4)

(i) Label the parts marked 1 to 4 and state their functions in transcription.

(ii) Which one of the two strands of DNA has nucleotide sequence similar to the mRNA that will be transcribed and why?

23. State in what ways Stanley Miller simulated the conditions of :

(i) Primitive atmosphere on earth.

(ii) Energy source at the time of origin of life, and

(iii) Formation of organic molecules of life to prove the theory of chemical evolution. 3

24. Draw a flow chart to depict the multiplication of an HIV virus in a host cell. 3

25. What are "flocs"? State their role in effluent treatment and their ultimate fate in sewage treatment tank. 3

26. Two of the steps involved in producing nematode resistant tobacco plants based on the process of RNAi are mentioned below. Write the missing steps in its proper sequence.

a. ....

↓

b. Using Agrobacterium as vector introduce it into tobacco

↓

c. ....

↓

d.

↓

e. Initiates RNA interference

↓

f. ....

↓

g. ....

↓

h. ....

27. An interesting property of restriction enzymes is molecular cutting and pasting. Restriction enzymes typically recognize a symmetrical sequence of DNA.

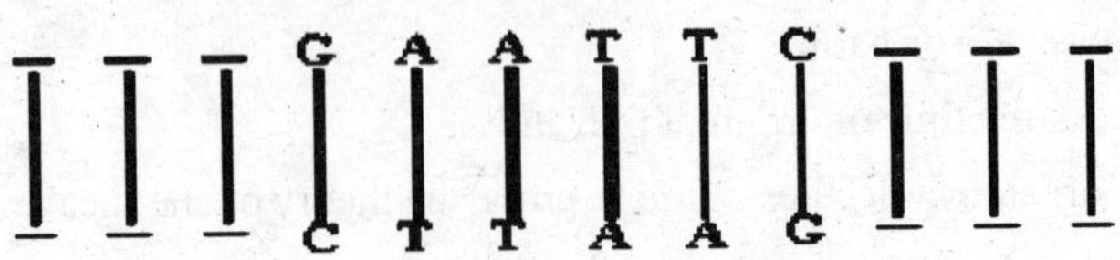

28. Notice that the top strand is the same as the bottom strand, but reads backward. When the enzyme cuts the strand between G and A, it leaves overhanging chains:

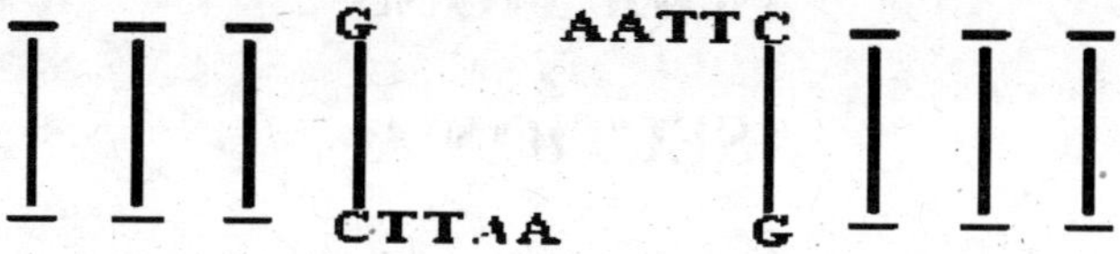

A. What is this symmetrical sequence of DNA known as?

B. What is the significance of these overhanging chains?

C. Name the restriction enzyme that cuts the strand between G and A 3

SECTION D

28. (i) A decade back, the enormous vehicular traffic in Delhi had made Delhi rank 4th among polluted cities of the world. Two measures taken by the Delhi Government brought marked improvement in air quality by 2005. What were these two measures and how did they reduce air pollution? 3

(ii) What is the norm set by Euro II for petrol and diesel vehicles?

OR

How is the "sixth episode of extinction" of species on earth, now currently in progress, different from the five earlier episodes? What is it due to? Explain the various causes that have brought about this difference.

29. (a) Draw the embroyo sac of a flowering plant and label (i) central cell (ii) Chalazal end of the embryo sac (iii) synergids.

(b) Name the cell that develops into the embryo sac and explain how this cell leads to the formation of Embryo sac . Also mention the role played by the various cells of the embryo sac. 5

OR

Show diagrammatically the stages of embryonic development from zygote upto implantation in humans. 5

30. Name the genes that constitute an operon. How does lac operon get switched on in the presence of lactose? 5

OR

With the advent of rDNA technology a powerful tool is available to identify a criminal or to the real parents. Name this technique. Write the missing steps in the procedure given below. Three steps are mentioned in the flow chart: Extraction of DNA from the cells - (ii)....................→(iii) DNA is cut into fragments by restriction enzymes → (iv)................→ (v)...............→ (vi).................→ (vii) Autoradiography.

SAMPLE QUESTION PAPER - III
SOLUTIONS

SECTION-A

1. Sea/Forest/Large tree ½ + ½ = 1
Upright

2. When the environment remains unchanged 1

3. Embryonic life ½ + ½ = 1
When the sperm enters the egg/at the time of fertilization

4. Fallopian tube/oviduct; ZIFT/zygote intra fallopian transfer ½ + ½ = 1

5. 1 : 1 : 1 : 1 : ; Test cross ½ + ½ = 1

6. Bacterial transformation/transfer of genetic material/by acquiring genes for smooth coat 1

7. a: Trichoderma - Biocontrol agent of several plant pathogens/ produces Cyclosporin A which is used as an immunosuppressive agent in organ transplant patients

b. Nucleopolyhedrovirus - Narrow spectrum insecticide ½ + ½ = 1

8. Increase in nutritional quality/Vitamain B_{12} check disease causing microbes in the stomach
½ + ½ = 1

9. A. Conformers
B. Regulators 1+1 = 2

10. A. Androgen/Testosterone/male hormone
B. Spermatogenesis
C. Sertoli Cells ½ x 4 = 2
D. Spermiogenesis
Stop marking at incorrect entry

11. (a) (i) GUU
(b) (i) CCU
(ii) TACAAATACGGACAAAGAATT ½ x 4 = 2
(iii) UAA stands as stop signal.

I^Ai A Blood group	$I^A I^B$ - AB blood group
I^Bi - B blood group	ii - O Blood group

12. (A) i. Water Hyacinth / Algal growth
ii. Fish / Aquatic animals

(B) i. Excessive growth of algae triggered by nitrates and phosphates from agricultural land run off water.

ii. Algal bloom / Eutrophication ½ x 4 = 2

13. (a) Blastocyst.

(b) Trophoblast. It helps in attachment of the blastocyst to the endometrium of uterine wall.

(c) The inner cell mass gets differentiated as the embryo.

(d) The inner cell mass contains certain cells called stem cells which have the potency to give rise to all the tissues and organs.

14. It produces 6-8 eggs instead of one egg which they normally yield per cycle It is either mated with an elite bull or artificially inseminated ½ x 4

Fertilised eggs at 32 cell stage are recovered non-surgically

Transferred to surrogate mothers

15. (a) Cancer ; Radiography / Computerised tomography / Magnetic Resonace Imaging/ any other correct ones ½ x 4

(b) Activate the immune system and help in destroying the cancer cells

16. (a) Technique where charged molecules are separated on their molecular weight, Gel acts as a sieve. ½ x 4

(b) DNA figerprinting / Cloning of rDNA / any other correct two points

17. i. GEAC—Genetic Engineeering Approval Committee

ii. Makes decisions regarding validity of GM research; checks safety of introducing GM-organisms for public services, may harm living organisms. GMO has unpredictable results

½ x 4

18. Allergy

Allergens

Mast Cells

Histamine / Serotonin ½ x 4

19. It is a tropical rain forest

A. Speciation is a fuction of time, unlike temporate regions, tropics have remained relatively undisturbed for millions of years and thus had long evolutionary time for species diversification.

B. Tropical environments are more constant, predictable and less seasonal. Variations such constant envi-ronments promote niche specialisation and lead to a greater diversity

1½ x 2

C. More solar energy available - higher productivity - greater diversity (Any two hypotheses)

20. (a) i. In the ovary

ii. In the isthmus - ampullary junction of Fallopian tube

iii. Same as (ii) ½ x 4

iv. In the uterus

(b) fully developed foetus and placenta; Oxytocin/Pitocin

21. (a) Case of dominance where allele T is dominant over allele t that is both heterozygous and homozygous dominant express the dominant trait.

(b) Case of incomplete dominance 1 : 2 : 1/ Codominance 1 : 2 : 1 ½ + ½

22 (i) 1. Template strand

2. Promoter ½ x 4 = 2

3. Coding strand

4. Terminator

(ii) Coding strand because both mRNA and the coding strand are complementary to template strand.

23. (i) In a closed flask containing NH_3, CH_4, H_2 and water vapour to simulate primitive atmosphere

(ii) Electric discharge to simulate on primitive earth

(iii) Formation of compounds like amino acids from simple molecules like NH_3, CH_4, H_2

1x3

24. a. HIV enters the macrophage (human cell)

b. Viral RNA genome replicates into DNA with the help of reverse transcription

c. Viral DNA is incorporated into host DNA

d. Viral DNA directs infected cell to produce viral particles

e. Virus comes out while infected cell continues producing HIV particles

f. New HIV particles infect Helper T cells which lead to decrease in Helper T cells.

½ x 6

25. (a) Masses of aerobic bacteria associated with fungal filaments

(b) While growing they consume large amount of organic matter of the effluents reducing BOD

(c) When effluent goes to settling tank and flocs are allowed to sediment for activated sludge, they get digested by anaerobic bacteria 1 + 1 + 1

26. (a) Isolate Nematode specific genes

(b) Produces sense and antisense RNA in the host cells

(c) Being complementary sense and antisense RNA form double stranded RNA (ds RNA)

(d) Silence the specific mRNA of the Nematode

(e) Parasite cannot survive in the transgenic tobacco host expressing RNAi

(f) Thus the transgenic plant tobacco is protected from nematode

27. A. (i) Insertional activation : A recombinant DNA is inserted within the coding sequence of an enzyme -galactosidase, results in inactivation of the enzyme

(ii) The bacterial colonies whose plasmids do not have the insert produce blue colour but those with an insert do not produce colour

B. Simple and easier method of selecting recombinants from non-recombinants.

28. (a) Palindromic nucleotide sequence / Recognition sequence.

(b) DNA fragments from two different molecules which have the same kind of sticky ends overhanging chains can be joined together (end to end) by DNA ligases. 1 x 3

(c) EcoRI

29. 1. Changing of all buses to run on CNG

a. CNG burns most efficiently

b. Cheaper than petrol or diesel

c. Cannot be siphoned off by thieves / adulterated like petrol or diesel

2. a. Phasing out of old vehicles ½ x 8

b. use of unleaded petrol / use of low sulphur petrol / diesel ½ + ½

c. Use of catalytic converters in vehicles norms or any other correct two points each

Euro II

a. stipulates that sulphur to be controlled at 350 ppm in diesel and 150 ppm in petrol.

b. Aromatic hydrocarbons are to be contained at 42% of the concerned fuel.

OR

1. The difference is that 6th episode of extinction is taking place at a 100 to 1000 times faster than the earlier ones. ½

2. It is largley due to human activities ½

The various causes are:

a. Habitat loss and fragmentation

b. Overexploitation $1 \times 4 = 4$

c. Introduction / Invasion of alien species

d. Coextinctions $1 + 4 = 5$

30. (a) Three correct labels

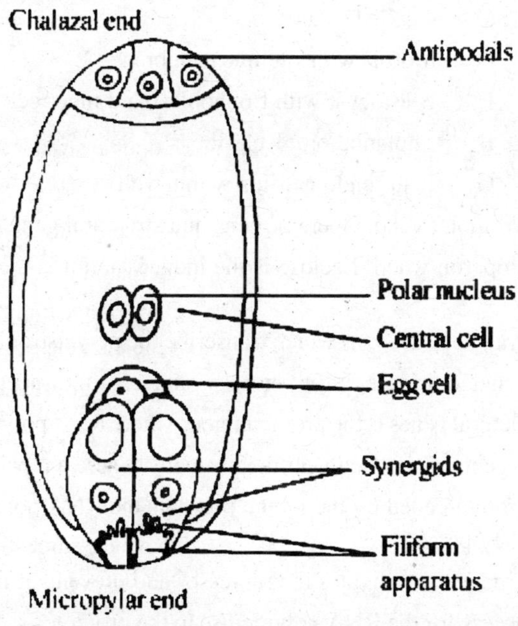

(b) i. The functional megaspore developes into embryo sac

ii. Nucleus undergoes mitotic division and the two cells move to the opposite poles

iii. Two successive mitotic division - an eight nucleate embryo sac ½ × 3

iv. Cell wall formation takes place after nuclear divisins ½ × 7

v. Three cells group together at the micropylar end—egg apparatus with an egg cell and two synergids

vi. Three cells group together at the chalazal end—antipodal cells

vii. The remaining two nuclei move to the centre - fuse to form secondary nucleus. 5

OR

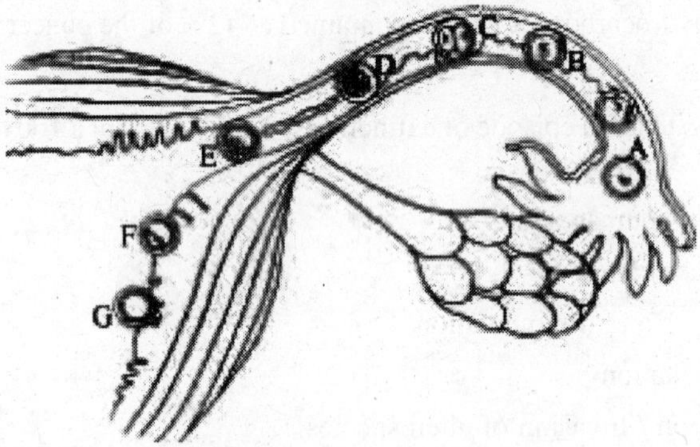

Zygote ———	A		½
Cleavage ——	B	2 celled stage	½
	C	4 celled stage	½
	D	Morula with vitelline membrane	1
	E	Blastocyst with trophoblast and inner cell mass	1
	F	Implantation of blastocys	½
	G	In the endometrium within wall	½

30. i. Regulator gene, Promoter gene. Operator gene and structural gene

1. An inducible operon where Lactose is the inducer and it is the substrate for the enzyme B-galactosidase
2. Three structural genes (z, y, a) which transcribe the polycistronic mRNA
3. z codes for - galactosidase, y for permease and a for transacetylase
4. Near the structural genes is the promoter gene where RNA polymerase binds for transcription
5. An operator gene as a switch near the promoter where a repressor always binds.
6. Repressor protein coded by the i gene prevents the RNA polymerase from transcribing by binding to the operator
7. Lactose, an inducer inactivates the repressor and prevents it from binding to the operator.
8. Allows an access for the RNA polymerase to the promoter

9. Transcription takes place

10. The substrate lactose regulates the lac-operon. ½ × 10 = 5

OR

DNA finger printing ;

(ii) Amplification by polymerase chain reaction

(iv) — Separation of DNA fragments by gel electrophoresis

(v) — Southern blotting

(vi) — Hybridization using probe tragment

(viii) Matching of DNA fragment photographs and interpretation. 1 × 5 = 5

□□□

SAMPLE PAPER FOR PRACTICE - I

Time allowed : 3 hours *Maximum Marks : 70*

General Instructions:

(i) *All questions are compulsory.*

(ii) *The question paper consists of four Sections* ***A, B, C*** *and* ***D****. Section* ***A*** *contains* ***8*** *questions of* **one** *mark each, Section* ***B*** *is of* ***10*** *questions of* ***two*** *marks each, Section* ***C*** *is of* ***9*** *questions of* **three** *marks each and Section* ***D*** *is of* ***3*** *questions of* ***five*** *marks each.*

(iii) *There is no overall choice. However, an internal choice has been provided in* **one** *questions of* ***2*** *marks, one question of* ***3*** *marks and all the three questions of* ***5*** *marks weightage. A student has to attempt only one of the alternatives in such questions.*

(v) *Wherever necessary, the diagrams drawn should be neat and properly labelled.*

SECTION A

1. List the changes the primary oocyte undergoes in the tertiary follicular stage in the human ovary. 1

2. Why are cattle and goats not seen browsing on *Calotropis* growing in the fields? 1

3. Mention how is mutation theory of Hugo de varies different from Darwin's theory of natural selection. 1

4. Why are some organisms called as eurythermals and some others as stenohaline? 1

5. Mention the type of allele that expresses itself only in homozygous state in any organism. 1

6. Malaria, typhoid, pneumonia and amoebiasis are some of the human infectious diseases. Which ones of these are transmitted through mechanical carriers? 1

7. Name any two techniques that serve the purpose of early diagnosis of some bacterial/viral human diseases. 1

8. Name the phenomenon and the cell responsible for the development of a new individual without fertilisation as seen in honey bees. 1

SECTION B

9. In a dihybrid cross white eyed, yellow bodied female *Drosophila* crossed with red eyed, brown bodied male *Drosophila* produced in F_2 generation 1.3 percent recombinants and 98.7 percent progeny with parental type combinations. This observation of Morgan deviated from Mendelian F_2 phenotypic dihybrid ratio. Explain, giving reasons, Morgan's observations. 2

10. How are recombinant vectors created? Why is only one type of restriction endonuclease required for creating one recombinant vector? 2

11. Bear hibernates whereas some species of zooplanktons enter diapause to avoid stressful external conditions. How are these two ways different from each other? 2

12. The figure below shows the relative contribution of four green house gases to global warming: 1

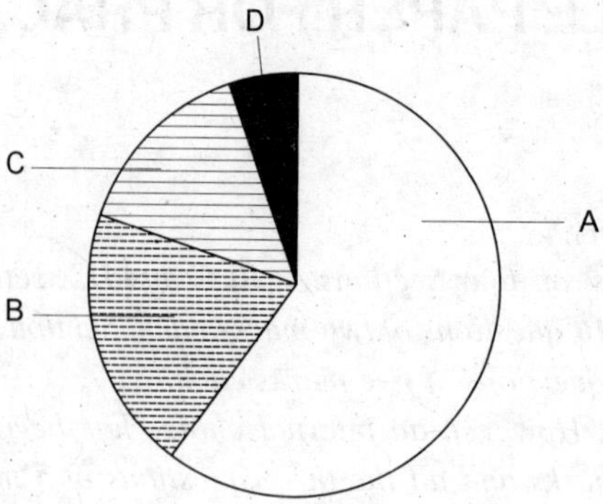

(*i*) Identify the gases A and C.

(*ii*) Why are these four gases called the green house gases?

13. At the time of Independence, the population of India was 350 million, which exploded to over 1 billion by May 2000. List any two reasons for this rise in population and any two steps taken by the Government to check this population explosion. 2

14. Explain the function of 'reservoir' in a nutrient cycle. List the two types of nutrient cycles in nature. 2

OR

Explain with the help of two examples, how the pyramid of numbers and the pyramid of biomass can look inverted. 2

15. A list of three flowering plants is given below. Which ones out of them are (*i*) monoecious and (*ii*) bearing pistillate flowers: 2

List — Datepalm, Cucurbits and Pea.

16. Name the organism from where the thermostable DNA polymerase is isolated. State its role in genetic engineering. 2

17. Study the flow chart given below:

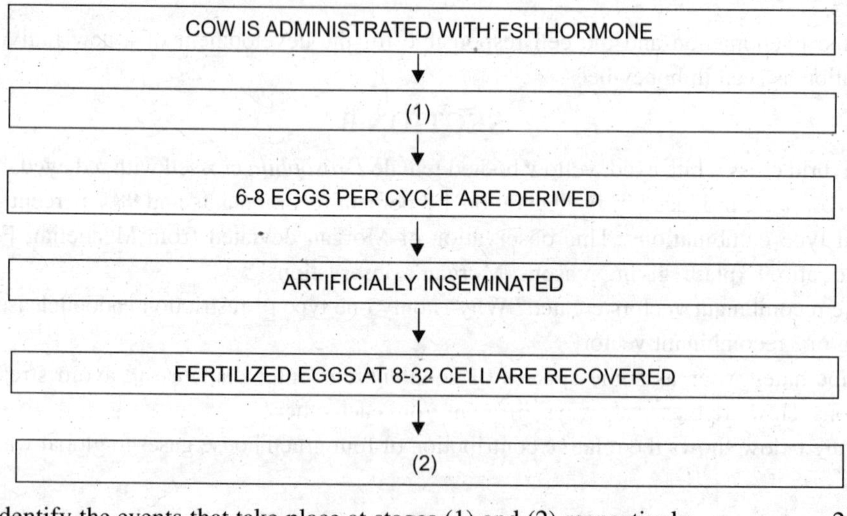

(*i*) Identify the events that take place at stages (1) and (2) respectively. 2

(*ii*) State the importance of the technology explained above.

18. Give the scientific name of the microbes from which cyclosporin A and statin are obtained. Write one medical use of each one of these drugs. 2

SECTION C

19. Draw a labelled diagram of the microscopic structure of a human sperm. 3

20. Government evolution and divergent evolution are the two concepts explaining organic evolution. Explain each one with the help of an example. 3

21. (*a*) Name a drug used (*i*) as an effective sedative and pain killer (*ii*) for helping patients to cope with mental illnesses like depression, but often misused.

(*b*) How does the moderate and high dosage of cocaine affect the human body? 3

22. Given below is a schematic representation of lac operon:

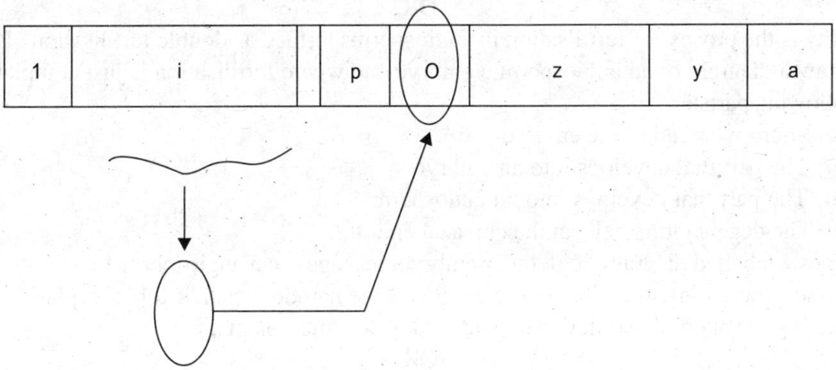

(*a*) Identify *i* and *p*.

(*b*) Name the 'inducer' for this operon and explain its role. 3

23. Explain the different steps involved in sewage treatment before it can be released into natural water bodies.

24. Study the three different age pyramids for human population given below and answer the questions that follow: 3

Post-reproductive

Reproductive

Pre-reproductive

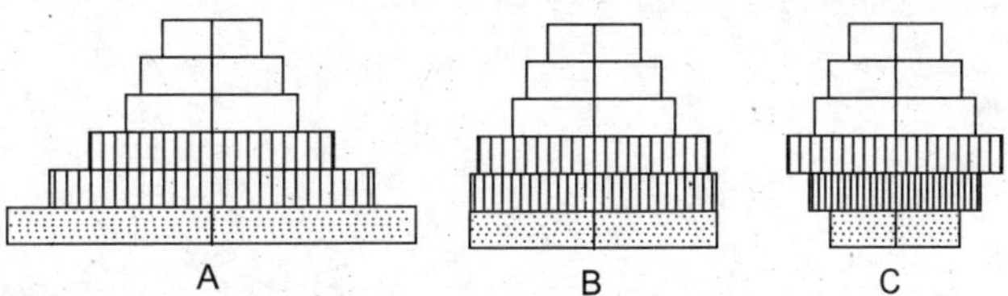

(*a*) Write the names given to each of these age pyramids.

(*b*) Mention the one which is ideal for human population and why.

25. Name a disorder, give the karyotype and write the symptoms a human suffers from as a result of monosomy of the sex chromosome. 3

26. Explain, giving one example, how co-extinction is one of the causes of loss of biodiversity. List the three other causes also (without description). 3

OR

Eutrophication is the natural aging of a lake. Explain. 3

27. IARI has released several varieties of crop plants that are biofortified. Give three examples of such crops and their biofortifications. 3

SECTION D

28. (*a*) Draw a diagram of an enlarged view of T.S. of one microsporangium of an angiosperm and label the following parts:

(*i*) Tapetum

(*ii*) Middle layer

(*iii*) Endothecium

(*iv*) Microspore mother cells.

(*b*) Mention the characteristic features and function of tapetum.

(*c*) Explain the following giving reasons:

(*i*) Pollen grains are well preserved as fossils.

(*ii*) Pollen tablets are in use by people these days. 5

OR

(*a*) Why is the process of fertilisation in angiosperms termed as double fertilisation? Explain.

(*b*) Draw a diagram of an angiospermic embryo-sac where fertilisation is just completed. Label the following parts:

(*i*) Micropylar end of the embryo-sac

(*ii*) The part that develops into an embryo

(*iii*) The part that develops into an endosperm

(*iv*) The degenerating cells at the chalazal end

(*c*) Draw a labelled diagram of globular embryonic stage of an angiosperm. 5

28. Name the process involved in the production of nematode-resistant tobacco plants, using genetic engineering. Explain the strategy adopted to develop such plants. 5

OR

Describe the various stages involved in gene transfer for the commercial production of human insulin by li Lilly. 5

❑❑❑

SAMPLE PAPER FOR PRACTICE - II

Time allowed : 3 hours *Maximum Marks : 70*

General Instructions:

(i) *All questions are compulsory.*

(ii) *The question paper consists of four Sections **A, B, C** and **D**. Section **A** contains **8** questions of **one** mark each, Section **B** is of **10** questions of **two** marks each, Section **C** is of **9** questions of **three** marks each and Section **D** is of **3** questions of **five** marks each.*

(iii) *There is no overall choice. However, an internal choice has been provided in **one** questions of **2** marks, one question of **3** marks and all the three questions of **5** marks weightage. A student has to attempt only one of the alternatives in such questions.*

(v) *Wherever necessary, the diagrams drawn should be neat and properly labelled.*

SECTION A

1. Name the embryonic stage that gets implanted in the uterine wall of a human female. 1

2. State the importance of biofortification. 1

3. Biotechnologists refer to *Agrobacterium tumifaciens* as a natural genetic engineer of plants. Give reasons to support the statement.
1

4. How do algal blooms affect the life in water bodies? 1

5. Name the common ancestor of the great apes and man. 1

6. Write a difference between net primary productivity and gross productivity. 1

7. Mention the contribution of genetic maps in human genome project. 1

8. Name the phase all organisms have to pass through before they can reproduce sexually. 1

SECTION B

9. Name the enzyme produced by *Streptococcus* bacterium. Explain its importance in medical sciences. 2

10. How is 'Rosie' considered different from a normal cow? Explain. 2

11. State the use of Biodiversity in modern agriculture. 2

12. Write the full form of VNTR. How is VNTR different from 'Probe'? 2

13. Differentiate between benign and malignant tumours. 2

14.

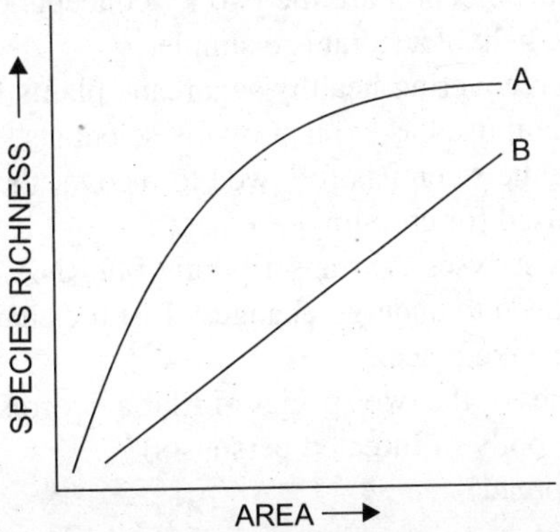

The above graph shows Species-Area relationship. Write the equation of the curve 'a' and explain. 2

OR

Differentiate between *in situ* and *ex situ* approaches of conservation of biodiversity.

15. The cell division involved in gamete formation is not of the same type in different organisms. Justify. 2

16.

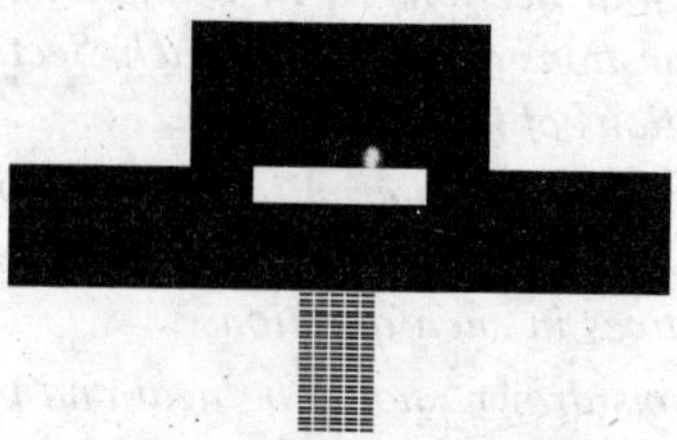

Identify the type of the given cological pyramid and give on example each of pyramid of number and pyramid of biomass in such cases. 2

17. Describe the Lactational Amenorrhea method of birth control. 2

18. Name the type of bioreactor shown. Write the purpose for which for which it is used. 2

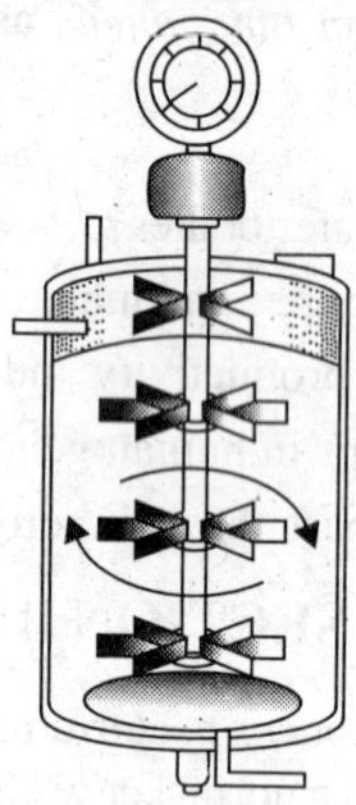

SECTION C

19. Draw a labelled diagram of the reproductive system in a human female. 3

20. Branching descent and natural selection are the two ky concepts of Darwinian Theory of Evolution. Explain each concept with the help of a suitable example. 3

21. Scientists have succeeded in recovering healthy sugarcane plants from a diseased on. 3

(*a*) Name the part of the plant used as explant by the scientists.

(*b*) Describe the procedure the scientists followed to recover the healthy plants.

(*c*) Name this technology used for crop improvement.

22. (*i*) Name the enzyme that catalyses the transcription of hnRNA. 3

(*ii*) Why does the hnRNA need to undergo changes? List the changes hnRNA undergoes and where in the cell such changes take place.

23. (*i*) Write the scientific names of the two species of filarial worms causing filariass. 3

(*ii*) How do they affect the body of infected persons(s)?

(*iii*) How dos the disease spread?

24. Name the gnus to which bauloviruses belong. Describe their role in the integrated pest management programmes. 3

25. Unambiguous, universal and degenerate are some of the terms used for the genetic code. Explain the salient features of each on of them.

26. Water is very essential for life. Write any three features both for plants and animals which noble them to survive in water scarce environment. 3

OR

How do organisms cope with stressful external environmental conditions which are localised or of short duration?

27. (*i*) State the consequence if the electrostatic precipitator of a thermal plant fails to function. 3

(*ii*) Mention any four methods by which the vehicular air pollution can be controlled. 3

SECTION D

28. Give reasons why: 5

(*i*) most zygotes in angiosperms divide only after certain amount of endosperm is formed.

(*ii*) groundnut seeds are exalbuminous and castor seeds of a seed.

(*iii*) Micropyle remains as a small pore in the seed coat of a seed.

(*iv*) integuments of an ovule harden and the water content is highly reduced, as the seed matures.

(*v*) apple and cashew are not called true fruits.

OR

(*a*) Draw a labelled diagram of L.S. of an embryo of grass (any six labels).

(*b*) Give reason for each of the following:

(*i*) Anthers of angiosperm flowers are described as dithecous.

(*ii*) Hybrid seeds have to be produced year after year.

29. Describe the mechanism of pattern of inheritance of ABO blood groups in humans. 5

OR

(*a*) Why is haemophilia generally observed in human males? Explain the conditions under which a human female can be haemophilic.

(*b*) A pregnant human female was advised to undergo M.T.P. It was diagnosed by her doctor that the foetus she is carrying has developed from a zygote formed by an XX-egg fertilized by Y-carrying sperm. Why was she advised to undergo M.T.P.?

30. (*i*) Describe the characteristics a cloning vector must possess. 5

(*ii*) Why DNA cannot pass through the cell membrane? Explain. How is a bacterial cell made 'competent' to take up recombinant DNA from the medium?

OR

If a desired gene is identified in an organism for some experiments, explain the process of the following:

(*i*) Cutting this desired gene at specific location.

(*ii*) **nthesis of multiple copies of this desired gene.

❑❑❑

SAMPLE PAPER FOR PRACTICE - III

Time allowed : 3 hours *Maximum Marks : 70*

General Instructions:

(i) *All questions are compulsory.*

(ii) *The question paper consists of four Sections **A, B, C** and **D**. Section **A** contains **8** questions of **one** mark each, Section **B** is of **10** questions of **two** marks each, Section **C** is of **9** questions of **three** marks each and Section **D** is of **3** questions of **five** marks each.*

(iii) *There is no overall choice. However, an internal choice has been provided in **one** questions of **2** marks, one question of **3** marks and all the three questions of **5** marks weightage. A student has to attempt only one of the alternatives in such questions.*

(v) *Wherever necessary, the diagrams drawn should be neat and properly labelled.*

SECTION A

1. Name the type of cell division that takes place in the zygote of an organism exhibiting haplontic life cycle. 1

2. Write the scientific name of the microbe used for fermenting malted cereals and fuit juices. 1

3. Write the unit used for measuring ozone thickness. 1

4. Name the event during cell division cycle that results in the gain or loss of chromosome. 1

5. How can bacterial DNA be released from the bacterial cell for biotechnology experiments? 1

6. Write the importance of cryoprservation in conservation of biodiversity. 1

7. Mention the role of the codons AUG and UGA during protein synthesis. 1

8. Normally one embryo develops in one seed but when an organ seed is squeezed many embryos of different shapes and sizes are sen. Mention how it has happened. 1

SECTION B

9. How do histones acquire positive charge? 2

10. Why is CuT considered a good contraceptive device to space children? 2

11. Differentiate between albuminous and non-albuminous seeds, giving one example of each. 2

12. Explain the process of RNA interference. 2

13. List the key tools used in recombinant DNA technology. 2

14. Name the two types of immune systems in a human body. Why are cell mediated and humoral immunities so called? 2

OR

Write the scientific names of the causal organisms of elephantiasis and ringworm in humans. Mention the body parts affected by them.

15. Justify with the help of an example where a deliberate attempt by humans has led to the extinction of a particular species. 2

16. Identify A, D, E and F in the diagram of an antibody molecule given below: 2

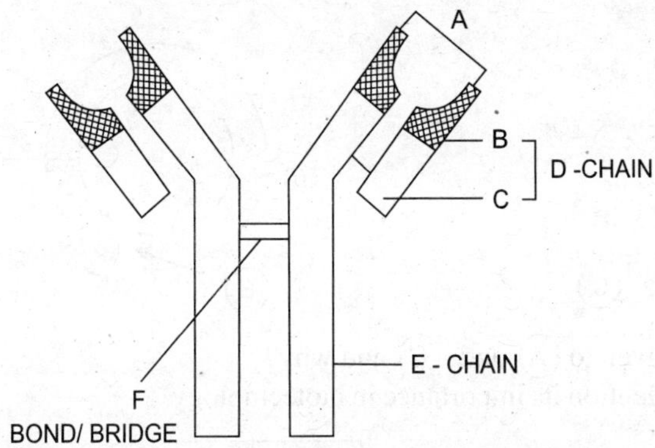

17. Study the graph given below. Explain how is oxygen concentration affected in the river when sewage is discharged into it. 2

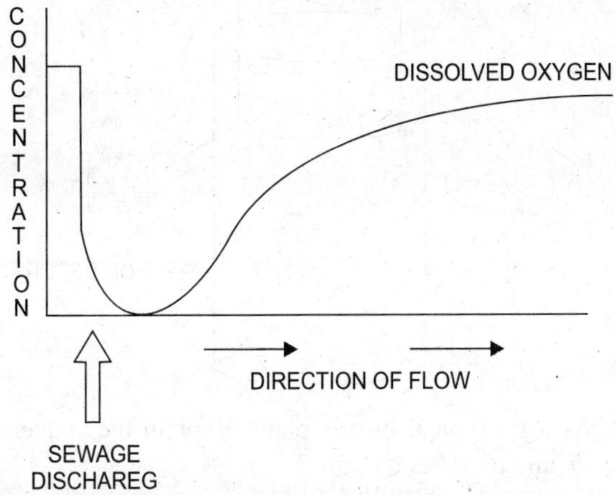

18. Explain how a hereditary disease can be corrected. Give an example of fist successful attempt made towards correction of such diseases. 2

SECTION C

19. Draw a diagram of a male gametophyte of an angiosperm. Label any **four** parts. Why is sporopollenin considered the most resistant organic material? 3

20. How are dominance, codominance and incomplete dominance patterns of inheritance different from each other? 3

21. The base sequence in one of the strands of DNA is TAGCATGAT. 3

(*i*) Give the base sequence of its complementary strand.

(*ii*) How are these base pairs held together in a DNA molecule?

(*iii*) Explain the base complementarity rules. Name the scientist who framed this rule.

22. (*a*) Sickle celled anaemia in humans is a result of point mutation. Explain. 3

(*b*) Write the genotypes of both the parents who have produced a sickle celled anaemic offspring.

23. What is inbreeding depression and how is it caused in organisms? Write any two advantages of inbreeding. 3

24. (*a*) Identify (A) and (B) illustrations in the following: 3

(*i*)

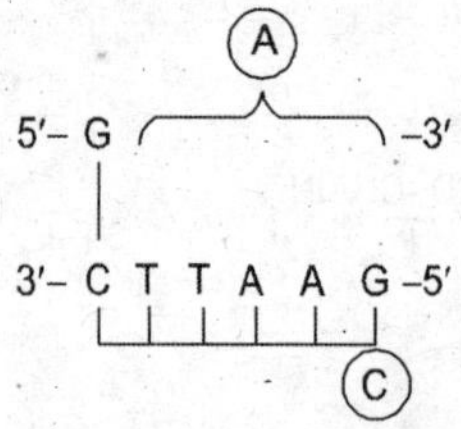

(*ii*)

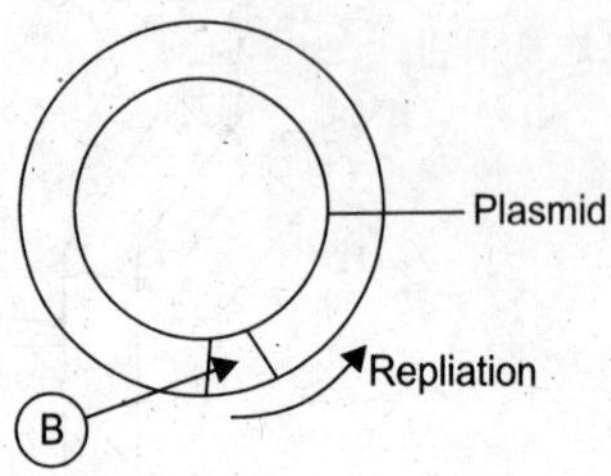

(*b*) Write the term given to (A) and (C) and why?

(*c*) Expland PCR. Mention its importance in biotectnology.

25.

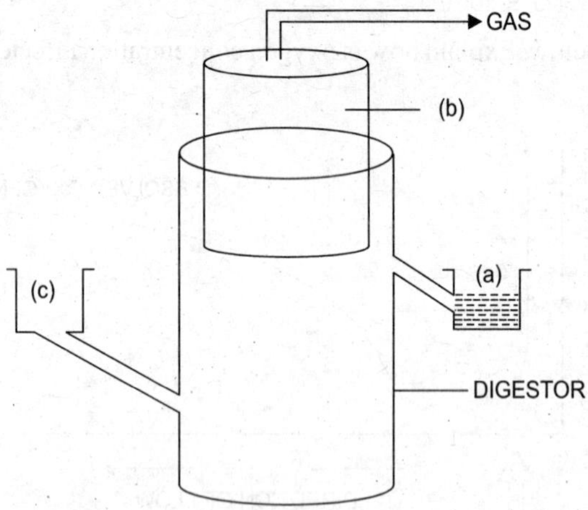

The diagram above is that of a typical biogas plant. Explain the sequence of events occurring in a biogas plant. Identify *a, b* and *c*. 3

26. How can crop varieties be made disease resistant to overcome food crisis in India? Explain. Name one disease resistant variety in India of: 3

(*a*) Wheat to leaf and stripe rust

(*b*) Brassica to white rust

OR

Write the source and the effect on the human body of the following drugs?

(*i*) Morphine

(*ii*) Cocaine

(*iii*) Marijuana

27. Name the type of interaction seen in each of the following examples: 3

(*i*) Ascaris worms living in the intestine of human

(*ii*) Wasp pollinating fig inflorescene

(*iii*) Clown fish living among the tentacles of sea-anemone

(*iv*) Mycorrhizae living on the roots of higher plants

(*v*) Orchid growing on a branch of a mango tree

(*vi*) Disappearance of smaller barnacles when Balanus dominated in the Coast of Scotland.

SECTION D

28. (*a*) Draw a labelled diagram of the human female reproductive system. 5

(*b*) enumerate the events in the ovary of a human female during:

(*i*) Follicular phase

(*ii*) Luteal phase of menstrual cycle

OR

(*a*) Write the specific location and the functions of the following cells in human males:

(*i*) Leydig cells

(*ii*) Sertoli cells

(*iii*) Primary spermatocyte

(*b*) Explain the role of any **two** accessory glands in human male reproductive system.

29. Explain the salient features of Hugo de Vris theory of mutation. How is Darwin's theory of natural selection different from it? Explain. 5

OR

(*a*) Name the primates that lived about 15 million years ago. List their characteristic features.

(*b*) (*i*) Where was the first man-like animal found?

(*ii*) Write the order in which Neanderthals, Homo habilis and Homo erectus appeared on earth. State the brain capacity of each one of them.

(*iii*) When did modern Homo sapiens appear on this planet?

30. (*a*) Explain primary productivity and the factors that influence it. 5

(*b*) Describe how do oxygen and chemical composition of detritus control decomposition.

OR

(*a*) What is EI Nino effect? Explain how it accounts for biodiversity loss.

(*b*) Explain any three measures that you as an individual would take, to reduce environmental pollution.

❑❑❑

SAMPLE PAPER FOR PRACTICE - IV

Time: 3 Hours **Max. Marks: 70**

SECTION-A

1. Mention the site where syngamy occurs in amphibians and reptiles respectively.
2. How is snow-blindness caused in humans?
3. Name one autosomal dominant and one autosomal recessive Mendelian disorder in humans.
4. How is the action of exonuclease different from that of endonuclease?
5. India has more than 50,000 strains of rice. Mention the level of biodiversity it represents.
6. Mention the information that the health workers derive by measuring BOD of a water body.
7. Name the enzyme involved in the continuous replication of DNA strand. Mention the polarity of the template strand.
8. Offsprings derived by asexual reproduction are called clones. Justify giving two reasons.

SECTION-B

9. Mention the role of ribosomes in peptide-bond formation. How does ATP facilitate it?
10. How do copper and hormone releasing IUDs act as contraceptives? Explain.
11. If you squeeze a seed of orange, you might observe many embryos of different sizes. How is it possible? Explain.
12. A recombinant DNA is formed when sticky ends of vector DNA and foreign DNA join. Explain how the sticky ends are formed and get joined.
13. (*i*) Mention the number of primers required in each cycle of polymerase chain reaction (PCR). Write the role of primers and DNA polymerase in PCR.

    (*ii*) Give the characteristic feature and source organism of the DNA polymerase used in PCR.
14. Define the term 'health'. Mention any two ways of maintaining it.

    OR

    Why does a doctor administer tetanus antitoxin and not a tetanus vaccine to a child injured in a roadside accident with a bleeding wound? Explain.
15. Giving two reasons explain why there is more species biodiversity in tropical latitudes than in temperate ones.
16. Name an opioid drug and its source plant. How does the drug affect the human body?
17. Mention the major cause of air pollution in metro cities. Write any three ways by which it can be reduced.
18. How did Eli Lilly synthesise the human insulin? Mention one difference between this insulin and the one produced by the human pancreas.

SECTION-C

19. (*i*) Write the characteristic features of anther, pollen and stigma of wind pollinated flowers.

(*ii*) How do flowers reward their insect pollinators? Explain.

20. (*i*) Why are grasshopper and *Drosophila* said to show male heterogamity? Explain.

(*ii*) Explain female heterogamty with the help of an example.

21. In a series of experiments with *Streptococcus* and mice F.Griffith concluded that R-strain bacteria had been transformed. Explain.

22. (a) How does the Hardy–Weinberg's expression ($p^2 + 2pq + q^2 = 1$) explain that genetic equilibrium is maintained in a population?

(b) List any two factors that can disturb the genetic equilibrium.

23. Mention the name of the causal organism, symptoms and the mode of transmission of the disease Amoebiasis.

24. (*i*) Mention the property that enables the explants to regenerate into a new plant.

(*ii*) A banana herb is virus-infected. Describe the method that will help in obtaining healthy banana plants from this diseased plant.

25. Mention the product and its use produced by each of the microbes listed beow:

(*i*) *Streptococcus*

(*ii*) *Lactobacillus*

(*iii*) *Saccharomyces cerevisiae*

26. (*i*) Name the organism in which the vector shown is inserted to get the copies of the desired gene.

(*ii*) Mention the area labelled in the vector responsible for controlling the copy number of the inserted gene.

(*iii*) Name and explain the role of a selectable marker in the vector shown.

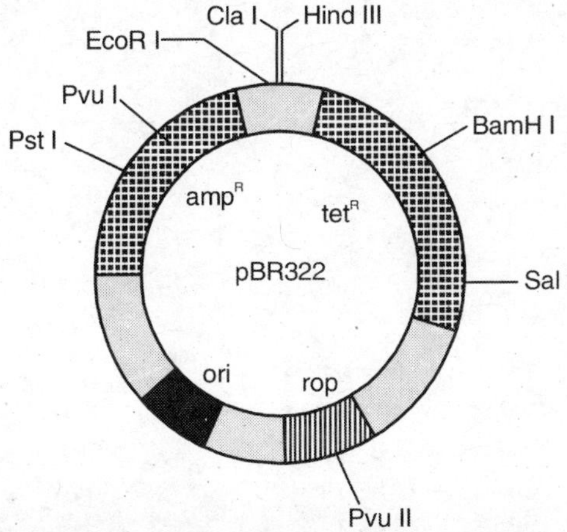

OR

Name the insect pest that is killed by the products of *cryIAc* gene. Explain how the gene makes the plant resistant to the insect pest.

27. How do organisms like fungi, zooplanktons and bears overcome the temporary short-lived climatic stressful conditions? Explain.

SECTION-D

28. Describe in sequence the events that lead to the development of a 3-celled pollen grain from microspore mother cell in angiosperms.

OR

(a) Give a schematic representation showing the events of spermatogenesis in human male.

(b) Describe the structure of a human sperm.

29. (a) State the law of independent assortment.

(b) Using Punnett Square demonstrate the law of independent assortment in a dihybrid cross involving two heterozygous parents.

OR

How did Alfred Hershey and Martha Chase arrive at the conclusion that DNA is the genetic material?

30. (a) Why are herbivores considered similar to predators in the ecological context? Explain.

(b) Differentiate between the following interspecific interactions in a population:

(*i*) Mutualism and Competition

(*ii*) Commensalism and Amensalism

OR

(a) Trace the succession of plants on a dry bare rock.

(b) How does phosphorus cycle differ from carbon cycle?